本书由教育部人文社会科学研究规划基金项目
「云贵川地区国家级非物质文化遗产的对外译介研究」
（项目编号：19YJA850009）资助

贵州省

国家级非物质文化遗产文献资料汇编

（汉英对照）

The Documentary Compilation of the State-level Intangible
Cultural Heritage of Guizhou Province
(Chinese-English Versions)

李新新　主编

李新新　译审

李新新　向晓红　于云飞　向兰　译

四川大学出版社
SICHUAN UNIVERSITY PRESS

图书在版编目（CIP）数据

贵州省国家级非物质文化遗产文献资料汇编：汉英
对照 / 李新新主编；李新新等译. -- 成都：四川大学
出版社，2024. 9. --（国家级非物质文化遗产文献资料
汇编）. -- ISBN 978-7-5690-7267-9

Ⅰ. G127.73

中国国家版本馆 CIP 数据核字第 2024M5D337 号

书　　名：贵州省国家级非物质文化遗产文献资料汇编（汉英对照）
　　　　　Guizhou Sheng Guojiaji Feiwuzhi Wenhua Yichan Wenxian Ziliao
　　　　　Huibian（Han-Ying Duizhao）
主　　编：李新新
译　　者：李新新　向晓红　于云飞　向　兰
丛 书 名：国家级非物质文化遗产文献资料汇编

丛书策划：刘　畅
选题策划：刘　畅　喻　震
责任编辑：刘　畅
责任校对：于　俊
装帧设计：墨创文化
责任印制：李金兰

出版发行：四川大学出版社有限责任公司
　　　　　地址：成都市一环路南一段 24 号（610065）
　　　　　电话：（028）85408311（发行部）、85400276（总编室）
　　　　　电子邮箱：scupress@vip.163.com
　　　　　网址：https://press.scu.edu.cn
印前制作：成都墨之创文化传播有限公司
印刷装订：四川煤田地质制图印务有限责任公司

成品尺寸：170 mm×240 mm
印　　张：18.75
插　　页：2
字　　数：456 千字

版　　次：2024 年 10 月 第 1 版
印　　次：2024 年 10 月 第 1 次印刷
定　　价：98.00 元

扫码获取数字资源

四川大学出版社
微信公众号

编者序

作为四大文明古国之一，中国拥有五千年的文明历史。作为统一的多民族国家，中国拥有 56 个民族共同造就的多姿多彩的文明。悠久的历史和灿烂的文明给中华民族留下了极其丰富的文化遗产，这既包括有形文化遗产（即物质文化遗产），又包括无形文化遗产（即非物质文化遗产，简称"非遗"）。我国政府历来重视文化遗产的保护工作，作为文化遗产的一种，非物质文化遗产的保护也受到高度重视。

当前，随着经济全球化和社会现代化，我国非物质文化遗产的生存环境渐趋恶化，尤其是濒临消亡的或人口数量少的民族的非物质文化遗产的抢救、挖掘、保护、保存及传承与发展面临极大挑战，现状堪忧。正是在这一新的时代背景下，我国政府加大对各省、市、县的非遗项目的抢救、挖掘与保护力度，其标志性事件是 2004 年我国政府正式批准联合国教科文组织通过的《保护非物质文化遗产公约》。第二年，国务院发布了《关于加强文化遗产保护的通知》，制定了"国家＋省＋市＋县"四级保护体系，为我国非遗确立了系统的保护体系。2011 年《中华人民共和国非物质文化遗产法》的通过，标志着我国非遗的抢救、挖掘、保护、保存、传承与发展有了成体系的法律保障。近年来，我国的非遗保护工作开展得如火如荼。2006、2008、2011 和 2014 年，国家文化部牵头分别组织了第一、二、三、四批次的国家级非遗名录的申报工作，提交国务院审批通过。我国各省、市、县也相继推出各级非遗名录，加大力度推进各级非遗的抢救、挖掘、保护、保存及传承工作。

迄今为止，我国非遗的挖掘、整理、保护、传承、传播等的相关研究已取得累累硕果，但大部分成果仅限于汉语文献，其传播也仅限于中华民族内部的非遗宣传。这种将已挖掘、整理和保护完善了的非遗珍宝围于国内的举措绝非智举，跟不上当下的中国文化"走出去"战略。为了扩大我国非遗研究前期阶段性成果的国际影响力，将中华文化精华对外传播至世界各地，弘扬光大，我国非遗的对外译介便成为当务之急。新的时代语境下，我国的非遗研究将迈入一个新阶段——深度对外译介阶段，即以前期阶段性成果为依托，将已

贵州省 国家级非物质文化遗产文献资料汇编（汉英对照）

The Documentary Compilation of the State-level Intangible Cultural Heritage of Guizhou Province (Chinese-English Versions)

挖掘、整理和保护完善了的非遗项目逐渐分批次、分阶段地译介给国际社会，这是新时代下非物质文化遗产保护的必由之路。正是在这一时代背景下，西华大学李新新副教授牵头，组建研究团队，以"云贵川地区国家级非物质文化遗产的对外译介研究"为题申报了2019年度教育部人文社会科学研究规划基金项目，并于2019年3月15日获得立项，项目编号：19YJA850009。该课题顺应了非遗研究的发展新趋势，是我国非遗对外译介迈出的尝试性的一步。《四川省国家级非物质文化遗产文献资料汇编（汉英对照）》［The Documentary Compilation of the State-level Intangible Cultural Heritage of Sichuan Province (Chinese-English Versions)］、《云南省国家级非物质文化遗产文献资料汇编（汉英对照）》［The Documentary Compilation of the State-level Intangible Cultural Heritage of Yunnan Province (Chinese-English Versions)］、《贵州省国家级非物质文化遗产文献资料汇编（汉英对照）》［The Documentary Compilation of the State-level Intangible Cultural Heritage of Guizhou Province (Chinese-English Versions)］正是该立项课题的研究成果。

这些研究成果主要是云、贵、川三省在前四批次中审批通过的国家级非遗名录项目已取得的阶段性成果的对外译介，是对这三省国家级非遗文献资料缺乏英译文现状的弥补。非物质文化遗产具有鲜明的民族性，云贵川地区分布着中华民族的55个少数民族，堪称是整个中华民族的缩影，蕴藏着我国的非遗"富矿"，这些丰富的非物质文化遗产便是中华民族文化精华的浓缩。在新的时代语境下，要深入推动中国文化"走出去"，使其发扬光大，离不开对云贵川地区这些民族文化浓缩精华的优质对外译介。作为我国非遗对外译介宏伟工程的先期研究，云贵川地区国家级非物质文化遗产的优质对外译介肩负着重要的历史使命，是对外弘扬、传播中华民族优秀传统文化必不可少的一部分。

本课题的成果主要涉及云、贵、川三省1—4批次348项国家级非物质文化遗产（含新增项目和扩展项目）的中英文版文献资料汇编，其中四川125项，云南113项，贵州110项。对应非遗项目的十个类别，《四川省国家级非物质文化遗产文献资料汇编（汉英对照）》［The Documentary Compilation of the State-level Intangible Cultural Heritage of Sichuan Province (Chinese-English Versions)］、《云南省国家级非物质文化遗产文献资料汇编（汉英对照）》［The Documentary Compilation of the State-level Intangible Cultural Heritage of Yunnan Province (Chinese-English Versions)］、《贵州省国家级非物质文化遗产文献资料汇编（汉英对照）》［The Documentary Compilation of the State-level Intangible Cultural Heritage of Guizhou Province (Chinese-English Versions)］除"引言"外，正文部分均分为十章，即"第一章民间文学""第二章传统音乐""第三章传统舞蹈""第四章传统戏剧""第五章曲艺""第六章传统体育、游艺与

杂技""第七章传统美术""第八章传统技艺""第九章传统医药""第十章民俗"。中文部分主要搜集整理了相关非遗项目目前已取得的阶段性成果，框架式地概述其基本内容，并附直观图片，为广大非遗爱好者和研究者们提供一个便于快速检索的文献资料集锦。英文部分为国际非遗爱好者提供了了解中国非遗文化，尤其是云贵川三省非遗文化的平台，使更多热爱中华文化的国际友人有机会了解中国的非遗文化，从而助力中国文化"走出去"。

课题负责人李新新副教授对云、贵、川三省所涉及的国家级非遗项目的中文介绍资料进行搜集、汇编、整理，并撰写"引言"。之后，和课题组成员一起进行翻译工作，具体的分工为：李新新副教授负责《四川省国家级非物质文化遗产文献资料汇编》的翻译；向晓红教授负责《贵州省国家级非物质文化遗产文献资料汇编》的翻译，由向兰协助；于云飞博士负责《云南省国家级非物质文化遗产文献资料汇编》的翻译。最后，李新新副教授负责所有译文的审校工作，并撰写"编者序"和"后记"，整理了书末的词汇表。

本课题的研究成果具有重要的学术价值和现实意义。首先，该系列成果系统整理了云、贵、川三省前四批次批准的国家级非物质文化遗产项目的中、英文文献资料，是对这三省国家级非遗文献资料缺乏英译文现状的弥补，具有重要的学术价值。这些成果将相关非遗在抢救、挖掘、整理、保护、传承、开发利用及传播等方面取得的前期阶段性成果转化为对外弘扬、传播这三个多民族聚居区所富含的中华民族优秀传统文化的外宣成果，能够在一定程度上促进我国非遗的保护、传承与传播向"深度对外译介"新阶段的转变，为最终实现对外弘扬、传播中华民族优秀传统文化和提升中国文化软实力作出基础性贡献。其次，作为我国非遗深度对外译介阶段的前期阶段性成果，这些成果可以为我国其他省、市、县少数民族非遗的对外译介提供一定的借鉴，助力各省、市、县的非遗对外译介向纵深推进，加快我国非遗的保护、传承与传播向"深度对外译介"新阶段实现转变，从而推动我国非遗的对外译介迈向高潮，为中国文化精华的深度对外译介打下一定的基础。最后，这些成果能够为英语国家的中国文化爱好者，尤其是中国非遗文化的爱好者提供深入了解中国非物质文化遗产及中国少数民族文化精髓的渠道。从这一层面来说，本课题的研究成果也具有重要的现实意义。

课题组在整理和翻译本系列文献资料汇编的过程中，主要遇到了三方面的困难。一是部分文献资料收集困难。在这些国家级非遗项目中，部分非遗项目的文字资料在权威的非物质文化保护中心官网、政府官网、新闻网上的介绍过于简单，尤其是第四批次通过的非遗项目，资料很少，因此需要到非遗所在地进行现场搜集。但是，课题立项九个多月后便遇上三年的疫情，出行极为不便，这使得文献资料的现场采集陷入困境。鉴于此，课题负责人查阅了大量高质量的期刊论文，购买了一批与所涉非遗项目有关的书籍、省志、县志等，详细研读后，进行汇编整理，补充了缺失的文献资料。二是字数多，翻译任务重。由于该课题的成果涉及三个省348项国家级非物质文化遗产，文献资料字数很多，因此翻译任务繁重。三是汉语文化负载词多，翻译难度大，审校任务重。在这些文献资料中，独具中国特色，尤其是云贵川三省少数民族特色的文化负载词很多，翻译难度很大，因为要将这些国家级非遗蕴含的西南少数民族文化尽可能"不失真""不走样"地译介给英语读者，以达到优质地对外传播我国民族文化精髓和云、贵、川三省国家级非物质文化遗产的目的，译者必须查阅大量资料，求其准确含义，才能准确翻译，因此翻译工作十分耗时，难度很大，审校任务也很重。

本着译介、传播中国文化的目的，在翻译独具中国文化特色，尤其是云、贵、川三省少数民族特色的文化负载词时，课题负责人和团队成员灵活采用了多种翻译方法，以确保英译文既能最大程度展示中国的语言文字特点、文化内涵，又能让英语读者快速、准确地理解相关表达的含义。例如，在翻译"第九章传统医药"中的非遗文献资料时，会涉及很多中国少数民族特有的药材，这些药材名在英语中缺少对应的表达，但在拉丁语中却有相应的表达。鉴于此，课题负责人和团队成员主要采用了音译（汉语拼音）+直译+拉丁译文、音译（汉语拼音）+增译+拉丁译文、直译+音译（汉语拼音）+拉丁译文等翻译方法，这样翻译出的英译文既保证了相关药材名称翻译的科学性，又向英语读者传达了其汉语拼音的语言文字特点，而且还补充了必要的中药材文化信息。再如，在该章里有很多中药名，这些中药名也是中国文化所特有的，独具中国特色，因而在英语和拉丁语中都没有相对应的表达。鉴于此，课题负责人和团队成员主要采用了直译、音译（汉语拼音）+直译、直译+音译（汉语拼音）+直译、直译+音译（汉语拼音）+增译等翻译方法，这样翻译出的英译文或直译出原药名的字面意思，或既保留了原药名汉语拼音的语言文字特点又直译出其字面意思，又或在此基础上增补了必要的中医药文化信息。

在翻译这些非遗项目的文献资料时，课题组所采用的基本原则如下：

（1）有约定俗成译文的，则采用约定俗成的译文。如"同济堂"是中华老字号的医药品牌，闻名中外，其药品外包装Logo上的英文为"TONGJI TANG"。由于该中药品牌的英文已经被中外消费者广泛接受，故课题组便采用这一约定俗成的译文。

（2）有些独具少数民族特色的非遗名称，在翻译时则采用保留其少数民族音的译文。如"侗族大歌"译为"Al Laox of the Dong Nationality"，"苗族贾理"译为*"Jaxlil of the Miao Nationality"*，"刻道"译为*"Kheik Det (carved song stick) Epic"*等。

（3）如果采用直译法能准确传达原文化负载词之意的，则采用直译法。如"秦皮"译为"ash bark"，"小儿救急丹"译为"Infant Emergency Pellets"，"接骨消炎丸"译为"Pills for Bonesetting and Diminishing Inflammation"，"八味秦皮丸"译为"Eight-flavor Ash Bark Pills"等。

（4）如果采用直译法达不到预期效果，则采用其他灵活多变的组合式翻译方法，如音译（汉语拼音）+释译+直译法、音译（汉语拼音）+释译+增译法、音译（汉语拼音）+增译法、音译（汉语拼音）+直译法、音译（汉语拼音）+直译+增译法、音译（汉语拼音）+释译法。采用这些翻译方法可以使英译文既保留原文化负载词的汉语拼音，又能适当增补其所蕴含的独特的中国少数民族文化内涵，为英语读者呈现原汁原味的具有异域风味的中国文化负载词的英译文，从而达到在英语世界优质地传播我国云贵川地区少数民族文化，尤其是非物质文化遗产的目的。例如，课题组采用音译（汉语拼音）+释译+直译法，将"口弦音乐"译为"Kouxian (a kind of buccal reed) Music"；采用音译（汉语拼音）+释译+增译法，将"司岗里"译为"*Sigangli (Out of the Cliff-cave) Epic*"；采用音译（汉语拼音）+增译法，将"仰阿莎"译为"*Yang'asha Poem*"；采用音译（汉语拼音）+直译法，将"黄龙溪火龙灯舞"译为"Huanglongxi Fire Dragon Lantern Dance"；采用音译（汉语拼音）+直译+增译法，将"滚山珠"译为"Gunshan Bead (also called Gunshan Worm)"；采用音译（汉语拼音）+释译法，将"寨老"译为"Zhailao (a head of a stockaded village)"，将"坯胎"译为"Pitai (a product that already has the required shape but still needs processing)"，将"甑子"译为"Zengzi (a wooden container used for steaming)"等。

（5）对于查阅很多资料仍无法获得准确含义的文化负载词，课题组只能通过汉语拼音进行音译。虽然此举使得译文无法传达原文化负载词的字面含义及文化内涵，但至少保留了其原汁原味的汉语拼音特征，虽有遗憾，却是不得已而为之。

（6）原文逻辑欠妥之处，译文中采用增译或适度改译的方法，以确保英译文逻辑正确。由于篇幅有限，不一一举例赘述。

漫长而艰巨的资料搜集、整理、翻译、审校工作接近尾声，课题组成员的心情既激动又忐忑。激动的是，四年多来的辛苦耕耘即将收获，付梓问世；忐忑的是，担心拙译在广大读者的慧眼下显出不妥之处。课题组成员深知我们在非物质文化遗产方面的学识和翻译能力有限，因此拙译中疏漏、舛误在所难免，祈请国内外非遗专家、翻译家及同行不吝批评赐教。

李新新

2023 年 12 月 31 日于西华大学

引言

本书主要涉及贵州省 1—4 批国家级非物质文化遗产的文献资料汇编，搜集整理了贵州省相关非遗项目目前已取得的阶段性成果，框架式地概述了各项目的基本内容，并提供适当图片，以期为广大非遗爱好者和研究者们提供一个便于快速检索的贵州省 1—4 批国家级非遗文献资料集锦。

根据中华人民共和国中央人民政府分别于 2006 年 5 月 20 日、2008 年 6 月 16 日、2011 年 6 月 9 日和 2014 年 12 月 3 日公布的《国务院关于公布第一批国家级非物质文化遗产名录的通知》《国务院关于公布第二批国家级非物质文化遗产名录和第一批国家级非物质文化遗产扩展项目名录的通知》《国务院关于公布第三批国家级非物质文化遗产名录的通知》和《国务院关于公布第四批国家级非物质文化遗产代表性项目名录的通知》，贵州省第一、二、三、四批次分别入围 35 项，40 项（新增 24 项、扩展 16 项），20 项（新增 8 项、扩展 12 项）和 15 项（新增 7 项、扩展 8 项）。共计 110 项。

根据批次，贵州省国家级非物质文化遗产名录（1—4 批）的详细统计数据如表 1：

表 1　贵州省国家级非物质文化遗产名录（1—4 批）分批次汇总表

省份	批次				
	第一批（项）	第二批（项）	第三批（项）	第四批（项）	总计（项）
贵州省	35	40（其中新增项 24 项，扩展项 16 项）	20（其中新增项 8 项，扩展项 12 项）	15（其中新增项 7 项，扩展项 8 项）	110

根据项目类别，贵州省国家级非物质文化遗产名录（1—4 批）的详细统计数据如表 2：

表 2　贵州省国家级非物质文化遗产名录（1—4 批）分类别汇总表

序号	项目类别	数量（单位：项）
1	民间文学	7
2	传统音乐	13
3	传统舞蹈	13

贵州省国家级非物质文化遗产文献资料汇编（汉英对照）

The Documentary Compilation of the State-level Intangible Cultural Heritage of Guizhou Province (Chinese-English Versions)

序号	项目类别	数量（单位：项）
4	传统戏剧	13
5	曲艺	1
6	传统体育、游艺与杂技	1
7	传统美术	10
8	传统技艺	19
9	传统医药	7
10	民俗	26
	总计	110

针对本汇编的正文部分，特做如下说明：

第一，根据项目类别，本汇编分为十章，相同类别的非遗项目归属一章，将其文献资料汇总在一起。

第二，非遗项目的类型有两种：新增项目和扩展项目。前者指首次进入国家级非遗名录的非遗项目；后者指此前已进入上一批国家级非遗名录，而在后续批次申报时，由于申报地区和单位不同，只能将其列入扩展项目名录的非遗项目。

第三，对于两个名称相同，但分别属于新增项目和扩展项目两个不同类型的非遗项目，由于申报批次、申报地区和申报单位不同，仍按两个项目统计，因此在正文中也分项列出。但是，二者的文献资料是合二为一，还是分别单独介绍，将视情况而定。如果二者涉及的文献资料大致相同，则合二为一，汇总起来一并介绍；如果二者涉及的文献资料独具当地特色，则单独介绍。

第四，本汇编中涉及名称相同的两项非遗项目合二为一介绍的有：

（1）第二章"传统音乐"中的"第1项：侗族大歌"和"第2项：侗族大歌"，"第3项：侗族琵琶歌"和"第4项：侗族琵琶歌"，"第6项：苗族民歌（苗族飞歌）"和"第7项：苗族民歌（苗族飞歌）"；

（2）第三章"传统舞蹈"中的"第4项：苗族芦笙舞"和"第5项：苗族芦笙舞"；

（3）第四章"传统戏剧"中的"第2项：花灯戏"和"第3项：花灯戏"；

（4）第八章"传统技艺"中的"第8项：苗族银饰锻制技艺"和"第9项：苗族银饰锻制技艺"；

（5）第十章"民俗"中的"第1项：苗族鼓藏节"和"第2项：苗族鼓藏节"，"第6项：侗族萨玛节"和"第7项：侗族萨玛节"。

第五，本汇编中涉及名称相同的两项非遗项目分别单独介绍的有：

（1）第七章"传统美术"中的"第4项：苗绣"和"第5项：苗绣"；

（2）第八章"传统技艺"中的"第13项：苗族织锦技艺"和"第14项：苗族织锦技艺"。

本汇编涉及的非遗项目是在贵州省定居的各少数民族及汉族所创造的文化珍宝，具有多学科的研究价值：

第一章"民间文学"中，有7项非遗，其中5项均是苗族祖先所创作的文学珍宝，涉及苗族的古歌、古词、婚姻制度、神话故事、爱情故事、古规古理和亚鲁王英雄；1项是布依族祖先创作的传统民歌；1项是侗族民间故事。这些是研究苗、布依和侗等少数民族的史学、文学、婚姻习俗、古代法律的"活化石"，具有民族学、民俗学和哲学方面的重要研究价值。

第二章"传统音乐"中，有13项非遗，主要涉及侗、苗、布依、彝和土家等少数民族的民歌或山歌，是研究相关少数民族音乐学的重要资料，具有鲜明的民族音乐风格和地域特征。

第三章"传统舞蹈"中，有13项非遗，主要涉及苗、彝、瑶、布依和毛南等少数民族的传统舞蹈，体现了其民族性格、精神观念和审美情趣，对加强民族内的人际交往，增强民族团结具有重要作用。其中，很多舞蹈属于祭祀舞蹈，如锦鸡舞、鼓龙鼓虎－长衫龙、苗族芦笙舞和反排苗族木鼓舞等，被视为连接相关少数民族社会过去、现在和未来的重要文化纽带。

第四章"传统戏剧"中，有13项非遗，主要涉及土家、布依、汉、侗、彝和仡佬等民族的传统戏剧。其中，有些戏剧，如花灯戏、石阡木偶戏和黔剧等是贵州多民族文化融合的产物，体现了多民族文化相互交融的特点。而有些戏剧，如侗戏、布依戏和彝族撮泰吉是某一个少数民族所独有，极具民族特色和地域性。这些传统戏剧对研究相关民族的戏剧文化具有重要价值。

第五章"曲艺"中，仅有1项非遗，即布依族八音坐唱，是布依族独特的曲艺形式，是布依族文化不可或缺的组成部分，具有鲜明的布依族特色，是研究布依族曲艺的"活材料"。

第六章"传统体育、游艺与杂技"中，也仅有1项非遗，即赛龙舟，是铜仁和镇远多民族参加的传统游艺体育活动，体现了当地民众对"团结协作、奋勇争先"的龙舟精神的传承与发扬。

第七章"传统美术"中，有10项非遗，主要涉及苗族、水族和侗族三个少数民族的传统美术，体现了这三个民族独特的审美情趣、思想意识及观念信仰等，具有很强的实用价值。

第八章"传统技艺"中，有19项非遗，主要涉及苗、彝、瑶、侗等民族的传统技艺。其中，苗族最多，有10项，主要涉及蜡染、芦笙制作、银饰锻制和织锦技艺等，体现了苗族人民的聪明智慧和精湛多样的传统技艺。这些传统技艺是苗、彝、瑶、侗等少数民族智慧的结晶，是其传统文化的重要组成部分。

第九章"传统医药"中，有 7 项非遗，主要涉及汉、苗、侗、瑶和布依等民族的传统医药。其中，有些是传统中医药与少数民族民间医药的融合，如同济堂传统中药文化和廖氏化风丹制作技艺等；而有些则是少数民族独特的医药精华，如药浴疗法，骨伤蛇伤疗法、九节茶药制作工艺，过路黄药制作工艺和益肝草制作技艺等。

第十章"民俗"中，有 26 项非遗，主要涉及苗、侗、布依、水、仡佬、彝及汉民族的民俗活动。这些民俗活动是相关民族凝聚人心、加强团结的纽带，为增进民族团结、促进社会和谐发挥了积极作用，同时也为各民族文化的展示与传承提供了平台。这些民俗活动从侧面折射了相关民族独特的人生观和价值观，是研究其历史与文化的百科全书。

值得一提的是，本汇编中涉及的一些非遗项目，由于受到社会现代化进程加快的影响，年轻人不愿意学习和传承，因此面临濒危的境地；而有些则是濒临消亡的民族或人口基数小的民族所独有的珍奇非遗项目，其本身即存在传承乏人的困境。因此，对这些濒危非遗项目的尽早抢救、挖掘和保护便显得尤为重要。

Introduction

   This book mainly involves the documentary compilation of the state-level intangible cultural heritage of Guizhou Province (Batches 1-4), which has collected and sorted out the interim results that have been achieved currently concerning the related intangible cultural heritage items in Guizhou, outlining the basic content of each item and providing appropriate pictures. It aims to provide a collection of literature of the state-level intangible cultural heritage of Guizhou Province (Batches 1-4) that is easy for intangible cultural heritage lovers and researchers to access quickly.

   The Notice of the State Council on Publishing the 1st-batch State-level Intangible Cultural Heritage List, The Notice of the State Council on Publishing the 2nd-batch State-level Intangible Cultural Heritage List and the 1st-batch Extended Item List of the State-level Intangible Cultural Heritage, The Notice of the State Council on Publishing the 3rd-batch State-level Intangible Cultural Heritage List and The Notice of the State Council on Publishing the 4th-batch Representative Item List of the State-level Intangible Cultural Heritage were published on the official website of the Central People's Government of the People's Republic of China respectively on May 20th, 2006, June 16th, 2008, June 9th, 2011 and December 3rd, 2014. According to these four notices, 35 items, 40 items (24 new ones plus 16 extended ones), 20 items (8 new ones plus 12 extended ones) and 15 items (7 new ones plus 8 extended ones) of the intangible cultural heritage of Guizhou Province have been shortlisted respectively in the 1st, 2nd, 3rd and 4th batches. There are 110 items in total.

   According to the batches, the detailed statistics of the State-level Intangible Cultural Heritage List of Guizhou Province (Batches 1-4) are shown in Table 1:

·**贵州省**·国家级非物质文化遗产文献资料汇编（汉英对照）

The Documentary Compilation of the State-level Intangible Cultural Heritage of Guizhou Province (Chinese-English Versions)

Table 1: Summary Table of the State–level Intangible Cultural Heritage List

of Guizhou Province in Batches (Batches 1–4)

Province	Batch				
	Batch 1 (Items)	Batch 2 （Items）	Batch 3 （Items）	Batch 4 （Items）	Total （Items）
Guizhou	35	40 （24 New Items, 16 Extended Items）	20 （8 New Items, 12 Extended Items）	15 （7 New Items, 8 Extended Items）	110

According to the categories of items, the detailed statistics of the State-level Intangible Cultural Heritage List of Guizhou Province (Batches 1-4) are shown in Table 2:

Table 2: Summary Table of the State-level Intangible Cultural Heritage List

of Guizhou Province in Categories (Batches 1-4)

No.	Categories of the Items	Amount（Unit: items）
1	Folk Literature	7
2	Traditional Music	13
3	Traditional Dance	13
4	Traditional Opera	13
5	Quyi （a general term for all Chinese talking-and-singing art forms）	1
6	Traditional Sports, Recreations and Acrobatics	1
7	Traditional Fine Arts	10
8	Traditional Craft	19
9	Traditional Medicine	7
10	Folk Custom	26
	Total	110

For the main body of this compilation, some specifics are explained as follows:

Firstly, according to categories of the items, this compilation is divided into ten chapters, with the same category of intangible cultural heritage items falling under one chapter and their literature summarized together.

Secondly, intangible cultural heritage items are divided into two types: New Item and Extended Item. The former refers to the intangible cultural heritage items that have been shortlisted in the State-level Intangible Cultural Heritage List for the first time; and the latter refers to the ones that have been shortlisted in the State-level Intangible Cultural Heritage List of the previous batch but have to be listed again due to different application regions and units in the subsequent batches.

Thirdly, as to two intangible cultural heritage items which have the same name but fall under different types of New Item and Extended Item, they are counted as two items due to different application batches, application regions and application units. Consequently, they are listed separately in the body part. However, whether to introduce their literature together or separately depends on specific situations: if the literature concerning them is roughly the same, their literature will be introduced together; and if the literature involved has unique local characteristics, their literature will be introduced separately.

Fourthly, in this compilation, two items of intangible cultural heritage with the same name that are introduced together are:

(1)"Item 1: Al Laox of the Dong Nationality" and "Item 2: Al Laox of the Dong Nationality"; "Item 3: Pipa Songs of the Dong Nationality" and "Item 4: Pipa Songs of the Dong Nationality"; as well as "Item 6: Folk Songs of the Miao Nationality (Flying Songs of the Miao Nationality)" and "Item 7: Folk Songs of the Miao Nationality (Flying Songs of the Miao Nationality)" in Chapter Two "Traditional Music".

(2) "Item 4: Lusheng Dance of the Miao Nationality" and "Item 5: Lusheng Dance of the Miao Nationality" in Chapter Three "Traditional Dance".

(3) "Item 2: the Lantern Opera" and "Item 3: the Lantern Opera" in Chapter Four "Traditional Opera".

(4) "Item 8: the Craft of Making Silver Ornaments of the Miao Nationality" and "Item 9: the Craft of Making Silver Ornaments of the Miao Nationality" in Chapter Eight "Traditional Craft".

(5) "Item 1: the Drum Worship Festival of the Miao Nationality" and "Item 2: the Drum Worship Festival of the Miao Nationality"; as well as "Item 6: the Sama Festival of the Dong Nationality" and "Item 7: the Sama Festival of the Dong Nationality" in Chapter Ten "Folk Custom".

Fifthly, in this compilation, two items of intangible cultural heritage with the same name that are introduced separately are:

(1) "Item 4: Miao Embroidery" and "Item 5: Miao Embroidery" in Chapter Seven "Traditional Fine Arts";

(2) "Item 13: the Craft of Making Brocade of the Miao Nationality" and "Item 14: the Craft of Making Brocade of the Miao Nationality" in Chapter Eight "Traditional Craft".

The intangible cultural heritage items involved in this compilation are cultural treasures created by the ethnic minorities and the Han nationality living in Guizhou Province, having multi-disciplinary research value:

In Chapter One "Folk Literature", there are seven items of intangible cultural heritage. Among them, five items are literary treasures created by the Miao ancestors, which mainly involve the ancient songs, poems, marriage system, myths, love stories, ancient rules and principles, and the hero of King Yalu of the Miao nationality; one item is a traditional folk song created by the Buyi ancestors; and one item is a folk tale of the Dong nationality. All these are the "living fossils" for studying the history, literature, cultures, marriage customs and ancient laws of the ethnic minorities of Miao, Buyi and Dong, which are of great research value in ethnology, folklore and philosophy.

In Chapter Two "Traditional Music", there are 13 items of intangible cultural heritage, which mainly involve the folk songs or Mountain Songs of the ethnic minorities of Dong, Miao, Buyi, Yi, Tujia, etc. They are important material for studying the musicology of relevant ethnic minorities, having distinctive national musical style and regional features.

In Chapter Three "Traditional Dance", there are 13 items of intangible cultural heritage, which mainly involve the traditional dances of the ethnic minorities of Miao, Yi, Yao, Buyi, Maonan, etc. These traditional dances embody their national characters, spiritual concepts and aesthetic taste, playing an important role in strengthening interpersonal communication within the nation and enhancing national unity. Among them, many dances belong to sacrificial dances, such as the Golden Pheasant Dance, the Dragon-and-tiger Dance in Long Gowns, Lusheng Dance of the Miao Nationality and Fanpai Wooden-drum Dance of the Miao Nationality, which are regarded as an important cultural link connecting the past, present and future of the societies of related ethnic minorities.

In Chapter Four "Traditional Opera", there are 13 items of intangible cultural heritage, which mainly involve the traditional operas of the nationalities of Tujia, Buyi, Han, Dong, Yi, Gelao, etc. Among them, some operas, such as the Lantern Opera, Shiqian Puppet Play and Guizhou Opera, are products of the integration of multiple ethnic cultures in Guizhou Province, showing the characteristics of multiple ethnic cultures blending with each other. Others, such as Dong Opera, Buyi Opera and Cuotaiji Opera of the Yi Nationality are unique to certain ethnic minority, having both ethnic and regional characteristics. All these traditional operas are of great value to the research of the opera culture of related nationalities.

In Chapter Five "Quyi (a general term for all Chinese talking-and-singing art forms)", there is only one item of intangible cultural heritage, that is, Bayin Sitting-and-singing of the Buyi Nationality. It is a form of Quyi (a general term for all Chinese talking-and-singing art forms) unique to the Buyi nationality and an indispensable component of Buyi culture, with distinctive characteristics of the Buyi nationality, which is the "living material" for studying its Quyi (a general term for all Chinese talking-and-singing art forms).

In Chapter Six "Traditional Sports, Recreations and Acrobatics", there is also only one item of intangible cultural heritage, namely the Dragon-boat Racing. It is a traditional sport and recreation activity participated by people from many ethnic groups in Tongren City and Zhenyuan County, reflecting local people's inheriting and carrying forward of the dragon-boat spirit of "unity, cooperation and striving for the first".

In Chapter Seven "Traditional Fine Arts", there are ten items of intangible cultural heritage, which mainly involve the traditional fine arts of the three ethnic minorities of Miao, Shui and Dong. All of them reflect their unique aesthetic taste, ideology, concepts, belief, etc., having great utility value.

In Chapter Eight "Traditional Craft", there are 19 items of intangible cultural heritage, which mainly involve the traditional crafts of the nationalities of Miao, Yi, Yao, Dong, etc. Among them, the Miao nationality has the largest number, reaching as many as ten items, which mainly involve the crafts of Batik, Lusheng Musical Instruments making, Silver Ornaments making, brocade making, etc. They embody the wisdom and the superb and diverse traditional crafts of the Miao people. All these traditional crafts are the crystallization of the wisdom of the ethnic minorities of Miao, Yi, Yao, Dong, etc., being an important part of their traditional cultures.

In Chapter Nine "Traditional Medicine", there are seven items of intangible cultural heritage, which mainly involve the traditional medicine of the nationalities of Han, Miao, Dong, Yao, Buyi, etc. Among them, some are the integration of the traditional Chinese medicine and the folk medicine of ethnic minorities, such as the Traditional Chinese Medicine Culture of TONGJI TANG and the Craft of Making the Liao Family's Huafeng Pill. While some are the medical essence unique to ethnic minorities, such as the Therapy of Medicated Bath, the Therapies for Bone Injuries and Snakebites, the Craft of Making Jiujiecha Medicine, the Craft of Making Guoluhuang Medicine and the Craft of Making Liver-protecting Herb Medicine.

In Chapter Ten "Folk Custom", there are 26 items of intangible cultural heritage, which mainly involve the folk activities of the Miao, Dong, Buyi, Shui, Gelao, Yi and Han nationalities. These folk activities are ties for related nationalities to unite people and strengthen unity, playing a positive role in promoting national unity and social harmony, and providing a platform for exhibiting and inheriting the cultures of these nationalities. These folk activities reflect the unique outlook on life and values of related nationalities, and are encyclopedias for studying their history and culture.

It is worth mentioning that: for some items of intangible cultural heritage involved in this compilation, due to the impact of the accelerated process of social modernization, young people are not willing to learn and pass them on, so they are faced with an endangered situation; while some items are unique to the ethnic minorities that are on the verge of extinction or have very small populations, they themselves are in a dilemma of the lack of inheritors. Therefore, it is particularly important to rescue, document and protect the endangered intangible cultural heritage as early as possible.

目录 Contents

·贵州省·国家级非物质文化遗产文献资料汇编（汉英对照）

The Documentary Compilation of the State-level Intangible Cultural Heritage of Guizhou Province (Chinese-English Versions)

第四章　传统戏剧
Chapter Four　Traditional Opera ···················· 071

第五章　曲　艺
Chapter Five　Quyi (a general term for all Chinese talking-and-singing art forms) ·························· 101

第九章　传统医药
Chapter Nine　Traditional Medicine ················ 173

第十章　民　俗
Chapter Ten　Folk Custom ·············· 190

附录
Appendixes

后记
Postscript

第一章
民间文学

Chapter One
Folk Literature

第 1 项：
苗族古歌

苗族古歌演唱
Singing The Ancient Song of the Miao Nationality

项目序号：1	项目编号：Ⅰ-1	公布时间：2006（第一批）	类别：民间文学
所属地区：贵州省	类型：新增项目	申报地区或单位：贵州省台江县、黄平县	

　　苗族古歌是苗族先民在长期的生产劳动中创造出来的史诗，又称"苗族史诗"，流传于黔东南清水江流域的苗族聚居区，尤其是台江县和黄平县。

　　苗族古歌从宇宙的诞生、人类和物种的起源，一直唱到苗族的大迁徙、苗族的社会制度和日常生活，由金银歌、古枫歌、蝴蝶歌、洪水滔天和溯河西迁五大部分组成，共 1.5 万行，塑造了 100 多位有名有姓的人物。^① 多在苗族鼓社祭、婚表活动、亲友聚会和节日等场合演唱，演唱者多为老年人、巫师和歌手。酒席是演唱古歌的重要场合。^② 其特点是盘歌问答、歌骨歌花交替演唱。诗歌运用古今对比的方式叙述，每段歌词可以反复吟唱。分为神话类古歌、历史类古歌、诉讼类古歌和婚嫁类古歌四类。一般由四人组成两组对唱，先甲方提问，乙方重复甲方问题后再回答；乙方回答完后紧接着提出问题，甲方重复乙方问题后再回答，如此往复。苗族古歌属五言体结构，押苗语韵，大量运用比喻、夸张、排比、拟人和反问等修辞，生动地呈现了苗族先民对天地、万物及人类起源的解释和人们艰苦奋斗开创人类历史的功绩，充满浪漫主义色彩。^③

Item 1: The Ancient Song of the Miao Nationality

Item Serial Number: 1	Item ID Number: I -1	Released Date: 2006 (Batch 1)	Category: Folk Literature
Affiliated Province: Guizhou Province	Type: New Item	Application Province or Unit: Taijiang County and Huangping County of Guizhou Province	

The Ancient Song of the Miao Nationality is the epic created by the Miao ancestors in the process of the long-term production and labor, also known as "the epic of the Miao nationality". It is spread in areas inhabited by the Miao people in the Qingshui River Basin of southeast Guizhou, especially Taijiang County and Huangping County.

The Ancient Song of the Miao Nationality involves the content from the birth of the universe, the origin of human beings and species, to the great migration, social system and daily life of the Miao nationality. It consists of five parts: Gold and Silver Song, Ancient Maple Song, Butterfly Song, Terrible Floods and Upstream Migration to the West, with a total of 15,000 lines, portraying more than 100 famous

---

① 《苗族古歌》，中华人民共和国国家民族事务委员会网，http://www.seac.gov.cn/seac/mzwh/201807/1084173.shtml，检索日期：2019 年 8 月 29 日。

② 《苗族古歌》，中国非物质文化遗产网，http://www.ihchina.cn/Article/Index/detail?id=12178，检索日期：2019 年 8 月 26 日。

③ 《苗族古歌》，中华人民共和国国家民族事务委员会网，http://www.seac.gov.cn/seac/mzwh/201807/1084173.shtml，检索日期：2019 年 8 月 29 日。

people with names. It is usually sung on the occasions of the Drum Worship Festival of the Miao nationality, weddings, gatherings of relatives and friends, and other festivals. Performers are mainly elderly people, necromancers and singers. Banquets are important occasions for singing **The Ancient Song of the Miao Nationality**. Its characteristics are singing in antiphonal style by asking and answering questions, and singing the main song and chorus alternately. It narrates stories by means of contrasting ancient times with modern times, and each paragraph of lyrics can be sung repeatedly. It is divided into four categories: mythological Ancient Song, historical Ancient Song, litigant Ancient Song and marriage Ancient Song. Generally, four singers form two groups: party A and party B. Party A asks a question first, and Party B repeats Party A's question before answering it. After answering it, Party B asks a question, and Party A repeats Party B's question, and then answers it. The cycle goes repeatly. **The Ancient Song of the Miao Nationality** adopts the five-character structure, using rhyme of the Miao language and a large number of rhetoric devices of analogies, hyperbole, parallelism, personification, rhetorical question, etc. It vividly presents the Miao ancestors' interpretation of the origins of the heaven, the earth, mankind and all things on earth, as well as their exploits of struggling hard to create human history, which is full of romantic color.

·贵州省·国家级非物质文化遗产文献资料汇编（汉英对照）

The Documentary Compilation of the State-level Intangible Cultural Heritage of Guizhou Province (Chinese-English Versions)

《刻道》演唱表演
the Performance of *Kheik Det (carved song stick) Epic*

第 2 项：
刻道

项目序号：5	项目编号：I -5	公布时间：2006（第一批）	类别：民间文学
所属地区：贵州省	类型：新增项目	申报地区或单位：贵州省施秉县	

　　刻道，苗语为"kheik det"，亦称"刻木"或"歌棒"。其材质以枫木为尊，这和苗族人民自古对枫木的崇拜有关，一般分三面镌刻，一面 9 个符号，共计 27 个符号。符号多用象形、指事等造字法。[1] 刻道是居住在中国境内的苗族群体中唯一保留的刻木记事符号，是迄今为止苗族最早的记事实物和该支系最古老的文字工具。由此引出了作为一种文化载体的名词——《刻道》，主要流传于贵州省施秉县杨柳塘镇飞云大峡谷的一个山坡洼地里。

　　《刻道》，汉语译为《苗族开亲歌》，是一部口耳相传的史诗，产生于苗族母系氏族过渡到父系氏族后的一段时期内，主要记载了苗族婚仪中的礼数，是苗族的"婚姻法典"，主要在婚礼、年节等酒席上，两男两女以盘歌形式进行对唱。与那些反映创世、开天辟地、人类起源等的古歌古词神话不同，《刻道》反映的主要是舅权制下的婚姻状况，是一部具有浓郁民族气息的苗族婚姻叙事长诗，是苗族古歌中历史最长、规模最大、流传最广的酒歌，有一万多行歌词。其对环境的描写，对人物语言、行动、心理和性格的刻画栩栩如生。《刻道》更是一部规模宏大、历史悠久的苗族古籍，有很高的文学艺术成就。[2]

---

① 《吴通贤：用"刻道"传承苗族古老歌谣》，贵州省非物质文化遗产保护中心官网，http://www. gzfwz. org. cn/xwdt/201804/t20180416_3119653. html，检索日期：2019 年 8 月 20 日。

② 《刻道》，中国非物质文化遗产网，http://www. ihchina. cn/Article/Index/detail?id=121 83，检索日期：2019 年 8 月 29 日。

Item 2: *Kheik Det (carved song stick) Epic*

Item Serial Number:5	Item ID Number: I-5	Released Date: 2006 (Batch 1)	Category: Folk Literature
Affiliated Province: Guizhou Province	Type: New Item	Application Province or Unit: Shibing County, Guizhou Province	

In the Miao language, " 刻道 " is written as "kheik det", which is also called "the Carved Stick" or "the Song Stick". Maple wood is the best material for it, which is related to the Miao people's worship of maple wood since ancient times. It is generally engraved on three sides, with nine notations on each side and 27 in total. Notations are often made by using the methods of pictographic characters and self-explanatory characters. "Kheik det" is the only wood-carved notations for recording events preserved among the Miao people living in China, the earliest material object used to keep a record of events of the Miao nationality and the oldest tool for writing of this branch up to now. This leads to a noun as a cultural carrier, *"Kheik Det"*, which is mainly spread in a low-lying land on the mountain slope of Feiyun Grand Canyon in Yangliutang Township, Shibing County, Guizhou Province.

Kheik Det (carved song stick) Epic refers to *Kaiqin Song of the Miao Nationality* in Chinese, which is an epic passed down orally, originating in the period after the Miao nationality's transition from matriarchal clan to patriarchal clan. It mainly records the etiquette in the wedding ceremony of the Miao nationality, being "the Marriage Code" of the Miao people. It is sung mainly at banquets on the occasions of weddings, festivals, etc. by two men and two women who perform antiphonal singing in the form of asking and answering questions. Different from myths in ancient songs that reflect the creation of the world, the creation of the heaven and the earth, the origin of human beings, etc., *Kheik Det (carved song stick) Epic* mainly reflects the marital status in the system of the power of mother's brother. It is a long narrative poem concerning the Miao people's marriage with strong ethnic flavor, and also a toasting song with the longest history, on the largest scale and circulated most widely, among the ancient songs of the Miao nationality. It has over 10,000 lines of lyrics. It vividly describes the environment and portrays characters' words, actions, psychology and personalities. *Kheik Det (carved song stick) Epic* is an ancient book of the Miao nationality with a large scale and a long history, having high literary and artistic achievements.

贵州省国家级非物质文化遗产文献资料汇编（汉英对照）

The Documentary Compilation of the State-level Intangible Cultural Heritage of Guizhou Province (Chinese-English Versions)

《仰阿莎》大型雕像
Large-sized Sculpture of Yang'asha

第3项：
仰阿莎

项目序号：548	项目编号：Ⅰ-61	公布时间：2008（第二批）	类别：民间文学
所属地区：贵州省	类型：新增项目	申报地区或单位：贵州省黔东南苗族侗族自治州	

　　《仰阿莎》是流传于贵州省黔东南苗族侗族自治州及毗邻地区的苗族长篇叙事歌，长达万余行，是迄今为止发现的苗族最长的叙事歌[①]，也是苗族民间古代神话爱情叙事诗。

　　《仰阿莎》以神话故事为蓝本，采用比兴的诗体语言手法，讲诉了一个叫仰阿莎的苗族美神和太阳、月亮之间的故事，借此歌颂苗族人民对美好生活的向往和对真挚爱情的追求，在苗族族群中享有较高声誉，被称为"最美丽的歌"。全诗共十章，从仰阿莎的出生写起，然后到游方谈情、嫁给太阳、私奔月亮，到最后获得完满婚姻，用苗文纪录、演唱传播。[②]《仰阿莎》以盘歌形式演唱，具有鲜明的苗民族特色，在苗族文学史上居于较高的地位，对苗族的歌谣，特别是叙事歌的发展具有重大的促进作用。其版本有上百种，内容、人物和细节上多有区别，但仰阿莎美丽、善良、勇敢的核心形象却是一致的。许多口传版本一般为五言韵文体，语言质朴、想象奇丽。[③]不同的口头版本唱法

---

① 《仰阿莎》，中国非物质文化遗产网，http://www.ihchina.cn/Article/Index/detail?id=12294，检索日期：2019年8月29日。

② 李珺、唐善林，《苗族神话〈仰阿莎〉的叙述主题及美学价值》，载《贵州社会科学》，2017年第8期，第76-81页。

③ 吴佳妮，《"仰阿莎"文化价值挖掘与文化品牌建设研究》，载《贵州民族研究》，2018年第4期，第88-92页。

不同，演唱曲调与演唱习俗直接相关，大大丰富了苗族音乐的内容和形式。^①

Item 3: *Yang'asha Poem*

Item Serial Number: 548	Item ID Number: I -61	Released Date: 2008 (Batch 2)	Category: Folk Literature
Affiliated Province: Guizhou Province	Type: New Item	Application Province or Unit: Qiandongnan Miao and Dong Autonomous Prefecture, Guizhou Province	

Yang'asha Poem is a long narrative song of the Miao nationality circulated in Qiandongnan Miao and Dong Autonomous Prefecture and its adjacent areas in Guizhou Province. With more than 10,000 lines, it is the longest narrative song of the Miao nationality discovered so far, and also a narrative poem of the ancient folk mythological love of the Miao nationality.

Based on mythological stories, *Yang'asha Poem* tells the story about the god of beauty of the Miao nationality named Yang'asha, the sun and the moon. It adopts Bi (analogy) and Xing (borrowing) techniques of the poetic language, and sings the praises of the Miao people's longing for a better life and their pursuit of sincere love. It is called "the most beautiful song", enjoying a high reputation among the Miao ethnic group. The whole poem consists of ten chapters, starting with Yang'asha's birth, traveling around to pursue love, marrying the sun, eloping with the moon, and then finally getting a perfect marriage, which is recorded, sung and transmitted in the Miao language. *Yang'asha Poem* is sung in the form of asking and answering questions, which has a distinct ethnic feature of the Miao nationality. It enjoys a high position in the literary history of the Miao nationality, and plays an important role in promoting the development of Miao ballads, especially narrative songs. It has over a hundred versions, in which many differences exist in content, characters and details, but Yang'asha's core images of beauty, kindness and bravery are the same. Many orally-transmitted versions are generally five-character literary compositions in rhyme, with simple language and singular and beautiful imagination. Different oral versions are sung by using different methods, and their singing tunes are directly related to singing customs, which has greatly enriched the music of the Miao nationality in content and form.

---

① 《仰阿莎》，中国非物质文化遗产网，http://www. ihchina. cn/Article/Index/detail?id= 12294，检索日期：2019 年 8 月 29 日。

第4项：布依族盘歌

户外演唱布依族盘歌
the Outdoor Singing of Pange Songs of the Buyi Nationality

项目序号：549	项目编号：Ⅰ-62	公布时间：2008（第二批）	类别：民间文学
所属地区：贵州省	类型：新增项目	申报地区或单位：贵州省盘县	

　　布依族盘歌是布依族的传统民歌和口传史诗，是一种用布依语创作并传唱的民间文学作品，流传于贵州省北盘江流域的布依村寨，六盘水市盘县羊场布依族白族苗族乡的布依族盘歌最具代表性。[①]

　　布依族盘歌主要有古歌、酒歌、情歌、祭祀歌和礼教歌等，内容涉及劳作、时政、仪式、爱情、生活环境和历史传说等方面，主要在婚丧嫁娶、迎来送往、生产劳动、休闲娱乐和谈情说爱等场合演唱。羊场布依族盘歌由三组"套歌"和"户外歌"组成，分为四个类型：丧祭仪式歌、婚礼仪式歌、友情仪式歌和"户外歌"。[②] 每位布依人都是歌手，大家在劳动、生活和节日中反复传唱，形成多种版本的布依族盘歌。毕摩、婚媒等在婚嫁、祭祀和葬仪等活动中有较规范的唱法。用布依语传唱，是布依族盘歌传承的一大特征，可以独唱、对唱、一人领唱众人合唱。领唱者唱诗词内容，众人唱衬词。大多采用"喜调""老人调""悲调"等传唱，可以清唱，也可以用乐器伴奏演唱。常用伴奏乐器有月琴、竹笛、箫筒、木叶等。[③] 布依族盘歌被喻为布依族的"无字百科全书"，集人类起源、布依族源、生产劳作、待人接物、伦理道德、婚嫁建房和丧葬祭祀等为一体，是布依族历史、文化的重要载体。

[①]　《布依族盘歌》，中国非物质文化遗产网，http://www.ihchina.cn/Article/Index/detail?id=12295，检索日期：2019年8月29日。

[②]　吴秋林，《歌唱的生存——羊场布依族盘歌综论》，载《民族文学研究》，2012年第2期，第130-142页。

[③]　李如海，《盘县"布依族盘歌"的内涵及传承发展》，载《贵州民族报》，2015年10月29日，第C03版。

Item 4: Pange Songs of the Buyi Nationality

Item Serial Number: 549	Item ID Number: I -62	Released Date: 2008 (Batch 2)	Category: Folk Literature
Affiliated Province: Guizhou Province	Type: New Item	Application Province or Unit: Panxian County, Guizhou Province	

Pange Songs of the Buyi Nationality are traditional folk songs and orally-transmitted epics of the Buyi people. They are folk literary works created, sung and transmitted in the Buyi language, spread in Buyi villages in the Beipanjiang River Basin of Guizhou Province. **Pange Songs of the Buyi Nationality** in Yangchang Buyi, Bai and Miao Township of Panxian County, Liupanshui City are the most representative.

Pange Songs of the Buyi Nationality mainly include ancient songs, toasting songs, love songs, sacrificial songs and etiquette songs, the content of which covers laboring, current politics, ceremonies, love, living environments, historical legends, etc. They are mostly sung on the occasions of weddings, funerals, welcoming visitors and seeing them off, production and labor, leisure and entertainment, loving dates, etc. **Pange Songs of the Buyi Nationality** in Yangchang Buyi, Bai and Miao Township consist of three sets of "group songs" and "outdoor songs". They are divided into four types: songs for funeral ceremonies and sacrifices, songs for wedding ceremonies, friendship songs and "outdoor songs". All Buyi people are singers, and they sing these songs repeatedly when they do manual labor, in their daily life and at festivals, thus forming various versions of **Pange Songs of the Buyi Nationality**. Bimo (the high priest in the traditional religion of the Yi nationality) and matchmakers sing these songs in a normative way at the wedding ceremony, sacrificial ceremony and funeral ceremony. Singing in the Buyi language is a major feature of the inheritance of **Pange Songs of the Buyi Nationality**. There are three singing forms: solo singing, antiphonal singing, and one person leading the singing with others singing in chorus. The leading singer sings the poem and others sing foil words. Mostly, **Pange Songs of the Buyi Nationality** are sung in "joyful tune", "elderly tune", "sad tune", etc., and can be sung without music accompaniment or to the accompaniment of musical instruments. The commonly used accompaniment instruments are Yueqin (a four-stringed plucked musical instrument with a full-moon-shaped sound box), bamboo

贵州省·国家级非物质文化遗产文献资料汇编（汉英对照）

The Documentary Compilation of the State-level Intangible Cultural Heritage of Guizhou Province (Chinese-English Versions)

flutes, Xiaotong flutes, Muye (leaves), etc. **Pange Songs of the Buyi Nationality** are likened to "an encyclopedia without words" of the Buyi nationality, integrating the origin of humankind, the origin of the Buyi nationality, production and labor, the manner of dealing with people, ethics and morals, marriages, house building, funerals and sacrifices, etc. They are important carriers of the history and culture of the Buyi nationality.

珠郎娘美雕塑
Sculptures of Zhulang and Niangmei

第 5 项：
珠郎娘美

项目序号：560	项目编号：Ⅰ-73	公布时间：2008（第二批）	类别：民间文学
所属地区：贵州省	类型：新增项目	申报地区或单位：贵州省从江县、榕江县	

　　《珠郎娘美》是一个侗族民间故事，起源于贵州省榕江县，后流传于贵州省黎平、从江等县的侗族聚居地，再后流传到广西三江、龙胜、融水和湖南通道等侗族聚居县。①

　　《珠郎娘美》是发生在清乾隆年间的真人真事。乾隆年间，榕江侗族青年珠郎与娘美为寻求美满自由婚姻，不畏权势，敢于冲破封建约束双双远走他乡，在如今的贯洞村落脚相依为命，后珠郎被当地财主设计害死，娘美在乡亲的帮助下为珠郎复仇后毅然留在贯洞侗乡传教侗歌一生。在故事发生地从江县贯洞镇和庆云乡等地至今还保留有"娘美井""江剑坡"等遗迹。清乾隆年间以来，《珠郎娘美》凄美的爱情故事一直在侗乡广泛流传，脍炙人口，妇孺皆知。②这个爱情故事曾被改编成侗族曲艺、侗戏，并拍成同名舞台艺术片在全国放映。《珠郎娘美》是侗族传统民间艺术作品的代表。③

---

① 《珠郎娘美》，中国非物质文化遗产网，http://www.ihchina.cn/Article/Index/detail?id=12309，检索日期：2019 年 8 月 29 日。

② 《国家非遗〈珠郎娘美〉侗戏剧本原稿现世从江加紧抢救保护整理"完整版"》，贵州省非物质文化遗产保护中心官网，http://www.gzfwz.org.cn/xwdt/201804/t20180416_3122884.html，检索日期：2019 年 8 月 30 日。

③ 《珠郎娘美》，中国非物质文化遗产网，http://www.ihchina.cn/Article/Index/detail?id=12309，检索日期：2019 年 8 月 29 日。

贵州省 国家级非物质文化遗产文献资料汇编（汉英对照）

The Documentary Compilation of the State-level Intangible Cultural Heritage of Guizhou Province (Chinese-English Versions)

Item 5: *Zhulang and Niangmei Folktale*

Item Serial Number: 560	Item ID Number: I –73	Released Date: 2008 (Batch 2)	Category: Folk Literature
Affiliated Province: Guizhou Province	Type: New Item	Application Province or Unit: Congjiang County and Rongjiang County of Guizhou Province	

Zhulang and Niangmei Folktale is a folk story of the Dong nationality, which originates from Rongjiang County of Guizhou Province. Later, it has been spread to areas inhabited by the Dong nationality in Liping and Congjiang counties, and then farther to counties where the Dong people live in Sanjiang, Longsheng and Rongshui of Guangxi Zhuang Autonomous Region, as well as Tongdao of Hunan Province.

It is a true story that happened during the reign of Emperor Qianlong of the Qing Dynasty. During Emperor Qianlong's reign, two young people of the Dong nationality in Rongjiang County, Zhulang and Niangmei, both left home in order to pursue a happy and free marriage, bravely defying great power and daring to break through feudal constraints. They settled down in today's Guandong Village and lived together depending on each other for survival. Later, a local landlord made a conspiracy and killed Zhulang. After taking revenge for Zhulang with the help of villagers, Niangmei resolutely stayed in Guandong, the area inhabited by the Dong people, to teach folk songs of the Dong nationality all her life. In Guandong Township, Qingyun Township, etc. of Congjiang County, where the story took place, there are still relics of "Niangmei Well", "Jiangjian Slope", etc. Since the reign of Emperor Qianlong of the Qing Dynasty, this poignant and beautiful love story has been widely circulated in areas inhabited by the Dong people, winning universal praise and even well-known to women and children. This love story has once been adapted into Quyi (a general term for all Chinese talking-and-singing art forms) of the Dong nationality and Dong Opera, made into a stage play with the same name and screened nationwide. *Zhulang and Niangmei Folktale* is the representative of traditional folk artistic works of the Dong nationality.

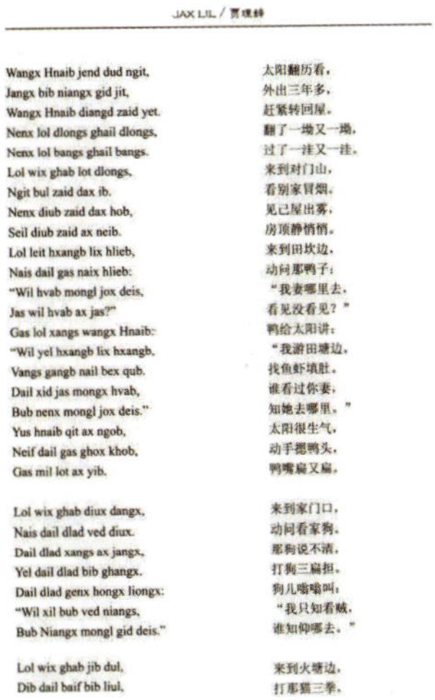

JAX LIL / 贾理辞

Wangx Hnaib jend dud ngit,	太阳翻历看，
Jangx bib niangx gid jit,	外出三年多，
Wangx Hnaib diangd zaid yet.	赶紧转回屋。
Nenx lol dlongs ghail dlongs,	翻了一坳又一坳，
Nenx lol bangs ghail bangs.	过了一洼又一洼。
Lol wix ghab lot dlongs,	来到对门山，
Ngit bul zaid dax ib.	看别家冒烟。
Nenx diub zaid dax hob,	见己屋出雾，
Seil diub zaid ax neib.	房顶静悄悄。
Lol leit hxangb lix hlieb,	来到田坎边，
Nais dail gas naix hlieb:	动问那鸭子：
"Wil hvab mongl jox deis,	"我妻哪里去，
Jas wil hvab ax jas?"	看见没看见？"
Gas lol xangs wangx Hnaib:	鸭给太阳讲：
"Wil yel hxangb lix hxangb,	"我游田塘边，
Vangs gangb nail bex qub.	找鱼虾填肚。
Dail xid jas mongx hvab,	谁看过你妻，
Bub nenx mongl jox deis."	知她去哪里。"
Yus hnaib qit ax ngob,	太阳很生气，
Neif dail gas ghox khob,	动手摁鸭头，
Gas mil lot ax yib.	鸭嘴扁又扁。
Lol wix ghab diux dangx,	来到家门口，
Nais dail dlad ved diux.	动问看家狗。
Dail dlad xangs ax jangx,	那狗说不清，
Yel dail dlad bib ghangx.	打狗三扁担。
Dail dlad genx hongx liongx:	狗儿嗡嗡叫：
"Wil xil bub ved niangs,	"我只知看贼，
Bub Niangx mongl gid deis."	谁知仰哪去。"
Lol wix ghab jib dul,	来到火塘边，
Dib dail baif bib liul,	打那猫三拳，

第 6 项：苗族贾理

苗族贾理节选（苗汉双语对照）

an Excerpt from Jaxlil of the Miao Nationality (Miao-Han Bilingual Versions)

项目序号：563	项目编号：Ⅰ-76	公布时间：2008（第二批）	类别：民间文学
所属地区：贵州省	类型：新增项目	申报地区或单位：贵州省黔东南苗族侗族自治州	

贾理，苗语叫“jaxlil”，是苗族以栽岩立法、理老司法和鼓社执法来维护苗族社会稳定和发展而形成的古规古理①，广泛流传于贵州黔东南州苗族支系。②

苗族贾理是黔东南苗族地区经典的历史文化记忆集成，集创世神话、族源传说、支系谱牒、知识技艺、原始宗教信俗、民俗仪礼、伦理道德、诉讼理辞和典型案例于一身，荟萃了苗族的原典文化，集中反映了苗族的精神情感和智慧意识。苗族贾理内容丰富，如《浑水与蝌蚪》以童话形式告诉人们，风有时候会造成一个个小的不和谐，但如风不吹，严冬常在，那就是最大的不和谐，天下就要大乱，风吹是为了复归于和谐。《曼朵多》则以一例两条人命案的故事来启发人们思想感情上更深层次的道德倾向与是非价值的判断。贾理是苗族言史述典的范本，也是苗族栽岩议榔、举行祭祀盛典和重大节庆活动的依据，

① 《苗族贾里的主要内容》，贵州文明网，http://gz.wenming.cn/zt/20170614_mzjl/20170614_jlwz/201706/t20170616_4300669.shtml，检索日期：2019 年 8 月 29 日。

② 《〈苗族贾理〉的特征和价值》，贵州文明网，http://gz.wenming.cn/zt/20170614_mzjl/20170614_jlwz/201706/t20170616_4300675.shtml，检索日期：2019 年 8 月 29 日。

· 贵州省 · 国家级非物质文化遗产文献资料汇编（汉英对照）

The Documentary Compilation of the State-level Intangible Cultural Heritage of Guizhou Province (Chinese-English Versions)

更是苗族先民言行必遵的神圣准则，在传承固有文化、塑造族人性格、促成民族认同、增强内聚力、实现对苗族社区的有效管理、推动苗族社会的有序发展等方面具有极其重要的作用。①

Item 6: Jaxlil of the Miao Nationality

Item Serial Number: 563	Item ID Number: I -76	Released Date: 2008 (Batch 2)	Category: Folk Literature
Affiliated Province: Guizhou Province	Type: New Item	Application Province or Unit: Qiandongnan Miao and Dong Autonomous Prefecture, Guizhou Province	

" 贾理 " is transcribed as "*Jaxlil*" in the Miao language. It is the ancient rules and principles formed to maintain the stability and development of the Miao society by means of planting rocks for legislation, performing judicial administration by leaders of stockaded villages and enforcing the law through drum communes. It is widely spread among the branches of the Miao nationality in Qiandongnan Miao and Dong Autonomous Prefecture, Guizhou Province.

Jaxlil of the Miao Nationality is a classic integration of the historical and cultural memory of the Miao areas in Qiandongnan Miao and Dong Autonomous Prefecture, which integrates the creation mythology, legends of the origin of the Miao nationality, genealogy of branches, knowledge and skills, primitive religious beliefs and customs, folk customs and etiquette, ethics and morals, litigation arguments and typical cases. It gathers the original classic culture of the Miao nationality and reflects its spiritual emotion and wisdom consciousness. **Jaxlil of the Miao Nationality** has rich content. For example, *Muddy Water and Tadpoles* tells people in the form of a fairy tale that wind sometimes causes small discord, but if wind stops blowing, the severe winter will last forever, which is the biggest disharmony, and then the world will be in chaos. Therefore, wind blows to restore harmony. *Manduoduo* inspires people's deeper moral inclination and judgment of right and wrong values at ideological and emotional levels through a murder case that involves the killing

---

① 《苗族贾理》，中国非物质文化遗产网，http://www. ihchina. cn/Article/Index/detail? id=12313，检索日期：2019 年 8 月 29 日。

of two people. **Jaxlil of the Miao Nationality** is an exemplary model for recording history and narrating classics of the Miao nationality, and also a basis for the Miao people to plant rocks and perform Yilang activity, and to hold grand sacrificial ceremonies and festival celebrations. What's more, it is a sacred criterion that the Miao ancestors must abide by in words and deeds. It plays an extremely important role in inheriting the intrinsic culture, shaping the ethnic character, promoting the ethnic identity, enhancing cohesive force, realizing the effective management of the Miao community and promoting the orderly development of the Miao society.

第 7 项：
亚鲁王

祭祀祖先亚鲁王
Offering Sacrifices to King Yalu, the Ancestor

项目序号：1062	项目编号：Ⅰ-118	公布时间：2011（第三批）	类别：民间文学
所属地区：贵州省	类型：新增项目	申报地区或单位：贵州省紫云苗族布依族自治县	

　　《亚鲁王》是苗族的一部英雄史诗，长 2.6 万余行。公元前 2033 年至公元前 1562 年，苗族史诗《亚鲁王》就有了雏形。

　　史诗唱述亚鲁王国 17 代王创世、立国、创业及发展的故事；还描述在公元前 221 年至公元前 202 年，亚鲁王带领王国的苗民迁徙到贵州，先后开发定都于"商都卜"（贵阳）和"阿代卜"（安顺），最后定都麻山的历史。史诗主要描述亚鲁王国 200 多个王族后裔的谱系及其迁徙征战的故事，涉及古代人物 1 万余人，古苗语地名 400 余个，古战场 20 余个，至今口头传承于麻山苗族地区的 3000 多名歌师中，常在麻山一带苗族丧葬仪式中唱诵，是对亡灵返回亚鲁王国时代历史的神圣唱诵。史诗的吟唱，用的是西部苗族语言，表现形式灵活多变。有时用叙事形式朗读吟唱，有时用道白形式问答，大量出现反复、重叠和比兴的表现手法，诗以散文诗为主，歌唱的曲调低沉悲凉。[1] 该史诗以口口相传的形式为苗族的古代史提供了不朽的民族记忆，传递了艰苦卓绝、自强不息的求生存、求发展的民族精神，为已有的世界史诗谱系增添了一种新的样式。[2]

---

[1]　《亚鲁王》，中国非物质文化遗产网，http://www.ihchina.cn/Article/Index/detail?id=12366，检索日期：2019 年 8 月 29 日。

[2]　《"非遗"〈亚鲁王〉：一部活在口头的英雄史诗》，中国非物质文化遗产网，http://www.ihchina.cn/Article/Index/detail?id=8047，检索日期：2019 年 8 月 29 日。

Item 7: *King Yalu*

Item Serial Number: 1062	Item ID Number: I -118	Released Date: 2011 (Batch 3)	Category: Folk Literature
Affiliated Province: Guizhou Province	Type: New Item	Application Province or Unit: Ziyun Miao and Buyi Autonomous Prefecture, Guizhou Province	

King Yalu is a heroic epic of the Miao nationality, with over 26,000 lines. It began to take shape from 2033 BC to 1562 BC.

The epic narrates the story of creating the world, establishing the kingdom, setting up a career and developing it of the 17th-generation king of the Kingdom of Yalu. It also narrates the history about how King Yalu led the Miao people to migrate to Guizhou from 221 BC to 202 BC, exploited and established the capital of the kingdom in Shangdubu (now called Guiyang City) and Adaibu (now called Anshun City) successively, and finally settled down in Mashan (now called Mashan Township). This epic mainly describes the genealogy of over 200 royal descendants in the Kingdom of Yalu and their stories of migration and wars, involving more than 10,000 ancient figures, more than 400 names of ancient places in the Miao language, and more than 20 ancient battlefields. Up to now, it has been orally inherited by over 3,000 singers in the Miao Region of Mashan. It is often sung in the funeral ceremony of the Miao nationality in Mashan, being a sacred chanting of the history of the souls of the deceased returning to the Kingdom of Yalu. The epic is sung in western Miao language, with flexible and varied forms of expression. Sometimes, it is read aloud and sung in narrative form, while sometimes it is performed through asking and answering questions in the form of Daobai (spoken parts in an opera). It uses a large number of techniques of expression, such as repetition, overlapping, Bi (analogy) and Xing (borrowing) techniques. *King Yalu* is mainly a prose poem, and its singing tune is low and sad. This epic provides an immortal ethnic memory for the ancient history of the Miao nationality by word of mouth, and conveys the national spirit of striving for survival and development through arduous efforts and continuous self-improvement, which has added a new form to the existing epic genealogy of the world.

第二章
传统音乐

Chapter Two
Traditional Music

第 1-2 项:
侗族大歌

侗族大歌比赛
the Singing Competition of Al Laox of the Dong Nationality

项目序号：59	项目编号：Ⅱ-28	公布时间：2006（第一批）	类别：传统音乐
所属地区：贵州省	类型：新增项目	申报地区或单位：贵州省黎平县	

项目序号：59	项目编号：Ⅱ-28	公布时间：2008（第二批）	类别：传统音乐
所属地区：贵州省	类型：扩展项目	申报地区或单位：贵州省从江县、榕江县	

　　侗族大歌，侗语称"嘎老"，"嘎"即歌，"老"既有大之意，又有人多、声多、古老之意，是中国侗族南部方言区由民间歌队演唱的一种民间合唱音乐，流行于黎平、从江和榕江等县。

　　侗族大歌一般在村寨或氏族之间集体做客的场合中演唱，是侗人文化和情感交流的核心内容，主要包括鼓楼大歌、声音大歌、叙事大歌、情歌、伦理大歌、礼俗大歌、儿歌、戏曲大歌和老人歌等形式。每首歌均由"歌头""歌身"和"歌尾"三部分组成。声部通常为二声部，侗族民间称为"雄音"（高声部）和"雌音"（低声部）。侗族大歌最小的结构单位称"角"（jogx，汉译为"句"）；若干"角"构成一"省"（sengh，汉译为"段"）；若干"省"构成一"枚"（meix，汉译为"首"）。如此累加聚合，形成分节歌性质的多段联缀体，体现出各类大歌的基本结构。侗族大歌绝大多数无需乐器伴奏。除叙事歌外，男声演唱侗族大歌均可用大琵琶伴奏。[1] 侗族大歌多用真嗓演唱，旋律优美动听，被誉为世界"最美的天籁之音"。作为多声部民曲，它在多声思维、多声形态、合唱技艺、文化内涵等方面所达到的水平均为世所罕见。代表曲目有《耶老歌》《嘎高胜》《嘎音也》《嘎戏》《蝉歌》等。侗族没有文字，大歌全靠"桑嘎"（歌师）口头教唱，世代传承。[2]

Items 1-2: Al Laox of the Dong Nationality

Item Serial Number: 59	Item ID Number: Ⅱ-28	Released Date: 2006 (Batch 1)	Category: Traditional Music
Affiliated Province: Guizhou Province	Type: New Item	Application Province or Unit: Liping County, Guizhou Province	

Item Serial Number: 59	Item ID Number: Ⅱ-28	Released Date: 2008 (Batch 2)	Category: Traditional Music
Affiliated Province: Guizhou Province	Type: Extended Item	Application Province or Unit: Congjiang County and Rongjiang County of Guizhou Province	

Al Laox of the Dong Nationality is pronounced as "al laox" in the Dong language. The word "al" refers to songs, and "laox" means "big", "many people", "multiple sounds" and "antiquity". It is a kind of folk choral music performed by folk

---

① 《侗族大歌》，中国非物质文化遗产网，http://www.ihchina.cn/Article/Index/detail?id=12467，检索日期：2019 年 9 月 7 日。

② 《侗族大歌》，中国非物质文化遗产网，http://www.ihchina.cn/Article/Index/detail?id=12465，检索日期：2019 年 8 月 18 日。

song teams in the southern dialect area of the Dong nationality in China, very popular in Liping, Congjiang and Rongjiang counties.

Al Laox of the Dong Nationality is generally sung on the occasion of paying a group visit between different stockaded villages or clans, which is the core content of the Dong people's cultural and emotional communication. It mainly includes the Drum Tower al laox, sound al laox, narrative al laox, love songs, ethical al laox, etiquette-and-custom al laox, children's songs, opera al laox and old people's songs. Each song consists of three parts: "song head", "song body" and "song tail". Usually, there are two voice parts, which are called "male voice" (high voice part) and "female voice" (low voice part) by the Dong people. The smallest structural unit of **Al Laox of the Dong Nationality** is called "jogx" in the Dong language, which is translated as "句 (sentence)" in Chinese. Several "jogx" constitute a "sengh" in the Dong language, which is translated as "段 (passage)" in Chinese; and then several "sengh" compose a "meix" in the Dong language, which is translated as "首 (a piece)" in Chinese. Accumulated and aggregated in this way, the multi-segment combinations in strophic form are formed, which embodies the basic structure of various kinds of al laox. The majority of **Al Laox of the Dong Nationality** need no accompaniment of musical instruments. Except narrative songs, the male singing of **Al Laox of the Dong Nationality** can be performed to the accompaniment of Big Pipa (a plucked string instrument with a fretted fingerboard). **Al Laox of the Dong Nationality** is often sung by using real voice with a beautiful melody, acclaimed as "the most beautiful sound of nature" in the world. As a kind of multi-voice folk song, it has reached an extremely high level in multi-voice thinking, multi-voice form, choral technique, cultural connotation, etc. The representative songs include "Yelao Song", "Gagaosheng", "Gayinye", "Gaxi" and "A Song of Cicadas". The Dong nationality has no written language, so al laox is taught to be sung orally by "Sangga" (the singer), passed down from generation to generation.

第 3–4 项：

侗族琵琶歌

侗族琵琶歌演奏
the Performance of Pipa Songs of the Dong Nationality

项目序号：60	项目编号：Ⅱ-29	公布时间：2006（第一批）	类别：传统音乐
所属地区：贵州省	类型：新增项目	申报地区或单位：贵州省榕江县、黎平县	

项目序号：60	项目编号：Ⅱ-29	公布时间：2011（第三批）	类别：传统音乐
所属地区：贵州省	类型：扩展项目	申报地区或单位：贵州省从江县	

　　侗族琵琶歌分布于侗族南部方言区，分为抒情琵琶歌和叙事琵琶歌两类。歌唱内容涵盖侗族历史、神话、传说、故事、古规古理、生产经验、婚恋情爱、风尚习俗和社会交往等方面。由于各地琵琶歌使用的琵琶型号和定弦的不同，土语不同，演唱场所不同，运用嗓音不同，形成了多种风格的琵琶歌。贵州省流传的侗族琵琶歌主要有五种：三宝琵琶歌、晚寨琵琶歌、六洞琵琶歌、榕江琵琶歌和平架琵琶歌，均属于抒情琵琶歌。

　　（1）三宝琵琶歌。用中型四弦琵琶伴奏，外加牛腿琴协奏，由男子操琴，男奏男唱或男奏女唱，男声用本嗓，女声用小嗓，在行歌坐夜的场合演唱，主要流行在榕江县三宝侗寨及周边地区。（2）晚寨琵琶歌。男声用三弦或五弦的大中型琵琶伴奏，女声用三弦或五弦的中小型琵琶伴奏，均为自弹自唱。主要流行在榕江、黎平两县毗连的四十八寨地区和榕江县的七十二寨地区。（3）六洞琵琶歌。用四弦小琵琶伴奏，男弹男唱或男弹女唱，在行歌坐夜的场合演唱，原先男女声均用假嗓，现在也有改用本嗓的，主要流行在黎平、从江两县泛称为"六洞""千五"和"十洞"的地区。（4）榕江琵琶歌。

抒情、叙事兼具，演唱形式、演唱场所和演唱内容与六洞弹唱相同，主要流行在广西壮族自治区三江县、融水县溶江河段和黎平县以"四脚牛"为中心的地区。（5）平架琵琶歌。由男子用三弦小琵琶伴奏，男弹男唱或男弹女唱，男女声均用假嗓，主要流行在黎平县洪州镇的平架村。其最大特征是男女均用假嗓高音演唱，曲调悠扬，歌词丰富，种类包括情歌、孝敬老人歌和叙事歌等。[①]侗族琵琶歌的唱词体现了侗族诗歌的最高水平。

Items 3-4: Pipa Songs of the Dong Nationality

Item Serial Number: 60	Item ID Number: Ⅱ-29	Released Date: 2006 (Batch 1)	Category: Traditional Music
Affiliated Province: Guizhou Province	Type: New Item	Application Province or Unit: Rongjiang County and Liping County of Guizhou Province	

Item Serial Number: 60	Item ID Number: Ⅱ-29	Released Date: 2011 (Batch 3)	Category: Traditional Music
Affiliated Province: Guizhou Province	Type: Extended Item	Application Province or Unit: Congjiang County, Guizhou Province	

Pipa Songs of the Dong Nationality are distributed in the southern dialect area of the Dong nationality, which can be divided into two categories: lyrical Pipa songs and narrative Pipa songs. Their content covers the history, myths, legends, stories, ancient rules, production experience, marriage and love, prevailing custom, social contacts, etc. of the Dong nationality. Due to the differences in types of Pipa (a plucked string instrument with a fretted fingerboard), tuning up, local dialects, singing places and usage of voices for the performance of Pipa songs in different localities, various styles of Pipa songs have been formed. There are five kinds of **Pipa Songs of the Dong Nationality** circulated in Guizhou Province: Sanbao Pipa songs, Wanzhai Pipa songs, Liudong Pipa songs, Rongjiang Pipa songs and Pingjia Pipa songs, all of which belong to lyrical Pipa songs.

(1) Sanbao Pipa songs. They are performed to the accompaniment of medium

---

① 《侗族琵琶歌》，中国非物质文化遗产网，http://www.ihchina.cn/Article/Index/detail?id=12469，检索日期：2019 年 8 月 13 日。

four-stringed Pipa (a plucked string instrument with a fretted fingerboard) as well as Niutui Lute (a bow-and-string instrument of the Dong nationality, named for its slender body looking like cattle's thigh), all played by men. Singers can be either male or female. Male singers use their own voices, while female singers use small voices. They are sung on the occasion of Xingge Zuoye (singing songs while sitting through the night, a custom of the Dong nationality for young men and women to sing love songs and get to know each other), mainly spread in Sanbao Dong Stockaded Villages and the surrounding areas in Rongjiang County. (2) Wanzhai Pipa songs. The male voice is accompanied by large- and medium-sized Pipa (a plucked string instrument with a fretted fingerboard) with three or five strings, and the female voice is accompanied by medium- and small-sized Pipa (a plucked string instrument with a fretted fingerboard) with three or five strings. All are played and sung by singers themselves. They are mainly popular in the 48 stockaded villages bordering Rongjiang and Liping counties and the 72 stockaded villages in Rongjiang County. (3) Liudong Pipa songs. Their singing is accompanied by small four-stringed Pipa (a plucked string instrument with a fretted fingerboard) played by men, and singers can be male or female. They are sung on the occasion of Xingge Zuoye (singing songs while sitting through the night, a custom of the Dong nationality for young men and women to sing love songs and get to know each other). At first, both male and female singers used false voices, but now some singers use their real voices. Liudong Pipa songs are mainly spread in areas commonly referred to as "Liudong", "Qianwu" and "Shidong" in Liping and Congjiang counties. (4) Rongjiang Pipa songs. They are both lyrical and narrative. Their singing forms, places and content are the same as those of Liudong playing and singing. They are mainly circulated in Sanjiang County and the Rongjiang River section of Rongshui County in Guangxi Zhuang Autonomous Region, as well as areas centered on "Four-legged Cattle District" in Liping County. (5) Pingjia Pipa songs. They are sung to the accompaniment of small three-stringed Pipa (a plucked string instrument with a fretted fingerboard) played by men, and singers can be male or female. Both male and female singers use false voices. Pingjia Pipa songs are mainly popular in Pingjia Village, Hongzhou Township, Liping County. Their greatest feature is that they are sung in high-pitched false voices by male and female singers with melodious tunes and rich lyrics. They are divided into love songs, songs of showing filial piety to the elderly, narrative songs, etc. The lyrics of **Pipa Songs of the Dong Nationality** reflect the highest level of the Dong poetry.

铜鼓十二调演奏
the Performance of Twelve Tunes of the Bronze Drum

第 5 项： 铜鼓十二调

项目序号：91	项目编号：Ⅱ-60	公布时间：2006（第一批）	类别：传统音乐
所属地区：贵州省	类型：新增项目	申报地区或单位：贵州省镇宁布依族苗族自治县、贞丰县	

　　铜鼓是布依族古老的打击乐器之一，用青铜铸造而成，常与唢呐、皮鼓、大镲、铙钹、锣和木棍混合敲击吹奏，保存了古代乐器的演奏风格，具有布依族的民族特色，被布依族人视为传家宝和氏族、宗教团结的象征，敬若神灵，年年施祭。布依族铜鼓十二调源于古代，流传在扁担山、丁旗镇、大山乡、城关镇、六马乡、沙子乡、良田乡和募役乡等布依族聚居区，并辐射到周边的布依族地区，形成了一个覆盖几县的布依族民间铜鼓文化圈。

　　布依族铜鼓十二调主要由"喜鹊调""散花调""祭鼓调""祭祖调""三六九调""祭祀调"和"喜庆调"组成，在庆典、祭祖和祭祀等仪式中演奏。贞丰县是一个多民族聚居的地区，其中布依族聚居的自然村寨有四百多个。贞丰布依族称铜鼓十二调为"铜鼓十二则"。布依族没有文字，"铜鼓十二则"以家族方式传承，一代代通过口传心授沿袭下来。作为民族文化和区域文化的重要组成部分，铜鼓始终与布依族的生活、文化样式联系在一起。铜鼓十二调是内容丰富的古代音乐作品和古代音乐信息的宝库。[①]

---

①　《铜鼓十二调》，中国非物质文化遗产网，http://www.ihchina.cn/Article/Index/detail?id=12584，检索日期：2019 年 8 月 26 日。

Item 5: Twelve Tunes of the Bronze Drum

Item Serial Number: 91	Item ID Number: Ⅱ-60	Released Date: 2006 (Batch 1)	Category: Traditional Music
Affiliated Province: Guizhou Province	Type: New Item	Application Province or Unit: Zhenning Buyi and Miao Autonomous County and Zhenfeng County of Guizhou Province	

The Bronze Drum is one of the ancient percussion instruments of the Buyi nationality, made of bronze, which is often played with Suona Horn (a woodwind instrument), the Leather Drum, big cymbals, cymbals, gongs and wooden sticks. It preserves the playing style of ancient musical instruments and has ethnic characteristics of the Buyi nationality. It is regarded as an heirloom and a symbol of the clan and religious unity by the Buyi people, respected like a deity and worshiped every year. **Twelve Tunes of the Bronze Drum** of the Buyi nationality originated from ancient times. They are circulated in areas inhabited by the Buyi people, such as the Biandan Mountain, Dingqi Township, Dashan Township, Chengguan Township, Liuma Township, Shazi Township, Liangtian Township and Muyi Township, and radiate to the surrounding Buyi regions, which have formed a folk bronze-drum culture circle of the Buyi nationality covering several counties.

Twelve Tunes of the Bronze Drum of the Buyi nationality are played in ceremonies of celebrations, ancestor worship, offering sacrifices, etc. They are composed of "Magpie Tune", "Sanhua Tune", "Drum Worship Tune", "Ancestor Worship Tune", "3-6-9 Tune", "Sacrifice-offering Tune" and "Festive Tune". Zhenfeng County is a multi-ethnic area where there are more than 400 natural stockaded villages inhabited by the Buyi nationality. The Buyi people in Zhenfeng County refer to **Twelve Tunes of the Bronze Drum** as "Twelve Musical Pieces of the Bronze Drum". The Buyi nationality has no written language, so "Twelve Musical Pieces of the Bronze Drum" are passed down within families from generation to generation through oral instruction. As an important part of the national and regional cultures, the Bronze Drum is always associated with the life and cultural forms of the Buyi nationality. **Twelve Tunes of the Bronze Drum** are a treasure trove of ancient music works and ancient music information that are rich in content.

第6-7项：
苗族民歌（苗族飞歌）

苗族飞歌演唱
the Singing of Flying Songs of the Miao Nationality

项目序号：608	项目编号：Ⅱ-109	公布时间：2008（第二批）	类别：传统音乐
所属地区：贵州省	类型：新增项目	申报地区或单位：贵州省雷山县	

项目序号：608	项目编号：Ⅱ-109	公布时间：2011（第三批）	类别：传统音乐
所属地区：贵州省	类型：扩展项目	申报地区或单位：贵州省剑河县	

　　苗族飞歌，苗语为"HXak Yangt"，是苗族特有的民歌形式。贵州省的苗族飞歌主要流传于雷山县和剑河县等的苗族居住区。

　　苗族飞歌的演唱内容主要根据不同的活动来确定，田间劳作、结婚、嫁女、生子、起房造屋、谈情说爱、过年过节、走亲访友等都可以飞歌。[1] 其曲调高亢、豪迈奔放，演唱形式分独唱、对唱和合唱。苗族飞歌的起腔以真声为核心音调，明快动听，感染力极强；正腔运用假声，音调高昂，音色丰满响亮，气势雄浑，飞扬荡漾，故有"飞歌"之称。苗族飞歌节奏舒缓自由，旋律起伏性大，长音处尽量使气息延长，句间可自由休止，句内用滑音连续级进，句尾收腔使用甩音，歌唱结束时运用假嗓，附加一声高昂的"啊呼"，更显热情奔放。飞歌多采用五言诗句，主题鲜明，形式简短。代表作有《赞美家乡歌》《祝福老人歌》等。苗族飞歌综合运用词、曲、假声和真声等因素，通过对节奏缓急、停顿和延续等技巧的熟练把握，将词、曲、调熔于一炉，充分体现了诗、乐、舞三者合一的艺术境界。飞歌明快的音调、动听的旋律和直抒胸臆的表现方式展现了苗族音乐的基本特征。[2]

---

① 《苗族民歌（苗族飞歌）》，中国非物质文化遗产网，http://www.ihchina.cn/Article/Index/detail?id=12662，检索日期：2019年9月7日。

② 《苗族民歌（苗族飞歌）》，中国非物质文化遗产网，http://www.ihchina.cn/Article/Index/detail?id=12661，检索日期：2019年9月7日。

Items 6-7: Folk Songs of the Miao Nationality
(Flying Songs of the Miao Nationality)

Item Serial Number: 608	Item ID Number: II-109	Released Date: 2008 (Batch 2)	Category: Traditional Music
Affiliated Province: Guizhou Province	Type: New Item	Application Province or Unit: Leishan County, Guizhou Province	

Item Serial Number: 608	Item ID Number: II-109	Released Date: 2011 (Batch 3)	Category: Traditional Music
Affiliated Province: Guizhou Province	Type: Extended Item	Application Province or Unit: Jianhe County, Guizhou Province	

Flying Songs of the Miao Nationality, called "HXakYangt" in the Miao Language, is a unique folk song form of the Miao nationality. The **Flying Songs of the Miao Nationality** in Guizhou Province are mainly circulated in areas inhabited by the Miao people in Leishan County and Jianhe County.

The content for the singing of **Flying Songs of the Miao Nationality** is mainly determined according to different activities: field work, getting married, marrying off one's daughter, giving birth to a baby, building a house, dating and courting, celebrating the Spring Festival and other festivals, visiting relatives and friends, etc. Their tunes are high-pitched, bold and unrestrained, and their singing forms are divided into solo singing, antiphonal singing and chorusing. The starting tone of **Flying Songs of the Miao Nationality** takes real voice as the core tone, bright and melodious, with strong appeal. Their main tone uses false voice, with a high pitch, a full and loud timbre and vigorous momentum, flying and rippling, so they are referred to as "Flying Songs". **Flying Songs of the Miao Nationality** are soothing and free in rhythms, and fluctuate greatly in melody. When singing a long note, singers prolong the breath as long as possible. They can stop anywhere between sentences at will, use the glide note for continuous progression in sentences, and employ the flinging note at the end of the sentence. When the singing comes to an end, they will use false voice, with a high pitch of "ah-hoo" added, to make it more enthusiastic and unrestrained. **Flying Songs** often adopt five-character poems with distinct themes and short forms. The representative songs are "A Song of Praising

贵州省 国家级非物质文化遗产文献资料汇编（汉英对照）

The Documentary Compilation of the State-level Intangible Cultural Heritage of Guizhou Province (Chinese-English Versions)

the Hometown", "A Song of Blessing the Elderly", etc. **Flying Songs of the Miao Nationality** comprehensively use factors of lyrics, melodies, false voice, real voice, etc. Through skillfully mastering the skills of the slowing, quickening, pause and continuation of rhythms, they integrate lyrics, melodies and tunes into one, and fully embody the artistic realm of the combination of poetry, music and dance. The bright tunes, beautiful melodies and straightforward expression of emotions of Flying Songs display the basic characteristics of the Miao music.

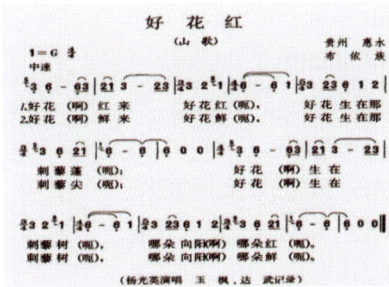

好花红调
Haohuahong Tune

第8项：
布依族民歌（好花红调）

项目序号：611	项目编号：Ⅱ-112	公布时间：2008（第二批）	类别：传统音乐
所属地区：贵州省	类型：新增项目	申报地区或单位：贵州省惠水县	

　　好花红调是布依族人叙唱情爱的歌曲，发源于贵州省惠水县好花红乡的布依族山寨，在惠水、青岩、花溪、龙里和贵定等地广泛流传。

　　好花红调中的"好花"指的是布依族村寨随处可见的刺藜花，过去布依族人演唱这一曲调是为了联络感情，寻找意中人，故必须选择场合，不能随口就唱。男女双方对唱情歌时，先唱敬客歌，再唱问候歌，然后唱抬爱歌。唱到"二八栏杆"时，双方经过试探，情意已相当融洽，即以"好花红"为歌头对唱。好花红调旋律简单，包括由四句构成的两个乐段。歌词七字四句，采用比兴手法抒情达意。曲子由"6、1、2、3、5"五音组成，第二乐段对第一乐段进行反复，形成并行乐段，旋律一直围绕"6"音展开，最后两个乐段的结束音都落在主音上。

　　好花红调在继承布依族民歌原有曲调的基础上，吸纳了汉族山歌七字四句的样式，逐渐形成具有独特地域风格的惠水山歌调，其简约明快、悠扬婉转的曲调和清新简练、寓意深远的歌词表现了布依族人民健康的生活情趣，成为布依族传统文化变迁的形象印证。①

---

① 《布依族民歌（好花红调）》，中国非物质文化遗产网，http://www.ihchina.cn/Article/Index/detail?id=12668，检索日期：2019年8月23日。

Item 8: Folk Songs of the Buyi Nationality (Haohuahong Tune)

Item Serial Number: 611	Item ID Number: II-112	Released Date: 2008 (Batch 2)	Category: Traditional Music
Affiliated Province: Guizhou Province	Type: New Item	Application Province or Unit: Huishui County, Guizhou Province	

Haohuahong Tune is the Buyi people's song of narrating and singing love, originated from the stockaded villages of the Buyi nationality in Haohuahong Township, Huishui County, Guizhou Province. It is widely circulated in Huishui County, Qingyan Ancient Town, Huaxi District, Longli County, Guiding County, etc.

"Haohua" in **Haohuahong Tune** refers to the prickly pear flowers that can be seen everywhere in the stockaded villages of the Buyi nationality. In the past, the Buyi people sang this tune for the purpose of making friendly contact to find the beloved, so they had to choose the occasion of singing and could not sing it casually. When the male and female parties perform the antiphonal singing of love songs, they begin with the song of respecting guests, then change to sing the song of greeting, and finally sing the song of favoring. After sounding out each other, both sides have arrived at "Erba Langan", which means that they have gained harmonious affections. At this time, they start their antiphonal singing with "Haohuahong" as the beginning of the song. The melody of **Haohuahong Tune** is simple, including two musical passages that are made up of four sentences. For the lyric, there are four sentences with each having seven words. Bi (analogy) and Xing (borrowing) techniques are adopted to express thoughts and feelings. The tune is composed of the five musical notes of "6, 1, 2, 3 and 5", with the second musical passage repeating the first to form parallel ones, and the melody always revolving around the musical note of "6". The final notes of the last two passages all fall on the main musical note.

Based on inheriting the original tunes of the Buyi folk songs, **Haohuahong Tune** has absorbed the seven-word-and-four-sentence style of the Mountain Songs of the Han nationality, and gradually developed the tune of Huishui Mountain Songs with unique regional characteristics. The simple, bright, melodious and tactful tunes, as well as the fresh and concise lyrics with profound implications show the healthy life interest of the Buyi people, and has become the vivid confirmation of the changes of the traditional Buyi culture.

苗族芒筒芦笙表演
the Performance of Mangtong and Lusheng of the Miao Nationality

第9项：
芦笙音乐（苗族芒筒芦笙）

项目序号：628	项目编号：Ⅱ-129	公布时间：2008（第二批）	类别：传统音乐
所属地区：贵州省	类型：新增项目	申报地区或单位：贵州省丹寨县	

　　苗族芒筒芦笙乐舞是一种独特的民族民间艺术，主要流传于贵州省丹寨县的苗族村寨和邻近的雷山、榕江、三都县及都匀市的部分地区。

　　芒筒芦笙是苗族人重要的乐器，定居于丹寨的苗民世代谨守传统风习，使芒筒芦笙乐舞一直保持着原初的宗教功能。苗族芒筒芦笙乐舞每队16人，共有芦笙3支、芒筒13支。吹奏时，芦笙领奏于前，芒筒随奏于后，沿顺逆时针方向围成圆圈，且吹且舞。众人以脚蹬地，发出整齐的舞步声，与乐音相应和。作为苗族古老的乐器，芒筒芦笙的主要功能是娱神，多用于大型庆典、祭祖和丧葬等活动，尤以丧葬场合使用最多。重大庆典时，芒筒芦笙往往在迎送祖鼓、斗牛场激牛和竞技场助威等活动中伴奏。其曲目众多，其中用于祭祀的曲调有"怀祖曲""邀约曲""离别曲"等，用于丧葬的曲调有"过路曲""进门曲""悲伤曲""送别曲""安慰曲""离别曲"等。苗族芒筒芦笙的演奏方式独特，曲调悲壮肃穆，在苗族文化生活中占有非常重要的地位。[①]

---

① 《芦笙音乐（苗族芒筒芦笙）》，中国非物质文化遗产网，http://www.ihchina.cn/Article/Index/detail?id=12729，检索日期：2019年8月23日。

贵州省·国家级非物质文化遗产文献资料汇编（汉英对照）

The Documentary Compilation of the State-level Intangible Cultural Heritage of Guizhou Province (Chinese-English Versions)

Item 9: Lusheng Music (Mangtong and Lusheng of the Miao Nationality)

Item Serial Number: 628	Item ID Number: II-129	Released Date: 2008 (Batch 2)	Category: Traditional Music
Affiliated Province: Guizhou Province	Type: New Item	Application Province or Unit: Danzhai County, Guizhou Province	

Mangtong-Lusheng Musical Dance of the Miao Nationality is a unique ethnic folk art, mainly spread in the villages of the Miao nationality in Danzhai County, and neighboring Leishan County, Rongjiang County, Sandu County, as well as parts of Duyun City in Guizhou Province.

Mangtong and Lusheng are important musical instruments of the Miao nationality. The Miao people who live in Danzhai County have kept the traditional custom for generations, which makes Mangtong-Lusheng Musical Dance maintain its original religious function. There are sixteen people, three Lusheng Musical Instruments and thirteen Mangtong in each team of Mangtong-Lusheng Musical Dance of the Miao Nationality. During the performance, with Lusheng Musical Instruments in the front of the team and Mangtong following, performers form a circle in the clockwise or counterclockwise directions, blowing the musical instruments while dancing. All performers stamp their feet and make neat dance steps in accordance with the music. As the ancient musical instruments of the Miao nationality, the main function of Mangtong and Lusheng is entertaining gods, mostly played in large-scale celebrations, ancestor worship, funerals, etc. Especially on the occasion of funerals, they are played most. In grand celebrations, they often act as the accompaniment musical instrument in the activities such as greeting and seeing off the Ancestral Drum, stimulating the bull in bullfighting and cheering in the arena. There are many tunes, among which the tunes used for offering sacrifices are "A Tune of Nostalgia for Ancestors", "A Tune of Invitation", "A Tune of Departure", etc.; and the tunes used for funerals are "A Tune of Passing by", "A Tune of Entering the Door", "A Tune of Sorrow", "A Tune of Bidding Farewell", "A Tune of Comforting", "A Tune of Departure", etc. **Mangtong and Lusheng of the Miao Nationality** are played in a unique way with solemn and tragic tunes, playing a very important role in the cultural life of the Miao nationality.

第10项：
布依族勒尤

布依族勒尤演奏
the Performance of Leyou Musical Instrument of the Buyi Nationality

项目序号：629	项目编号：Ⅱ-130	公布时间：2008（第二批）	类别：传统音乐
所属地区：贵州省	类型：新增项目	申报地区或单位：贵州省贞丰县、兴义市、镇宁布依族苗族自治县	

　　布依族勒尤是一种木制的双簧直吹乐器，流传于贵州省黔西南州兴义市及南北盘江沿岸的布依族聚居区。"勒尤"系布依语译音，意为"对情人发出信号的小喇叭"或"唤醒情人的小喇叭"。这种乐器古已有之，至今有200多年的历史。勒尤出现以后，为布依族八音坐唱乐班所采用，成为重要的演奏乐器。

　　勒尤管身长约40厘米，由共鸣筒、管身、铜箍、芯子和虫哨五部分组成，音域a-a1。演奏时主要采用自然换气法和循环换气法，技巧丰富，发音甜美，具有圆润流畅、优美动听的艺术风格，长于表情达意。勒尤演奏的曲调名为《勒尤调》，常以《思念调》《喊妹调》《浪哨调》等冠名，可分为两类：（1）用勒尤吹奏的器乐曲，代表作有《喊妹调》等；（2）用勒尤曲调填词演唱的声乐曲，代表作有《浪哨调》《勒尤的思念》等。勒尤演奏只在首尾稍稍表现出一些规律，其他部分相对自由，吹奏者可随意发挥，同一曲调每次吹奏都会有很大变化。布依族勒尤演奏艺术是布依人在长期生产生活中创造出的独特民族音乐形式，体现了布依族的生活观念和艺术才能。[1]

---

① 《布依族勒尤》，中国非物质文化遗产网，http://www.ihchina.cn/Article/Index/detail?id=12732，检索日期：2019年8月25日。

Item 10: Leyou Musical Instrument of the Buyi Nationality

Item Serial Number: 629	Item ID Number: Ⅱ-130	Released Date: 2008 (Batch 2)	Category: Traditional Music
Affiliated Province: Guizhou Province	Type: New Item	Application Province or Unit: Zhenfeng County, Xingyi City and Zhenning Buyi and Miao Autonomous County of Guizhou Province	

Leyou Musical Instrument of the Buyi Nationality is a kind of vertically-blowing double-reed wooden musical instrument, which is spread in Xingyi City, Qianxinan Prefecture and the areas inhabited by the Buyi people along the North and South Panjiang Rivers in Guizhou Province. "Leyou" is a transliteration of the Buyi language, meaning "a small horn that sends signals to a lover" or "a small horn that awakens a lover". This musical instrument has been in existence since ancient times, with a history of more than 200 years up to now. After its appearance, it has been adopted by the troupes of Bayin Sitting-and-singing of the Buyi Nationality, and has become an important musical instrument of performance.

The tube of **Leyou Musical Instrument** is about 40 cm in length, consisting of five parts: a resonance tube, the tube body, a copper hoop, the core and an insect whistle, with the register of a-a1. During the process of performance, players mainly adopt natural ventilation method and cyclic ventilation method, with diverse skills to produce sweet sound, which has the artistic style of being round, smooth, beautiful and pleasant to hear, skilled in conveying ideas and feelings. The tunes played by using **Leyou Musical Instrument** are called "Tunes of Leyou Musical Instrument", often named as "Tunes of Missing", "Tunes of Calling Girls" and "Langshao Tunes". They can be divided into two categories: (1) The instrumental music compositions played by using **Leyou Musical Instrument**. The representative song is "Tunes of Calling Girls", etc.; (2) The vocal music compositions sung by using Tunes of Leyou Musical Instrument. The representative songs are "Langshao Tunes", "Missing Leyou Musical Instrument", etc. The playing of **Leyou Musical Instrument** only shows some rules at the beginning and the end, and the other parts are relatively free, so players can blow it at will, with the same tune varying greatly every time they play it. The performance art of **Leyou Musical Instrument of the Buyi Nationality** is a unique ethnic musical form created by the Buyi people in their long-term production and life, displaying their life concepts and artistic talents.

第11项：
多声部民歌（苗族多声部民歌）

苗族多声部民歌比赛
the Singing Competition of Polyphonic Folk Songs of the Miao Nationality

项目序号：61	项目编号：Ⅱ-30	公布时间：2008（第二批）	类别：传统音乐
所属地区：贵州省	类型：扩展项目	申报地区或单位：贵州省台江县、剑河县	

苗族多声部民歌是流传于贵州省台江县、剑河县等地苗族村寨的一种原生态民歌，已有 700 余年的历史。

苗族多声部民歌以宫、商、羽、徵、角为主要音列，和音为纯五度、纯八度、大三度和大六度，节拍相对自由，多以 3/4、4/4、2/4 和 6/8 混合使用，曲调优美，情感细腻，具有民族和地域特色。其内容大多反映青年男女从接触到成婚的过程，包括"见面歌""赞美歌""单身歌""青春歌""求爱歌""相恋歌""分别歌""成婚歌""逃婚歌"和"离婚歌"等，各用不同曲调演唱，演唱时歌手一般两男两女以上。演唱方式有两种：主旋律男女对唱、主旋律男女合唱。一首完整的多声部民歌有 6～16 个乐句，以八乐句歌曲为例，开头 1～6 乐句为男声单声部，从第 7 乐句开始，女声部加入和声形成多声部，男声部唱完第 8 乐句后，女声部主唱第 2 段，男声部和音形成复调，从第 3 乐句开始为女声单声部，到第 2 乐段第 7 乐句，男声部加入和音形成多声部。如此反复相和，构成苗族复调音乐的雏形。代表作品有《假如你是一朵花》《阳春三月好风光》等。[①] 苗族多声部民歌是当地苗族现存传统文化最重要的组成部分。

---

① 《多声部民歌（苗族多声部民歌）》，中国非物质文化遗产网，http://www.ihchina.cn/Article/Index/detail?id=12478，检索日期：2019 年 8 月 11 日。

Item 11: Polyphonic Folk Songs (Polyphonic Folk Songs of the Miao Nationality)

Item Serial Number: 61	Item ID Number: II -30	Released Date: 2008 (Batch 2)	Category: Traditional Music
Affiliated Province: Guizhou Province	Type: Extended Item	Application Province or Unit: Taijiang County and Jianhe County of Guizhou Province	

Polyphonic Folk Songs of the Miao Nationality are a kind of original ecological folk song circulated in the stockaded villages of the Miao nationality in Taijiang County, Jianhe County, etc. of Guizhou Province, with a history of more than 700 years.

Polyphonic Folk Songs of the Miao Nationality takes Gong (one of the five ancient Chinese musical notes equal to "Do" in western musical scale), Shang (one of the five ancient Chinese musical notes equal to "Re" in western musical scale), Yu (one of the five ancient Chinese musical notes equal to "La" in western musical scale), Zhi (one of the five ancient Chinese musical notes equal to "Sol" in western musical scale) and Jue (one of the five ancient Chinese musical notes equal to "Mi" in western musical scale) as the main series of musical notes. The harmonies are perfect fifth, octave, major third and major sixth. Their beats are relatively free, mostly with 3/4, 4/4, 2/4 and 6/8 beats mixed in use. They have beautiful tunes, express delicate emotions, and bear ethnic and regional characteristics. The content mostly reflects the process of young men and women's falling in love to marriage, including "A Song of Seeing Each Other", "A Song of Praise", "A Song of Singleness", "A Song of Youth", "A Song of Courtship", "A Song of Falling in Love", "A Song of Parting", "A Song of Getting Married", "A Song of Escaping Marriage" and "A Song of Divorce". They are sung by using different tunes. When performing the singing, singers are generally more than two men and two women. There are two ways of singing: male and female singers' antiphonal singing of the main melody, as well as male and female singers' choral singing of the main melody. A complete polyphonic folk song ranges in musical phrases from 6 to 16. Take an 8-phrase song as an example, for 1-6 musical phrases, male single voice part is used. From the 7th one, female voice part is added to the harmony, forming the multi-voice parts. After the male voice part finishes singing the 8th musical phrase, the second musical passage is primarily sung by the female voice part, with the male voice part singing in harmony, forming polyphony. From the 3rd musical phrase, female single voice part is adopted. Until the 7th one in the 2nd musical passage, male voice part is added to the harmony, forming multi-voice parts. Such repeated harmonies constitute the embryonic form of the polyphonic music of the Miao nationality. The representative songs are "If You Were a Flower", "Beautiful Scenery in March", etc. **Polyphonic Folk Songs of the Miao Nationality** are the most important part of the existing traditional culture of the local Miao nationality.

贵州省 国家级非物质文化遗产文献资料汇编（汉英对照）

The Documentary Compilation of the State-level Intangible Cultural Heritage of Guizhou Province (Chinese-English Versions)

彝族山歌比赛
the Singing Contest of Mountain Songs of the Yi Nationality

第12项：彝族民歌（彝族山歌）

项目序号：612	项目编号：Ⅱ-113	公布时间：2011（第三批）	类别：传统音乐
所属地区：贵州省	类型：扩展项目	申报地区或单位：贵州省盘县	

　　盘县彝族山歌是彝族传统文化的重要组成部分，主要流传于贵州省六盘水市盘县盘北地区，其中以盘县淤泥乡的山歌最具代表性。

　　盘县彝族山歌按内容分为情歌、酒歌、劳动歌和叙事歌。按演唱形式，分为独唱、两人对唱、群体对唱、集体齐唱和二声部合唱。演唱时间和场合自由灵活。有不少歌词是半汉半彝的，部分歌词全是汉语的；歌词结构以七言四句最为常见，也有四句一问、四句一答的；曲调婉转悠扬，被当地人称为"拉山腔"。盘县彝族山歌有独特的演唱技巧，比如喉、头腔共振，真假声混合等，使其具有独特的魅力。老一辈人用口传心授的方式使彝族山歌巧妙的演唱技巧得以传承。盘县彝族山歌通过对唱的形式，倡导尊老爱幼、夫妻恩爱、邻里和睦、勤劳善良、人与自然和谐相处等理念，是彝人传承好客、友善优良传统的主要形式。[①]

Item 12: Folk Songs of the Yi Nationality (Mountain Songs of the Yi Nationality)

Item Serial Number: 612	Item ID Number: Ⅱ-113	Released Date: 2011 (Batch 3)	Category: Traditional Music

---

① 《彝族民歌（彝族山歌）》，中国非物质文化遗产网，http://www. ihchina. cn/Article/Index/detail?id=12670，检索日期：2019 年 8 月 26 日。

Affiliated Province:	Type:	Application Province or Unit:
Guizhou Province	Extended Item	Panxian County, Guizhou Province

Mountain Songs of the Yi Nationality in Panxian County are an important part of the traditional Yi culture, mainly spread in the northern area of Panxian County, Liupanshui City, Guizhou Province. Mountain Songs in Yuni Township are the most representative ones.

According to content, **Mountain Songs of the Yi Nationality** in Panxian County can be divided into love songs, toasting songs, labor songs and narrative songs. According to singing forms, they can be divided into: solo singing, two-person antiphonal singing, group antiphonal singing, collective chorusing and chorusing of two voice parts. Their singing time and occasions are free and flexible. Most of the lyrics are partly in Chinese and partly in the Yi language, and some are only in Chinese. The common structure of the lyrics is four sentences with each having seven words. Some are four sentences with one question, and four sentences with one answer. The tune is gentle and melodious, called "Lashan Tune" (high-pitched voice) by local people. For **Mountain Songs of the Yi Nationality** in Panxian County, there are unique singing techniques, such as the resonance of the larynx and head cavities, and the mixing of real and false voices, which make them possess a unique charm. Through the inheritance way of oral instruction, the older generations have passed down the ingenious techniques of singing **Mountain Songs of the Yi Nationality** from generation to generation. In the form of antiphonal singing, **Mountain Songs of the Yi Nationality** in Panxian County advocate the concepts of respecting the old and loving the young, love between husband and wife, harmonious neighborhood, diligence and kindness, harmonious coexistence between man and nature, etc. They are the main form for the Yi people to inherit the excellent traditions of hospitality and friendliness.

第13项：
土家族民歌

土家族民歌演唱
the Singing Performance of Folk Songs of the Tujia Nationality

项目序号：1250	项目编号：Ⅱ-156	公布时间：2014（第四批）	类别：传统音乐
所属地区：贵州省	类型：新增项目	申报地区或单位：贵州省沿河土家族自治县	

　　土家族民歌是土家族人在长期的生产生活及社会实践中逐渐形成的文学与音乐交融的结晶，主要流传于贵州省沿河土家族自治县。

　　土家族民歌种类较多，有砍柴歌、盘歌、采茶歌、情歌对唱、翻山调和赶马调等。根据活动性质，土家族民歌又可分为与宗教活动相关的民歌，与民俗活动相关的民歌和集会、田间地头歌唱的民歌三种。其艺术特征主要有三个：第一，演唱时注重运用特殊的润腔技巧，主要是甩腔、直音、滑音、喉音与颤音等五项技巧。其中甩腔的声音宏大、冲击力和致远力强；直音的爆发力和号召力强；滑音感性、粗犷、豪迈；喉音地域色彩鲜明；颤音具有抖动感。第二，演唱时注重唱腔特点，主要体现在用声和用气两个方面，有小嗓、大嗓和高腔三种唱法，其中小嗓唱法挂位高、泛音广；大嗓唱法音量宏大、冲击力强；高腔唱法结实明亮。第三，演唱中注重语言特点。土家人常将生活语言节奏化、旋律化，故土家族民歌的旋律节奏与语言节奏韵律基本一致，唱法接近自然语言状态，既有说唱又有喊唱，说中有唱、唱中有说的语言艺术特点非常突出。土家族民歌的传承方式有家族间的传承和群体间的传承两种。其旋律自由、慷慨优美，歌词通俗易懂、情感朴实。[①]

Item 13: Folk Songs of the Tujia Nationality

Item Serial Number: 1250	Item ID Number: Ⅱ-156	Released Date: 2014 (Batch 4)	Category: Traditional Music

① 余永霞，《贵州土家族民歌的传承与传播》，载《贵州民族研究》，2013 年第 4 期，第44-47 页。

Affiliated Province: Guizhou Province	Type: New Item	Application Province or Unit: Yanhe Tujia Autonomous County, Guizhou Province

Folk Songs of the Tujia Nationality are the crystallization of the integration of literature and music developed by the Tujia people in their long-term production, life and social practice, mainly circulated in Yanhe Tujia Autonomous County, Guizhou Province.

There are many kinds of **Folk Songs of the Tujia Nationality**: firewood-chopping song, question-answer song, tea-picking song, love song of antiphonal singing, mountain-crossing tune, horse-riding tune, etc. According to the nature of activities, they can also be divided into three categories: folk songs related to religious activities, folk songs related to folk activities, as well as folk songs sung at the gathering and in the fields. They have three artistic features. First, when singing them, singers attach importance to the use of special techniques of lubricating vocal cavity, which mainly include five techniques: Shuaiqiang (the flinging note), the straight note, the glide, the glottal and the tremolo. Among them, Shuaiqiang (the flinging note) is loud and far-spreading with strong impact force; the straight note has strong explosive force and appeal; the glide is perceptive, rough and bold; the glottal has distinctive regional features; and the tremolo has a trembling sensation. Second, in the process of singing, singers pay attention to the characteristics of singing tones, which is mainly reflected in two aspects: the use of voice and the use of breath. There are three singing methods: Xiaosang (head voice or light voice), Dasang (full voice) and high-pitched voice. Among them, singing by using Xiaosang (head voice or light voice) is at a high vocal position, with a wide range of harmonics; singing by using Dasang (full voice) is loud, having strong impact force; and singing by using high-pitched voice is solid and bright. Third, when singing them, singers highlight their linguistic features. The Tujia people often rhythmize and melodize the language of life, so the melodic rhythm of **Folk Songs of the Tujia Nationality** is basically consistent with the rhythm of speaking. Their singing is similar to the natural state of speaking, including not only speaking while singing, but also shouting while singing. Their artistic features of the language, namely speaking while singing and singing while speaking, are very prominent. There are two ways of inheriting **Folk Songs of the Tujia Nationality**: inter-family inheritance and inter-group inheritance. Their melodies are free, generous and beautiful, and their lyrics are easy to understand, expressing simple emotions.

第三章
传统舞蹈

Chapter Three
Traditional Dance

锦鸡舞
the Golden Pheasant Dance

第 1 项：
芦笙舞（锦鸡舞）

项目序号：126	项目编号：Ⅲ-23	公布时间：2006（第一批）	类别：传统舞蹈
所属地区：贵州省	类型：新增项目	申报地区或单位：贵州省丹寨县	

　　锦鸡舞发源于贵州省丹寨县排调镇，流传于苗族"嘎闹"支系中穿麻鸟型超短裙服饰的排调镇和雅灰乡等的苗族村寨。传说这支苗族的祖先因灾难辗转来到丹寨县定居，在此开荒种田。锦鸡帮其获得小米种，助其度过饥荒，故锦鸡被其视为吉星。于是，他们仿照锦鸡的模样打扮自己，模拟锦鸡的求偶步态跳起芦笙舞。

　　锦鸡舞是苗族人每十二年举行一次的祭祖活动使用的主要舞蹈形式。民间的婚庆、迎客礼仪和青年男女的"跳月"过程中也常表演锦鸡舞。以芦笙伴奏，表演时女性绾发高耸，头插锦鸡银饰，穿绣花超短百褶裙，戴全套银项圈手镯，脚穿翘尖绣花鞋，打扮得像美丽的锦鸡。男性吹芦笙作为前导，女性随后起舞，排成一字形，逆时针转圈跳舞。随芦笙曲调的快慢节拍，妇女头上的锦鸡银饰跃跃欲飞，银角冠一点一摇，腿边花带一飘一闪，百褶裙脚边的洁白羽毛银浪翻飞，舞者步履轻盈，似锦鸡在行乐觅食。舞蹈动作以四步为主，兼以六步转身，腰、膝自然摇动是其基本特点。每跳一步，舞者双膝自然向前颤动，双手于两侧悠然摇摆。锦鸡舞表现了苗族人温和娴静的性格，体现出人与自然和谐友好的精神状态，凸显了苗族人古老而绚烂的美感追求。[①]

Item 1: Lusheng Dance (the Golden Pheasant Dance)

Item Serial Number: 126	Item ID Number: Ⅲ-23	Released Date: 2006 (Batch 1)	Category: Traditional Dance
Affiliated Province: Guizhou Province	Type: New Item	Application Province or Unit: Danzhai County, Guizhou Province	

The Golden Pheasant Dance originated from Paidiao Township, Danzhai County, Guizhou Province, which is spread in the stockaded villages inhabited by the "Ganao" branch of the Miao nationality in Paidiao Township and Yahui Township, where people wear the Hemp Bird-type Miniskirts. It's said that the ancestors of this Miao branch came to settle down in Danzhai County because of disasters, and opened up wastelands for farming here. They got millet seeds with the help of golden pheasants, which helped them survive the famine. Thus, they regarded golden pheasants as lucky stars, imitated the appearance of golden pheasants to dress themselves, and learned the courtship gait of golden pheasants to perform Lusheng Dance.

The Golden Pheasant Dance is the major dance form in the activity of ancestral worship of the Miao nationality held every twelve years. In folk wedding ceremonies, guest-welcoming etiquette and the activity of the Moon Dance for young men and

---

① 《芦笙舞（锦鸡舞）》，中国非物质文化遗产网，http://www. ihchina. cn/Article/Index/detail?id=12954，检索日期：2019 年 8 月 19 日。

贵州省 国家级非物质文化遗产文献资料汇编（汉英对照）

The Documentary Compilation of the State-level Intangible Cultural Heritage of Guizhou Province (Chinese-English Versions)

women, it will be also performed often. To the accompaniment of Lusheng Musical Instruments, female dancers dress like beautiful golden pheasants when they perform this dance, wearing their hair in buns highly, with gold-pheasant silver ornaments inserted. They wear embroidered ultra-short pleated skirts, a complete set of silver collars and bracelets, as well as embroidered shoes with upturned tips on feet. The Male play Lusheng Musical Instruments, leading the way, and the female follow them, forming a line and dancing in a circle counterclockwise. To the slow or fast rhythm of Lusheng melody, the golden-pheasant silver ornaments on women's heads seem to fly, the silver horn crowns are shaking with dance steps, the flower belts besides the legs are floating and flashing, the white feathers on the feet of pleated skirts are flying, and dancers' gait is light, like golden pheasants having fun and foraging. The dance movements are mainly four steps, supplemented with six steps and one turn. The basic feature of this dance is the natural swinging of waists and knees. For the dancing of each step, dancers' both knees tremble forward naturally, with their both hands swaying leisurely on both sides. **The Golden Pheasant Dance** shows the gentle and quiet character of the Miao people, reflects the harmonious and friendly mental state of human and nature, and highlights the age-old and gorgeous aesthetic pursuit of the Miao people.

第2项： 芦笙舞（鼓龙鼓虎－长衫龙）

鼓龙鼓虎－长衫龙表演
the Performance of the Dragon-and-tiger Dance in Long Gowns

项目序号：126	项目编号：Ⅲ-23	公布时间：2006（第一批）	类别：传统舞蹈
所属地区：贵州省	类型：新增项目	申报地区或单位：贵州省贵定县	

　　鼓龙鼓虎－长衫龙是贵州省贵定县新埔乡谷撒村独有的一种苗族芦笙舞蹈，已有千余年的历史。

　　过去，鼓龙鼓虎－长衫龙仅在丧葬和祭寨神仪式中表演；现在，每逢重大节日集会、婚嫁、立房和跳月等传统民族活动都要表演此舞，成为开展娱乐竞赛、增进情谊的重要活动方式。此舞用于丧葬时，于出殡队伍最前列表演；用于祭寨神时，于阴历二月初一在杀牛祭祖踩场之际表演；用于立房时，在踩屋基时进行；用于跳月时，在正月初一至三十的"跳月场"活动中表演。鼓龙鼓虎－长衫龙包括男子双人舞、四人舞和群舞等形式，整个舞蹈分为三节，第一节群龙出现，第二节龙腾虎跃，第三节群龙抢宝。舞者身着黑色大襟长衫，头插两根野鸡翎，顶戴龙面牛角图腾，戴髯口，拴红色银饰腰带，手执芦笙，自吹自跳，随芦笙旋律做出"龙斗角""龙吐水""龙出洞""龙飞膀子""莲花""拜见"等动作。该舞伴奏乐器笙管粗长，声音低沉浑厚，舞蹈动作与音乐紧密结合为一体，形成一种独具魅力的艺术形式。[①]

---

① 《芦笙舞（鼓龙鼓虎－长衫龙）》，中国非物质文化遗产网，http://www.ihchina.cn/Article/Index/detail?id=12955，检索日期：2019 年 9 月 23 日。

贵州省·国家级非物质文化遗产文献资料汇编（汉英对照）

The Documentary Compilation of the State-level Intangible Cultural Heritage of Guizhou Province (Chinese-English Versions)

Item 2: Lusheng Dance (the Dragon-and-tiger Dance in Long Gowns)

Item Serial Number: 126	Item ID Number: III-23	Released Date: 2006 (Batch 1)	Category: Traditional Dance
Affiliated Province: Guizhou Province	Type: New Item	Application Province or Unit: Guiding County, Guizhou Province	

The Dragon-and-tiger Dance in Long Gowns is a Lusheng Dance of the Miao nationality unique to Gusa Village, Xinpu Township, Guiding County, Guizhou Province, which has a history of more than one thousand years.

In the past, **the Dragon-and-tiger Dance in Long Gowns** was only performed at funerals and the ceremony of offering sacrifices to the god of stockaded villages. At present, whenever there are any traditional ethnic activities, such as grand festival gatherings, weddings, building houses and performing the Moon Dance, this dance will be performed, which has become an important way to carry out entertainment competitions and enhance friendship. At funerals, this dance is performed in the front of the funeral procession. At the ceremony of offering sacrifices to the god of stockaded villages, it is performed on the first day of the second lunar month when it is the time of killing cattle and offering sacrifices to ancestors. In the building of a house, it is performed on the occasion of tamping the foundation of the house. In the Moon Dance, it is performed in the activity of the Moon Dancing Field from the 1st to the 30th days of the first month of the lunar calendar. **The Dragon-and-tiger Dance in Long Gowns** includes male double-person dance, four-person dance and group dance. The whole dance is divided into three sections: swarms of dragons appearing in the first section, dragons rising and tigers leaping in the second section, and swarms of dragons snatching treasures in the third section. Dancers are dressed in black long gowns with big Jin (two fronts of an upper garment), with two pheasant plumes inserted on their heads, wearing a dragon-face ox-horned totem and artificial whiskers. Red belts with silver ornaments tied around their waists, they hold Lusheng Musical Instruments in their hands, blowing and dancing. With the melody produced by Lusheng Musical Instruments, they perform the motions of "Dragons Fighting with Their Horns", "Dragons Spitting Water", "Dragons Flying out of the Cave", "Dragons Flapping Arms", "Lotus Flowers", "Paying a Formal Visit", etc.

The tubes of Lusheng Musical Instruments accompanying the dance are thick and long, producing a deep and solid sound. Its dance movements and music are closely integrated into one, forming an artistic form with a unique charm.

贵州省 国家级非物质文化遗产文献资料汇编（汉英对照）

The Documentary Compilation of the State-level Intangible Cultural Heritage of Guizhou Province (Chinese-English Versions)

第 3 项：

芦笙舞（滚山珠）

滚山珠表演

the Performance of Gunshanzhu Dance

项目序号：126	项目编号：Ⅲ-23	公布时间：2006（第一批）	类别：传统舞蹈
所属地区：贵州省	类型：新增项目	申报地区或单位：贵州省纳雍县	

　　滚山珠，原名"地龙滚荆"，流传在贵州省纳雍县猪场苗族彝族乡。据传苗族祖先大迁徙途中荆棘遍野，英勇的苗族青年们为了给乡亲们开辟通道，用自己的身躯从荆棘林中滚出一条路，后人为纪念他们，模仿他们用身躯滚倒荆棘的动作，编成芦笙舞，取名"地龙滚荆"。

　　滚山珠是集芦笙吹奏、舞蹈表演和杂技艺术为一体的苗族民间舞。表演时用 6 支长约 20 厘米的铁制梭镖头，镖尖向上插入地下，围成一个直径约 0.7 米的圆圈，或用 6 只对顶的饭碗装满水摆成圆圈代替梭镖亦可。表演者手执芦笙，边吹边跳，围着梭镖或水碗翻滚，表演技巧性强，异常惊险。滚山珠在发展过程中逐渐融进各种技巧，不断完善，后发展成由 6 ~ 8 人同时表演的舞蹈。表演者手执六管芦笙，头戴箐鸡翎帽，身着绣花白褂，吹奏芦笙舞曲，围绕梭镖或盛满水的碗跳舞表演，芦笙舞步与技巧运用难度随表演进程不断增加，展现了苗人在迁徙途中不畏艰险、勇往直前的惊险场面。苗族芦笙舞滚山珠体现了苗人坚韧顽强、不屈不挠的民族性格。该舞风格粗犷豪放，动作高难惊险，蕴含着深厚的苗族历史文化内涵。①

---

① 《芦笙舞（滚山珠）》，中国非物质文化遗产网，http://www.ihchina.cn/Article/Index/detail?id=12953，检索日期：2019 年 9 月 23 日。

Item 3: Lusheng Dance (Gunshanzhu Dance)

Item Serial Number: 126	Item ID Number: Ⅲ-23	Released Date: 2006 (Batch 1)	Category: Traditional Dance
Affiliated Province: Guizhou Province	Type: New Item	Application Province or Unit: Nayong County, Guizhou Province	

Gunshanzhu Dance, originally called "Dilong Gunjing (Earth Dragons Rolling on Thorns)", is circulated in Zhuchang Miao and Yi Township, Nayong County, Guizhou Province. It's said that during the great migration of the Miao ancestors, thorns stood everywhere in their way. In order to make a path for fellow villagers, the brave youths of the Miao nationality rolled their bodies across a forest of thistles and thorns, making a path. In memory of them, later generations imitated their actions of rolling down thorns with their bodies, and choreographed Lusheng Dance, named "Dilong Gunjing (Earth Dragons Rolling on Thorns)".

Gunshanzhu Dance is a folk dance of the Miao nationality integrating Lusheng Musical Instruments playing, dance performance and acrobatics into one. When performing it, six 20 cm-long iron-made dart heads are inserted into the ground, with dart tips upward, forming a circle about 0.7 meters in diameter, or six top-to-top bowls filled with water are placed on the ground and form a circle to take the place of darts. With Lusheng Musical Instruments in hand, performers blow and dance, rolling over around the darts or water bowls. The performance requires high level of skills, extremely thrilling. In the process of its development, **Gunshanzhu Dance** has gradually absorbed various skills, constantly improved, and later has developed into a dance performed by 6-8 people at the same time. The performers hold six-pipe Lusheng Musical Instruments in their hands, with pheasant-feather hats on their heads and embroidered white coats, playing Lusheng dance music while dancing around darts or bowls full of water. The difficulty of Lusheng dance steps and skill application increases with the process of the performance, reflecting the thrilling scene of the Miao people fearing no difficulties and advancing bravely during their migration. **Gunshanzhu Dance**, Lusheng Dance of the Miao nationality, embodies the tough and indomitable ethnic character of the Miao people. The style of this dance is rough and bold with highly difficult and thrilling actions, which contains profound historical and cultural connotations of the Miao nationality.

第 4-5 项：
苗族芦笙舞

苗族芦笙舞表演
the Performance of Lusheng Dance of the Miao Nationality

项目序号：126	项目编号：Ⅲ-23	公布时间：2008（第二批）	类别：传统舞蹈
所属地区：贵州省	类型：扩展项目	申报地区或单位：贵州省雷山县、关岭布依族苗族自治县、榕江县、水城县	

项目序号：126	项目编号：Ⅲ-23	公布时间：2014（第四批）	类别：传统舞蹈
所属地区：贵州省	类型：扩展项目	申报地区或单位：贵州省普安县	

　　苗族芦笙舞是苗族人民举行祭祖和节日、喜庆活动时所跳的传统民间舞蹈，源于古代播种前祈求丰收、收获后感谢神灵赐予和祭祀祖先的仪式性舞蹈，广泛流行于苗族地区，其中贵州的苗族芦笙舞主要分布在雷山、关岭、榕江、水城和普安等县。

　　各地苗族芦笙舞的舞曲和舞步大同小异。根据内容，芦笙舞曲分为礼乐曲、叙事曲、进行曲、歌体曲和舞曲等。芦笙舞有吹笙伴舞、吹笙领舞和吹笙自舞三种形式。前两种形式中，吹笙者不舞或在场中小舞，周围男女群众层层环绕舞蹈。芦笙舞动作有走、移、跨、转、立、踢、别、勾、翻等主要类型，反映了苗族人民多样的生活与文化形态。

　　雷山苗族芦笙舞因节日不同而舞姿各异，每种舞姿都包含一定的内容，表演起来优美自然、和谐圆融，带有鲜明的地域特色。关岭苗族芦笙舞是在长期的农耕狩猎生活中逐渐形成的，蕴涵了大量的原始农耕文化祭祀礼仪，承载着苗族许多重要的历史文化信息和原始记忆，西部方言苗族歪梳苗支系每年都要在"绕坡"活动中表演这种舞蹈。榕江滚仲苗族芦笙舞以滚仲苗寨为中心，分布于贵州榕江县八开、乐里、平永、塔石、兴华等乡镇，表演中芦笙种类和曲调都很多，音色高亢清亮，男性动作热烈欢快，女性动作飘逸轻盈。水城苗族芦笙舞又称"箐鸡舞"，是苗族同胞聚会时表演的一种集体竞技舞蹈，来源于苗族"老谱"在民族斗争和生产生活中的经历，以水城县南开乡小花苗支系芦笙手所跳舞蹈最具代表性。①

普安苗族芦笙舞又称"芦笙棒舞"，流传于贵州普安县龙吟、白沙等乡镇的苗族村寨，是一种依存于"蒙洒"苗人丧祭仪式的传统祭祀性舞蹈，其表演有一整套严格的仪式规范。舞蹈动作难度大，有"巧喝酒""蚯蚓滚沙""滚山珠""过门坎""猴子上树""叠罗汉""牛打架""斗鸡"等套路，表现了"蒙洒"苗人先民在远古时期迁徒时围猎搏杀，披荆斩棘开辟道路、开疆种地等历史族群记忆。②

Items 4-5: Lusheng Dance of the Miao Nationality

Item Serial Number: 126	Item ID Number: Ⅲ-23	Released Date: 2008 (Batch 2)	Category: Traditional Dance
Affiliated Province: Guizhou Province	Type: Extended Item	Application Province or Unit: Leishan County, Guanling Buyi and Miao Autonomous County, Rongjiang County and Shuicheng County of Guizhou Province	

Item Serial Number: 126	Item ID Number: Ⅲ-23	Released Date: 2014 (Batch 4)	Category: Traditional Dance
Affiliated Province: Guizhou Province	Type: Extended Item	Application Province or Unit: Pu'an County, Guizhou Province	

Lusheng Dance of the Miao Nationality is a traditional folk dance performed when the Miao people hold ancestral worship ceremony, festivals and festive activities. It originated from the ritual dance of praying for harvests before sowing, thanking the god after harvesting and offering sacrifices to their ancestors, widely popular in areas inhabited by the Miao nationality. Among them, **Lusheng Dance of the Miao Nationality** in Guizhou Province is mainly circulated in Leishan, Guanling, Rongjiang, Shuicheng, Pu'an, etc. counties.

---

① 《苗族芦笙舞》，中国非物质文化遗产网，http://www.ihchina.cn/Article/Index/detail?id=12959，检索日期：2019 年 8 月 19 日。

② 《苗族"惹捱德亘"（也称为：芦笙棒舞）》，黔西南州人民政府网，http://www.qxn.gov.cn/View/Article.1.2/110477.html，检索日期：2019 年 8 月 25 日。

贵州省 国家级非物质文化遗产文献资料汇编（汉英对照）

The Documentary Compilation of the State-level Intangible Cultural Heritage of Guizhou Province (Chinese-English Versions)

The dance music and steps of **Lusheng Dance of the Miao Nationality** are largely identical with only minor differences in different places. According to the content, Lusheng dance music is divided into ritual music, narrative music, march, song-style music, dance music, etc. In terms of forms, Lusheng Dance is divided into three kinds: accompanying the dance while playing Lusheng Musical Instruments, leading the dance while playing Lusheng Musical Instruments and dancing on one's own while playing Lusheng Musical Instruments. In the first two forms, Lusheng Musical Instruments players do not dance or dance mildly in the center, while the surrounding male and female masses dance around in several layers of circles. The actions of Lusheng Dance include the main types of walking, moving, striding, turning around, standing, kicking, parting, hooking and turning over, which reflect the diverse life and culture of the Miao people.

The dancing postures of **Lusheng Dance of the Miao Nationality** in Leishan County are varied due to different holidays. Each dancing posture contains certain meaning, beautiful, natural, harmonious and mellow with distinctive regional characteristics. **Lusheng Dance of the Miao Nationality** in Guanling County has been gradually developed from the long-time farming and hunting life, contains a lot of the sacrificial etiquette of the primitive farming culture, and carries much important historical and cultural information, as well as primitive memories of the Miao nationality. This kind of dance is performed by the Waishu Miao branch of the Miao nationality that speaks the western dialect in the activity of "circling the slope" every year. **Lusheng Dance of the Miao Nationality** of Gunzhong in Rongjiang County is centered around Gunzhong Miao Stockaded Village, which is spread in Bakai, Leli, Pingyong, Tashi, Xinghua, etc. townships. During the performance, there are many types of Lusheng Musical Instruments and tunes, with high-pitched tones and clear timbres. Male dancers' actions are warm and cheerful, and female dancers' actions are elegant and lissom. **Lusheng Dance of the Miao Nationality** in Shuicheng County, also known as "the Pheasant Dance", is a collective competitive dance performed by the Miao compatriots at the gathering. It comes from the experiences of the Miao ancestors in their national struggle as well as production and life. The most representative dance is the one performed by Lusheng performers of the Xiaohua Miao branch in Nankai Township, Shuicheng County.

Lusheng Dance of the Miao Nationality in Pu'an County, also called "Lusheng Stick Dance", is spread in the stockaded villages inhabited by the Miao nationality in Longyin, Baisha, etc. townships of Pu'an County, Guizhou Province. It is a traditional sacrificial dance based on the "Mengsa" Miao people's funeral ceremony, and its performance has a set of strict ritual norms. The difficulty of dance movements is great. The routines include "Drinking Skillfully", "Earthworms Rolling across Sand", "Gunshanzhu (Earth Dragons Rolling on Thorns)", "Crossing the Threshold", "Monkeys Climbing Trees", "Human Pyramid", "Bulls Fighting" and "Cockfighting", which display the historical ethnic memory of the "Mengsa" Miao people's ancestors during their migration in ancient times when they were hunting and fighting, cutting down thorns, making a path, expanding boundaries and cultivating the land.

·贵州省·国家级非物质文化遗产文献资料汇编（汉英对照）

The Documentary Compilation of the State-level Intangible Cultural Heritage of Guizhou Province (Chinese-English Versions)

第6项：
木鼓舞（反排苗族木鼓舞）

反排苗族木鼓舞表演
the Performance of Fanpai Wooden-drum Dance of the Miao Nationality

项目序号：128	项目编号：Ⅲ-25	公布时间：2006（第一批）	类别：传统舞蹈
所属地区：贵州省	类型：新增项目	申报地区或单位：贵州省台江县	

　　木鼓舞是流传在西南苗族、彝族和佤族人民中以敲击木鼓起舞祭祀的民间舞蹈。一般木鼓舞为族群全体参与的大型祭祀活动中的一部分，木鼓被作为族群的象征，以敲木鼓、跳木鼓为核心的祭祀活动充满着强烈的祖先崇拜、自然崇拜的寓意。流传于贵州省台江县苗族村寨的木鼓舞主要有反排木鼓舞和施洞、革东木鼓舞两大类，其中反排木鼓舞影响较大。

　　每逢丑年，十二年一次的祭鼓节到来时，反排木鼓舞便要大跳一次，与宰牛祭祀和盛大的节庆活动相配合。反排木鼓舞由"牛高抖""牛扎厦""厦地福""高抖大""扎厦耨"五个鼓点章节组成，采用单击、合击、交错敲击等演奏手法，鼓点错落有致，节奏明快，与舞蹈有机地结合在一起。该舞蹈采用递进方式，逐步把情节推向高潮。演员歌舞并进，五体皆动，甩同边手，踏二四拍，舞姿粗犷奔放，洒脱优美；头、手、脚开合度大，摆动幅度宽。反排木鼓舞启、承、转、合结构完整，舞蹈动作简练，组合丰富，风格热烈豪迈，表现先民的生活场面和地理环境，叙述先民的由来，是苗族祭鼓节重要的活动环节。①

Items 6: the Wooden-drum Dance (Fanpai Wooden-drum Dance of the Miao Nationality)

Item Serial Number: 128	Item ID Number: Ⅲ-25	Released Date: 2006 (Batch 1)	Category: Traditional Dance

---

① 《木鼓舞（反排苗族木鼓舞）》，中国非物质文化遗产网，http://www.ihchina.cn/Article/Index/detail?id=12964，检索日期：2019年8月21日。

Affiliated Province: Guizhou Province	Type: New Item	Application Province or Unit: Taijiang County, Guizhou Province

The Wooden-drum Dance is a folk dance performed by beating the Wooden Drum to offer sacrifices, popular among the Miao, Yi and Wa people in Southwest China. Generally, **the Wooden-drum Dance** is a part of the large-scale sacrificial activity participated by all members of the ethnic group. The Wooden Drum is regarded as the symbol of the ethnic group. The sacrificial activity, with beating and dancing around the Wooden Drum as the core, is full of strong ancestral worship and natural worship implications. **The Wooden-drum Dance** spread in the Miao stockaded villages in Taijiang County, Guizhou Province is mainly divided into two kinds: Fanpai Wooden-drum Dance, as well as Shidong and Gedong Wooden-drum Dance. Among them, Fanpai Wooden-drum Dance is more influential.

In the year of Chou (the second of the Twelve Earthly Branches), when the Drum-worship Festival comes every twelve years, Fanpai Wooden-drum Dance will be performed on a large scale, together with slaughtering cattle for sacrifice and grand celebration activity. Fanpai Wooden-drum Dance is composed of five chapters of beats: "Niugaodou" (dance steps to show the difficulties of ancestors in migration from east to west), "Niuzhaxia" (dance steps to express nostalgia for ancestor leaders in the migration), "Xiadifu" (happy dance steps to show the reunion of brothers, relatives and friends), "Gaodouda" (dance steps to display the settled-down ancestors who cut down thorns, opened up wastelands, lived and worked in peace) and "Zhaxianou"(a scene dance in memory of ancestors' hunting life). By using the playing techniques of single beating, joint beating and alternate beating, the drumbeats are well arranged and rhythmic, organically combined with the dance. This dance adopts a progressive approach, and gradually pushes the plot to a climax. The performers sing and dance at the same time, and their whole bodies move from head to toe, swinging their hands on the same side and treading to the beat of two or four. The dancing postures are rough, unrestrained, free and graceful, with their heads, hands and feet moving in a large range and swinging widely. **Fanpai Wooden-drum Dance** has a complete structure of the initiation, the continuation, the transition and the ending, with concise dance movements, rich combinations as well as warm and heroic style, which shows the living scene, the geographical environment and the origin of the Miao ancestors. It is an important part of the Drum-worship Festival of the Miao nationality.

第7项：
毛南族打猴鼓舞

毛南族打猴鼓舞表演道具
Props for Performing the Monkey Drum Dance of the Maonan Nationality

项目序号：660	项目编号：Ⅲ-63	公布时间：2008（第二批）	类别：传统舞蹈
所属地区：贵州省	类型：新增项目	申报地区或单位：贵州省平塘县	

　　打猴鼓舞是毛南族独有的一种民间舞蹈，流传在贵州省平塘县的毛南族聚居区。打猴鼓舞一直在不足10万人口的毛南族中传承，已有600多年的历史。

　　表演该舞蹈时，一人击铜鼓，一人击皮鼓，多人模仿猴子进行表演，动作滑稽诙谐。打猴鼓舞的表演有男子独舞、双人舞和多人舞三种形式，整个舞蹈显现出狂、野、粗、灵的风格特点。打猴鼓舞分"猴王出世""猴子敲桩""猴火引路"三段：第一段"猴王出世"表现毛南族先人自强不息的奋斗精神；第二段"猴子敲桩"表现毛南人顽强生存、团结勇敢的抗争精神；第三段"猴火引路"表现毛南人继承先人遗志、奋勇前进的开拓精神。表演打猴鼓舞时，表演者击打铜鼓、皮鼓以控制节奏，用鼓点的强弱、轻重、快慢引导舞蹈动作的变化，双腿蹲跳的动作贯穿表演始终。[①]其伴奏乐器以铜鼓和皮鼓为主，表演前，先吹牛角，再吹大号，在鼓声中依次表演。主要道具是木凳或竹编椅，代表树桩，表演者在地上和凳子上跳上跳下，在滚、翻时敲击木棒，动作幅度大，舞蹈语言丰富，表演幽默。

---

① 《毛南族打猴鼓舞》，中国非物质文化遗产网，http://www.ihchina.cn/Article/Index/detail?id=13049，检索日期：2019年8月23日。

Item 7: the Monkey Drum Dance of the Maonan Nationality

Item Serial Number: 660	Item ID Number: III-63	Released Date: 2008 (Batch 2)	Category: Traditional Dance
Affiliated Province: Guizhou Province	Type: New Item	Application Province or Unit: Pingtang County, Guizhou Province	

The Monkey Drum Dance is a folk dance unique to the Maonan nationality, spread in areas inhabited by the Maonan people in Pingtang County, Guizhou Province. It has been passed on among the Maonan people with a population of less than 100,000 for more than 600 years.

When performing this dance, one person beats the Bronze Drum and one person beats the Leather Drum, several people perform the dance by imitating monkeys, with comical and witty actions. There are three forms for the performance of **the Monkey Drum Dance**: one-male dance, two-male dance and many-male dance, and the whole dance shows the characteristics of craziness, wildness, coarseness and spirituality. This dance is divided into three sections: "the Birth of Monkey King", "Monkeys Knocking on Piles" and "Monkey Fire Leading the Way". The first section "the Birth of Monkey King" shows the unyielding spirit of self-improvement of the Maonan ancestors; the second section "Monkeys Knocking on Piles" displays the Maonan people's fighting spirit of surviving tenaciously and uniting together bravely; and the third section "Monkey Fire Leading the Way" expresses the Maonan people's pioneering spirit of inheriting their ancestors' will and advancing bravely. During the performance, performers beat the Bronze Drum and the Leather Drum to control the dancing rhythm. They use the strength and weakness, lightness and heaviness, as well as quickness and slowness of the drumbeats to guide the change of dance movements, with double-leg squatting and jumping running through the whole performance. Its accompaniment instruments are mainly the Bronze Drum and the Leather Drum. Before the performance, performers play the ox horn first, and then the tuba, and to the beat of the drum, they perform the dance in turn. The main props are wooden benches or bamboo chairs representing tree stumps. Performers jump up and down on the ground or on the benches, and knock on wooden sticks when rolling and turning over, with a large range of movements, rich dance language and humorous performance.

瑶族猴鼓舞表演
the Performance of the Monkey Drum Dance of the Yao Nationality

第8项：瑶族猴鼓舞

项目序号：661	项目编号：Ⅲ-64	公布时间：2008（第二批）	类别：传统舞蹈
所属地区：贵州省	类型：新增项目	申报地区或单位：贵州省荔波县	

　　瑶族猴鼓舞是白裤瑶先民为纪念祖先和与之密切相关的"先猴"而自发形成的一种仪式舞蹈，仅在贵州省荔波县的白裤瑶居住区流传。

　　据传白裤瑶祖先从广西迁徙经荔波捞村乡时遭遇危难，一群猴子为他们解危救难，后为纪念祖先的迁徙之苦和猴子护送之功，白裤瑶先民就模仿祖先爬山涉水和猴子们攀爬跳跃的神态起舞，形成了目前的猴鼓舞，并把该舞蹈作为丧葬祭祀的一个重要仪式。瑶族猴鼓舞以皮鼓和铜鼓为乐器，表演时由皮鼓手担任领舞和指挥。众人围着皮鼓站成一大圈，另一侧悬吊几面乃至十几面铜鼓。每面铜鼓配两名鼓手，一人击鼓，一人在鼓后手持形如饭甑的"共鸣箱"如戽水样一进一出，以使鼓声更加厚重深沉。皮鼓手围着皮鼓一边敲击，一边舞蹈跳跃。众人踩着鼓点纷纷起舞，模仿猴子的姿态和动作，攀爬跳跃，舞姿柔中有刚、轻重分明，显示出亢爽英武的风格。猴鼓舞是原始社会图腾崇拜的产物，缩影式地展示了荔波白裤瑶迁徙的历史，揭示了其不懈奋斗的坚强意志和不畏强暴的民族精神。①

---

① 《瑶族猴鼓舞》，中国非物质文化遗产网，http://www.ihchina.cn/Article/Index/detail?id=13050，检索日期：2019 年 8 月 22 日。

Item 8: the Monkey Drum Dance of the Yao Nationality

Item Serial Number: 661	Item ID Number: Ⅲ-64	Released Date: 2008 (Batch 2)	Category: Traditional Dance
Affiliated Province: Guizhou Province	Type: New Item	Application Province or Unit: Libo County, Guizhou Province	

The Monkey Drum Dance of the Yao Nationality is a kind of ritual dance spontaneously developed by the ancestors of the Baiku branch of the Yao nationality to commemorate their ancestors and "the earlier monkey" closely related to them, only popular in areas inhabited by the Baiku branch of the Yao nationality in Libo County, Guizhou Province.

It's said that, during their migration from Guangxi, the ancestors of the Baiku branch of the Yao nationality encountered a crisis when they arrived at Laocun Township of Libo County, and then they were rescued by a group of monkeys. Later, to commemorate their ancestors' hardship of migration and monkeys' contribution to escorting, the Miao ancestors of the Baiku branch imitated the bearing of their ancestors' climbing mountains and crossing rivers as well as monkeys' climbing and jumping to dance, and thus developed the current Monkey Drum Dance, which has been used as an important ritual at funerals and sacrifices. The accompaniment instruments of **the Monkey Drum Dance of the Yao Nationality** are the Leather Drum and the Bronze Drum. When performing it, the player of the Leather Drum acts as the leading dancer and the conductor. All dancers stand in a big circle around the Leather Drum. On the other side hangs several or even dozens of the Bronze Drums, with each requiring two drummers. One person beats the drum, and the other holds a "sound box" like a rice steamer in his hand behind the drum. The drum sound is sent out like drawing water with a bailing bucket for irrigation, and in this way, the drum sound becomes thicker and deeper. The player of the Leather Drum beats the drum while dancing around it. All people dance to the beat of drums, imitating monkeys' postures and movements, climbing and jumping. Their dancing postures are gentle yet firm, with a clear distinction between weight and lightness, which shows a vigorous and heroic style. **The Monkey Drum Dance** is the product of the totem worship in primitive society, epitomizes the migration history of the Baiku branch of the Yao nationality in Libo, and reveals their strong will of unremitting struggle and the ethnic spirit of defying brute force.

彝族铃铛舞表演
the Performance of the Small Bell Dance of the Yi Nationality

第9项: 彝族铃铛舞

项目序号：666	项目编号：Ⅲ-69	公布时间：2008（第二批）	类别：传统舞蹈
所属地区：贵州省	类型：新增项目	申报地区或单位：贵州省赫章县	

　　彝族铃铛舞是彝族人祭奠亡灵的一种传统民间舞蹈，主要流传于贵州省赫章县。其历史可追溯到公元前8世纪彝族先民笃尔帝分封六侯的时代。当时各诸侯部落全民皆兵，组建战马队伍，国王、首领举行祭祀追悼先王时，部下都要组织120人的兵马队伍和数十人的歌舞队，在祭祀歌舞场上展示骑士风采。舞动时要摇响手中的马铃控制节奏，铃铛舞由此得名。

　　跳彝族铃铛舞时，舞者先歌后舞，舞蹈动作豪放粗犷，两队舞者作跃马扬鞭状，相向而来，纵横有序，变幻无常。该舞蹈用鼓、铜铃铛打节拍，有很多高难动作，表现了战场上勇猛威武的彝山汉子的血性气概。跳铃铛舞时，舞者右手执马铃铛，左手执彩带，欣然起舞。过去只允许男青年跳，参演人数4～6人。后经改编，铃铛舞表演形式更多样化，舞台布局和队形穿插有较大调整，内容也有改变，主要表现彝族先民在与自然抗争中顽强生存，一代代男耕女织、繁衍生息的民族发展史，女子也得以参与其中。彝族铃铛舞保留着原始风貌，是彝族保存最完整、艺术价值最高、流传最广的民间舞蹈形式。[1]

Item 9: the Small Bell Dance of the Yi Nationality

Item Serial Number: 666	Item ID Number: Ⅲ-69	Released Date: 2008 (Batch 2)	Category: Traditional Dance

----

[1]　《彝族铃铛舞》，中国非物质文化遗产网，http://www. ihchina. cn/Article/Index/detail?id=13055，检索日期：2019年8月21日。

Affiliated Province: Guizhou Province	Type: New Item	Application Province or Unit: Hezhang County, Guizhou Province

The Small Bell Dance of the Yi Nationality is a kind of traditional folk dance for the Yi people to offer sacrifices to the dead, mainly spread in Hezhang County, Guizhou Province. It can be dated back to the eighth century B.C. when King Du'er, the ancestor of the Yi nationality, enfeoffed six vassal states. At that time, all people in the tribes of the vassal states were soldiers, so they built war-horse teams. When the king and the chieftain held a ceremony of offering sacrifices to mourn the former king, their subordinates would organize a war-horse team of 120 soldiers, and a singing and dancing team of dozens of people to show warriors' elegant demeanor on the Sacrificial-song Dance Hall. When dancing, they rang the horse bells in their hands to control the rhythm, hence the name, **the Small Bell Dance**.

When performing **the Small Bell Dance of the Yi Nationality**, dancers sing first and then dance. Their dance moves are bold and wild, and two teams of dancers make the postures of spurring the horses and flapping the whips, coming from opposite directions and dancing, being orderly vertically and horizontally, changing constantly and irregularly. This dance adopts the beats produced by beating the drum and ringing small copper bells, having many dance moves with great difficulty, which shows the courage and uprightness of the brave and mighty Yi men on the battlefield. When performing the Small Bell Dance, dancers hold the horse bells in their right hands and the colored ribbons in the left, dancing happily. In the past, only young males were allowed to dance, with the number of participants ranging from 4 to 6. After later adaptation, the performance forms of **the Small Bell Dance** have become more diversified, the stage layout and the alteration of formations have been adjusted to a larger extent. Its content has also been changed, which mainly shows the history of the development of the Yi nationality, depicting the tenacious survival of its ancestors in the struggle against nature, generations of men farming and women weaving, as well as their reproduction and flourishing. Women can also participate in the dancing. **The Small Bell Dance of the Yi Nationality** retains primitive style and features, and is a form of folk dance of the Yi nationality that has been preserved most completely and spread most extensively, with the highest artistic value.

贵州省·国家级非物质文化遗产文献资料汇编（汉英对照）

The Documentary Compilation of the State-level Intangible Cultural Heritage of Guizhou Province (Chinese-English Versions)

第10项：
布依族高台狮灯舞

布依族高台狮灯舞表演
the Performance of the High-platform Lion Lantern Dance of the Buyi Nationality

项目序号：108	项目编号：Ⅲ-5	公布时间：2008（第二批）	类别：传统舞蹈
所属地区：贵州省	类型：扩展项目	申报地区或单位：贵州省兴义市	

　　布依族高台狮灯舞是流传在贵州省兴义市马岭镇瓦嘎村的一种民族民间舞蹈。东汉时传入盘江流域，三国南北朝以后逐渐盛行，元明清时期在这一带的布依族中广泛流传。

　　表演时，用6张或8张八仙桌叠成高台，最上的一张翻转过来四脚朝天，狮子自下盘旋而上，时而转动，时而跳跃，在此过程中完成翻、滚、叠等惊险动作。上到顶部后，狮子在四只桌脚上凌空起舞。遇到这种凌空表演，瓦嘎的狮灯艺人会用高难度的"跳脚"技巧迅速准确地跳过去，表现出高超的功夫。高台狮灯的打击乐器称为"响器"，由马锣、钹、堂锣和鼓组成，打法有上百种，新颖别致，变化多端。① 瓦嘎布依族高台狮灯舞以"上高台"著称，搭台后，先由狮子头"圆台子"，再进行表演。以"杂脸子"（唐僧取经，一套20余人参与的表演）和"大脸子"（沙和尚）、狮子一对、猴子一对上台表演。高台狮灯舞常在布依族的传统节日、婚丧嫁娶、农闲时及贺新房时表演，生动展示了布依族的生产状况、生活习俗、宗教信仰和理想追求。舞狮者要有强健的体魄和一定的武术功底，动作要敏捷灵活，首尾舞者要配合默契。②

---

① 《狮舞（布依族高台狮灯舞）》，中国非物质文化遗产网，http://www.ihchina.cn/Article/Index/detail?id=12878，检索日期：2019年9月7日。

② 《布依族高台狮灯舞》，贵州百科信息网，http://gz.zwbk.org/MyLemmaShow.aspx?lid=4573，检索日期：2019年8月21日。

Item 10: the High-platform Lion Lantern Dance of the Buyi Nationality

Item Serial Number: 108	Item ID Number: Ⅲ-5	Released Date: 2008 (Batch 2)	Category: Traditional Dance
Affiliated Province: Guizhou Province	Type: Extended Item	Application Province or Unit: Xingyi City, Guizhou Province	

The High-platform Lion Lantern Dance of the Buyi Nationality is an ethnic folk dance popular in Waga Village, Maling Township, Xingyi City, Guizhou Province. It was introduced into the Panjiang River Basin in the Eastern Han Dynasty, gradually prevailed after the Three Kingdoms and the Northern and Southern dynasties, and then widely circulated among the Buyi people in this area in the Yuan, Ming and Qing dynasties.

During its performance, six or eight Baxian Tables (a kind of old-fashioned square table for eight people) are piled up into a high platform, with the top one turned over and its four legs upward. Lions spiral from bottom to top, sometimes turn around and sometimes jump, exhibiting the thrilling movements of turning around, rolling over, piling, etc. Arriving at the top, lions dance in the air on the four table legs like flying. In such aerial performances, Lion Lantern performers in Waga Village will jump over quickly and accurately by using the highly challenging technique of "jumping feet", showing their excellent Kung Fu. The percussion instruments of **the High-platform Lion Lantern Dance** are called "Xiangqi (sound-making instruments)", which is composed of Maluo (a kind of Chinese percussion instrument), earthen bowls, Tangluo (a copper percussion instrument) and drums with more than 100 kinds of playing methods, novel and unique, full of varieties and changes. **The High-platform Lion Lantern Dance of the Buyi Nationality** in Waga Village is famous for "climbing the high platform". After the high platform is piled, the lion head performer "moves around the platform" first, and then the performance begins. A team of more than 20 people performs a set of "Zalianzi" (Monk Tang's pilgrimage for Buddhist scriptures), and then "Dalianzi" (Monk Sha), a pair of lions and a pair of monkeys climb onto the high platform to perform the dance. **The High-platform Lion Lantern Dance** is often performed at the traditional festivals of the Buyi nationality, at weddings and funerals, as well as during the slack season and the

· 贵州省 · 国家级非物质文化遗产文献资料汇编（汉英对照）

The Documentary Compilation of the State-level Intangible Cultural Heritage of Guizhou Province (Chinese-English Versions)

new house celebration, which vividly shows the production situation, living customs, religious belief and ideal pursuit of the Buyi people. Lion dancers should have strong physiques and certain martial arts skills, and their movements should be agile and flexible, with the first and last dancers cooperating with each other tacitly.

雷山苗族铜鼓舞表演
the Performance of Leishan Bronze-drum Dance of the Miao Nationality

第11项：
铜鼓舞（雷山苗族铜鼓舞）

项目序号：129	项目编号：Ⅲ-26	公布时间：2008（第二批）	类别：传统舞蹈
所属地区：贵州省	类型：扩展项目	申报地区或单位：贵州省雷山县	

　　铜鼓舞是用一头有面、中空无底、呈平面曲腰状的铜鼓为打击乐器伴奏的舞蹈。雷山苗族铜鼓舞是苗族特有的民族民间舞蹈，主要流传在贵州省雷山县大塘乡的掌坳村。

　　苗族有崇拜鼓的风俗，每个支系都拥有一只铜鼓或木鼓，一般每隔12年就要过一次鼓藏节，宰水牯牛或猪来祭鼓。同时，还要跳起祭鼓舞来表示对祖先的尊重和追念。相传，雷山苗族铜鼓舞有12种，其中一种已经失传，目前能收集到的有捉蟹舞、翻身舞、迎客舞、获猎舞、鸭步舞、送客舞、祭鼓舞、放牧舞、捞虾舞、送鼓舞和共欢舞11种。每种舞均有鼓点鼓曲，舞姿各不相同。每种舞姿都包含一定的内容，有对动物的模仿，如鸭子走路等；有对生产生活行为的模仿，如捞虾捉蟹、狩猎生产等。雷山苗族铜鼓舞主要在鼓藏节和庆祝丰收、祭祖等活动中表演，往往因节庆活动不同而选择不同的舞蹈风格：鼓藏节时舞姿庄重厚实，庆祝丰收时舞姿粗犷奔放，模仿动物时舞姿夸张有趣。[①]雷山苗族铜鼓舞反映了苗族的自然崇拜和祖先崇拜。

Item 11: the Bronze-drum Dance (Leishan Bronze-drum Dance of the Miao Nationality)

Item Serial Number: 129	Item ID Number: Ⅲ-26	Released Date: 2008 (Batch 2)	Category: Traditional Dance

---

① 《铜鼓舞（雷山苗族铜鼓舞）》，中国非物质文化遗产网，http://www.ihchina.cn/Article/Index/detail?id=12968，检索日期：2019年9月7日。

Affiliated Province: Guizhou Province	Type: Extended Item	Application Province or Unit: Leishan County, Guizhou Province

The Bronze-drum Dance is a dance performed to the accompaniment of the Bronze Drum, one end of which has the drumhead, being hollow and bottomless, with a flat surface and a curved waist. **Leishan Bronze-drum Dance of the Miao Nationality** is an ethnic folk dance unique to the Miao nationality, mainly spread in Zhang'ao Village, Datang Township, Leishan County, Guizhou Province.

The Miao people have the custom of worshiping drums. In each branch of the Miao nationality, there is either a bronze drum or a wooden drum. Every twelve years, the Drum Worship Festival will be held once, in which male buffaloes or pigs are slaughtered to offer sacrifices to drums. At the same time, they perform the Drum Worship Dance to express their respect for and remembrance of ancestors. It's said that there are twelve kinds of **Leishan Bronze-drum Dance of the Miao Nationality**, among which one has been lost. At present, eleven kinds have been collected, namely, the Crab-catching Dance, the Dance of Turning Over, the Guest-welcoming Dance, the Dance of Hunting, the Duck-step Dance, the Dance of Seeing Off Guests, the Drum Worship Dance, the Herding Dance, the Shrimp-fishing Dance, the Drum-sending Dance and the Dance of Rejoicing Together. For each dance, there are drumbeats and drum music, with different dance postures. Each dance posture embodies specific content, including the imitation of animals, such as duck walking, as well as the imitation of production and life behaviors, such as catching shrimps and crabs, hunting and production. **Leishan Bronze-drum Dance of the Miao Nationality** is mainly performed at the Drum Worship Festival and in the activities of harvest celebration, ancestor worship, etc. Generally, due to different festival celebrations, different dancing styles will be chosen. At the Drum Worship Festival, dancing postures are solemn and thick. In harvest celebrations, dancing postures are vigorous and forceful. When imitating animals, they are exaggerating and interesting. **Leishan Bronze-drum Dance of the Miao Nationality** reflects the natural worship and ancestor worship of the Miao nationality.

阿妹戚托表演

the Performance of Amei Qituo Dance

第12项：阿妹戚托

项目序号：1277	项目编号：Ⅲ-124	公布时间：2014（第四批）	类别：传统舞蹈
所属地区：贵州省	类型：新增项目	申报地区或单位：贵州省晴隆县	

　　阿妹戚托为彝语音译，意为"姑娘出嫁舞"，俗称"跳脚舞"，起源于贵州省晴隆县三宝彝族乡，以令人震撼的艺术魅力和"以足传情"的特殊表现形式，被誉为"东方踢踏舞"。①

　　阿妹戚托是无音乐伴奏的彝族婚俗舞蹈，新婚姑娘临出嫁时，寨中及邻寨女伴纷纷前来跳这支欢快的舞蹈，为新娘送行，表达女伴们依依难舍的心情，同时告诫新娘坐家之后，要勤俭持家、孝敬公婆、相夫教子、尊重寨邻；祝福新娘与丈夫全家和睦相处、兴旺发达。表演场地在新娘家的堂屋中；参与者须为双数，可为6人、8人或12人；参与者多为年轻人，男女合跳或分别独跳。舞蹈动作主要是依靠膝关节、髋关节、踝关节等带动形成的各种踢踏来展示美。主要由12个动作组成：插秧、翻脚板、转脚尖、打脚板、男左女右、背和背、喂狗饭、踢鸡冠、鸭喝水、跨三步、耍克膝和踢板壁，依次从第一个动作开始至最后一个动作结束，舞者边歌边舞，唱词对应相关舞段，以此反复。由于缺乏文字记载，阿妹戚托仅靠口传身授的方式在本族内传承，传承方式为父母传子女、姊妹互传、兄弟互传和朋友互传等。②

---

① 陈亚林，《晴隆举办"阿妹戚托"舞蹈大赛庆新春》，http://www.gzfwz.org.cn/xwdt/201804/t20180416_3119393.html，检索日期：2019年8月22日。

② 杨军，《彝族舞蹈"阿妹戚托"传承问题研究——以贵州省晴隆县三宝彝族乡为个案分析》，载《贵州师范大学学报·社会科学版》，2011年第5期，第73-76页。

·**贵州省**·国家级非物质文化遗产文献资料汇编（汉英对照）

The Documentary Compilation of the State-level Intangible Cultural Heritage of Guizhou Province (Chinese-English Versions)

Item 12: Amei Qituo Dance

Item Serial Number: 1277	Item ID Number: Ⅲ-124	Released Date: 2014 (Batch 4)	Category: Traditional Dance
Affiliated Province: Guizhou Province	Type: New Item	Application Province or Unit: Qinglong County, Guizhou Province	

Amei Qituo Dance is the transliterated version of the Yi language, which means "the Girl's Dance of Getting Married", commonly called "the Foot Dance". It originated from Sanbao Yi Township, Qinglong County, Guizhou Province. It is acclaimed as "the Oriental Tap Dance" for its amazing artistic charm and special form of "expressing feelings with feet".

Amei Qituo Dance is a marriage-custom dance of the Yi nationality performed without musical accompaniment. When the bride is about to get married, her female friends in the village and from neighboring villages come to join this joyful dance to see the bride off and express their reluctance to separate from the bride. This dance also exhorts the bride to manage the household industriously and thriftily, show filial obedience to her parents-in-law, assist her husband and educate the children, as well as respect village neighbors after she arrives at home. It expresses the wishes and blessings for the bride and her husband to live in harmony and prosperity. The performance venue is the main hall of the bride's house. The number of participants must be even, with 6, 8 or 12 people. Most participants are young people, with male and female ones dancing together or dancing separately. Its dance movements mainly rely on the various kicks and taps formed by the movements of knee joints, hip joints, ankle joints, etc. to show its beauty, which primarily consist of twelve ones: transplanting rice seedlings, turning over soles of feet, turning the tips of toes, tapping soles of feet, male left and female right, back and back, feeding the dog, kicking the cockscomb, duck drinking water, striding three steps, playing with knees and kicking the wooden partition. Dancers perform this dance while singing, starting with the first movement and ending with the last one. The lyrics correspond to relevant dance segments, with the dance movements repeated over and over again. Due to the lack of written records, **Amei Qituo Dance** is imparted and inherited within the family only by oral transmission and personal teaching. Its inheriting ways involve parent-to-child transmission, sister-to-sister transmission, brother-to-brother transmission and transmission between friends.

布依族转场舞表演
the Performance of Zhuanchang Dance of the Buyi Nationality

第13项：布依族转场舞

项目序号：1278	项目编号：Ⅲ-125	公布时间：2014（第四批）	类别：传统舞蹈
所属地区：贵州省	类型：新增项目	申报地区或单位：贵州省册亨县	

布依族转场舞是流传于贵州省册亨县布依族聚居村寨的传统舞蹈。每年的农历三月初三和春节期间，布依族村寨男女老少都会身着盛装聚集在村寨晒坝场跳转场舞，寓意布依族人对祖先和自然的崇拜，也是布依人民团结、友爱和对美好生活向往的象征。

该舞蹈起初是一种祭祀性舞蹈，现逐渐演变成布依人欢迎远方来客、祈求风调雨顺、四季平安和男女青年"浪哨"的民间习俗性身体舞蹈，具有很强的娱乐和健身性。其传统的表演程式包括祭祀、开场请师、情景表演和跳转场四个内容。转场舞目前有八式传统动作：踏歌迎客、并肩祈福、罗盘定安康、挑山顶梁、蛙步闹春、穿针引线、龙舞凤飞和欢庆丰收。[1]布依人在春耕即将来临的时节跳转场舞向神灵行吉礼祈福，以求一年农事顺利，五谷丰登。通过跳转场舞，布依族人在愉悦中了解到一些本民族的历史文化、风俗习惯，接受感恩、尊重、团结等的教育。该舞蹈蕴藏着布依族人的信仰、社交礼仪、生活态度、道德观念和教育方式等诸多要素。[2]

---

[1] 李景繁、向其英、罗毅，《黔西南布依族转场舞传承叙事》，载《武术研究》，2016年第1期，第92-94页。

[2] 《布依族转场舞》，黔西南州人民政府网，http://www.qxn.gov.cn/View/Article.1.2/110476.html，检索日期：2019年8月21日。

 贵州省 国家级非物质文化遗产文献资料汇编（汉英对照）

The Documentary Compilation of the State-level Intangible Cultural Heritage of Guizhou Province (Chinese-English Versions)

Item 13: Zhuanchang Dance of the Buyi Nationality

Item Serial Number: 1278	Item ID Number: Ⅲ-125	Released Date: 2014 (Batch 4)	Category: Traditional Dance
Affiliated Province: Guizhou Province	Type: New Item	Application Province or Unit: Ceheng County, Guizhou Province	

Zhuanchang Dance of the Buyi Nationality is a traditional dance popular in the stockaded villages inhabited by the Buyi nationality in Ceheng County, Guizhou Province. On the 3rd day of the 3rd lunar month and during the Spring Festival every year, all people, men and women, old and young, in Buyi stockaded villages gather on the Threshing Ground to dance, wearing splendid attire. The dance shows the Buyi people's worship for their ancestors and nature, so it is also a symbol of the Buyi People's unity, friendship and yearning for a better life.

This dance was originally a kind of sacrificial dance. At present, it has gradually evolved into a folk customary body dance for the Buyi people to welcome guests from afar, and pray for timely wind and rain as well as peace in four seasons, and for young men and women to take part in "Langshao activity (having a love affair)", with a strong feature of entertainment and fitness. Its traditional performing procedures include four kinds of content: offering sacrifices, opening the show and inviting the master, performing on the scene and dancing on vacant lots. There are eight traditional movements: welcoming guests by dancing while singing, praying for blessings side by side, determining the well-being with a compass, shouldering mountains and beams, celebrating spring by dancing frog gait, threading the needle, dragon dancing and phoenix flying, as well as celebrating the harvest. In the upcoming season of spring plowing, the Buyi people perform this dance to offer auspicious salute to gods for blessings of a smooth year of farming and a bumper grain harvest. Through performing **Zhuanchang Dance**, the Buyi people learn about their own history, culture, customs and folkways, and accept the education of gratitude, respect, unity, etc. This dance contains many elements of the Buyi people's beliefs, social etiquette, life attitudes, moral concepts, educational methods, etc.

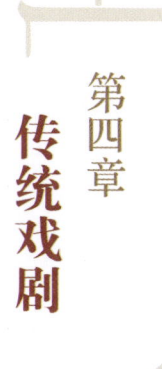

第四章
传统戏剧

Chapter Four
Traditional Opera

第 1 项：
思南花灯戏

思南花灯戏表演
the Performance of Sinan Lantern Opera

项目序号：222	项目编号：Ⅳ-78	公布时间：2006（第一批）	类别：传统戏剧
所属地区：贵州省	类型：新增项目	申报地区或单位：贵州省思南县	

　　贵州花灯戏是在当地民间歌舞基础上发展起来的。最初叫采花灯，只有歌舞，后在歌舞中加入小戏，又受外来戏曲影响，发展为演出本戏。贵州花灯戏

主要流行于独山、遵义、毕节、安顺、铜仁等地，各地有不同的称谓。黔北、黔西一带叫"灯夹戏"，独山一带叫"台灯"，思南、印江等地叫"花灯戏"。①

思南花灯戏以土家族花灯歌舞为基础，吸取了土家族傩堂戏、湘剧、辰河戏及其他戏剧的表演形式，于清朝道光年间形成了独特的民族剧种。② 其表演形式多样，最初是二人转，明末清初发展为三人出场，一男二女称为"双凤朝阳"；二男一女称为"双狮戏球"。现在出场人数不受限制，多达二三十人，而且由女性扮演旦角，改变了男扮女装的传统。思南花灯戏的音乐有浓郁的民族风情和地方特色，曲调分灯调、正调、杂调、小调等四大类，传统上有二十四大类曲牌。由于其曲调繁多，风格各异，各地有不同特色。思南花灯戏的伴奏乐器主要有马锣、大锣、二胡、月琴、三弦等。表演时载歌载舞、歌舞穿插，其舞蹈形式活泼多样，舞姿健康优美。

Item 1: Sinan Lantern Opera

Item Serial Number: 222	Item ID Number: IV-78	Released Date: 2006 (Batch 1)	Category: Traditional Opera
Affiliated Province: Guizhou Province	Type: New Item	Application Province or Unit: Sinan County, Guizhou Province	

Guizhou Lantern Opera was formed on the basis of local folk songs and dances, originally called Picking the Lantern, which only had singing and dancing. Later, small-scale opera was added to the singing and dancing. Influenced by foreign operas, it has developed into the current Lantern Opera. Guizhou Lantern Opera is mainly popular in Dushan County, Zunyi City, Bijie City, Anshun City, Tongren City, etc., with different names in different places. It is called "the Lantern plus Opera" in northern and western Guizhou, "the Stage Lantern" in Dushan County, and "the Lantern Opera" in Sinan County, Yinjiang County, etc.

Sinan Lantern Opera is a unique national opera formed during the reign of Emperor Daoguang of the Qing Dynasty, which is based on the singing and dancing

---

① 《花灯戏（思南花灯戏）》，中国非物质文化遗产网，http://www. ihchina. cn/Article/Index/detail?id=13339，检索日期：2019 年 8 月 19 日。

② 《思南土家花灯戏》，中国铜仁门户网，http://www. tongren. gov. cn/2013/0128/67. shtml，检索日期：2020 年 8 月 21 日。

of Tujia Lantern and has absorbed the performance forms of Nuotang Opera of the Tujia nationality, Hunan Opera, Chenhe Opera and other operas. Its performance forms are diversified. At first, it was two-person singing and dancing, and developed into three-person performance on the stage in the late Ming and early Qing dynasties, with one actor and two actresses, called "Double Phoenixes Facing the Sun"; or with two actors and one actress, called "Double Lions Playing with a Ball". Now the number of performers on the stage is unlimited, reaching as many as 20 or 30 ones, with women playing the role of Dan Character (a female role), which has changed the tradition of males being dressed as females. The music of **Sinan Lantern Opera** bears rich ethnic customs and local characteristics. Its tunes are divided into four categories: the lantern tune, the formal tune, the miscellaneous tune and the minor tune. It has 24 kinds of traditional Qupai (the tune name of a melody). Due to various tunes and different styles, **Sinan Lantern Opera** in different places has different characteristics. Its accompaniment instruments are mainly Maluo (a kind of Chinese percussion instrument), big gongs, Erhu (a two-stringed bowed instrument), Yueqin (a four-stringed plucked musical instrument with a full-moon-shaped sound box), Sanxian (a three-stringed plucked musical instrument), etc. During the performance, performers sing and dance, with singing and dancing interspersed with each other. Their dance forms are lively and diverse, and their dance postures are robust and beautiful.

贵州省 国家级非物质文化遗产文献资料汇编（汉英对照）

The Documentary Compilation of the State-level Intangible Cultural Heritage of Guizhou Province (Chinese-English Versions)

独山花灯戏展演
the Performance of the Lantern Opera in Dushan

第 2−3 项：花灯戏

项目序号：222	项目编号：Ⅳ−78	公布时间：2008（第二批）	类别：传统戏剧
所属地区：贵州省	类型：扩展项目	申报地区或单位：贵州省独山县	

项目序号：222	项目编号：Ⅳ−78	公布时间：2011（第三批）	类别：传统戏剧
所属地区：贵州省	类型：扩展项目	申报地区或单位：贵州省花灯剧团	

　　贵州花灯戏主要流行于独山、遵义、毕节、安顺、铜仁等地，各地称谓有所不同。独山县的花灯戏，又叫"台灯"，是贵州南路花灯的代表。遵义、毕节、安顺和铜仁等市的花灯戏属黔西花灯戏，是黔西北地区花灯的代表。

　　独山花灯最早是"地灯"，源于正月闹元宵玩灯的习俗，是一种不择场所徒步于地上表演的艺术形式。多以扇、帕为道具载歌载舞，后被"还愿"习俗借用，形成"愿灯"，内容是娱神、酬神了愿，驱魔去邪、消灾化劫。"愿灯"逐渐形成一整套程序，其中要扎灯、搭台、唱灯，就形成了"台灯"，这也标志着独山花灯戏的形成。目前，已有两百多年的历史。"台灯"表演分为两部分：开台的第一个节目是《踩新台》，接着是《打头台》，俗称"打花折"，之后才出折子戏（正戏）。独山花灯戏有 140 多种剧目，包括《金铃记》《蟒蛇记》等 85 种早期条纲戏剧目，《铡美案》等 27 种移植剧目和《七妹与蛇郎》等 27 种新创剧目。独山花灯戏兼容并蓄、地域特色鲜明、舞姿优美、曲调独特，是独山人特殊的生活方式、民族个性与文化多样性的展现，体现其勤劳勇敢、淳朴善良、达观进取的精神气质。[①]

　　贵州省花灯剧团申报的花灯戏属于黔西花灯戏。20 世纪初，黔西花灯戏

---

① 《花灯戏》，中国非物质文化遗产网，http://www.ihchina.cn/Article/Index/detail?id=13341，检索日期：2019 年 8 月 18 日。

加入了武功表演、音乐曲调"桐子树"、舞蹈耍双扇、衬词运用等艺术表现形式，在贵州其他几路花灯中已不常见，独具黔西特色。代表剧目有《拜年》《姐妹观花》《三访亲》《刘三妹挑水》《放牛拦妻》等。[①]

Items 2-3: the Lantern Opera

Item Serial Number: 222	Item ID Number: IV-78	Released Date: 2008 (Batch 2)	Category: Traditional Opera
Affiliated Province: Guizhou Province	Type: Extended Item	Application Province or Unit: Dushan County, Guizhou Province	

Item Serial Number: 222	Item ID Number: IV-78	Released Date: 2011 (Batch 3)	Category: Traditional Opera
Affiliated Province: Guizhou Province	Type: Extended Item	Application Province or Unit: the Lantern Troupe of Guizhou Province	

Guizhou Lantern Opera is mainly popular in Dushan County, Zunyi City, Bijie City, Anshun City, Tongren City, etc., with various names in different places. **The Lantern Opera** in Dushan County is also called "the Stage Lantern", which is the representative of the Southern-school Lantern Opera of Guizhou Province. **The Lantern Operas** in Zunyi City, Bijie City, Anshun City, Tongren City, etc. belong to **the Lantern Opera** of Western Guizhou, which are the representatives of **the Lantern Opera** in northwest region of Guizhou Province.

The Lantern Opera in Dushan was originally "the Ground Lantern", originating from the custom of playing with lanterns during the Lantern Festival in the first month of the lunar calendar. It was an artistic form performed on the ground at any place. Usually, using fans and handkerchiefs as props, actors sang and danced. Later, the opera borrowed the custom of "redeeming a vow to a god", and developed into "the Willing Lantern", the content of which was to amuse gods, fulfill one's vows, exorcise evil spirits and eliminate disasters. "The Willing Lantern" gradually formed a complete set of procedures, including making lanterns, setting up the stage

---

① 《花灯戏》，中国非物质文化遗产网，http://www. ihchina. cn/Article/Index/detail? id=13346，检索日期：2019 年 8 月 18 日。

贵州省 国家级非物质文化遗产文献资料汇编（汉英对照）

The Documentary Compilation of the State-level Intangible Cultural Heritage of Guizhou Province (Chinese-English Versions)

and singing **the Lantern Opera**, and thus "the Stage Lantern" came into being, marking the beginning of **the Lantern Opera** in Dushan. At present, it has had a history of over two hundred years. The performance of "the Stage Lantern" is divided into two parts: the first one is "Stepping on the New Stage", followed by "Beginning the First Stage", called "Dahuazhe" by local people, and then comes the main plays (Zhezi Opera). **The Lantern Opera** in Dushan consists of more than 140 plays, including 85 early-stage Tiaogang plays, such as "The Story of the Golden Bell" and "The Story of the Python"; 27 transplanted plays, such as "The Case of Beheading Chen Shimei"; and 27 newly-created plays, such as "Sister Qi and Snake Boy". **The Lantern Opera** in Dushan is inclusive, with distinctive regional characteristics, beautiful dance postures and unique melody, which shows Dushan people's special way of life, their national personality and cultural diversity, and reflects their hardworking, brave, honest, kind, optimistic and enterprising spirit.

The Lantern Opera declared by the Lantern Troupe of Guizhou Province belongs to **the Lantern Opera** of western Guizhou. In the early 20th century, the artistic forms of martial arts performance, music tune "the Tongzi Tree", playing with double fans in dance, using lining words, etc. were added to **the Lantern Opera** of Western Guizhou, which have been rarely seen in other schools of Guizhou Lantern Opera, having the unique feature of Western Guizhou. The representative plays are "Paying a New Year's Call", "Sisters Watch Flowers", "Three Visits to Relatives", "Liu Sanmei Carries Water", "Herding Cattle to Meet His Wife", etc.

侗戏《珠郎娘美》
the Dong Opera of "Zhulang and Niangmei"

第4项：侗戏

项目序号：227	项目编号：Ⅳ-83	公布时间：2006（第一批）	类别：传统戏剧
所属地区：贵州省	类型：新增项目	申报地区或单位：贵州省黎平县	

侗戏由黎平县腊洞村侗族歌师吴文彩始创，已有150多年的历史，主要流行于贵州省的黎平、从江和榕江县侗族村寨。

侗戏主要曲调有【平板】（又称【普通板】、【胡琴板】）和【哀调】（又称【哭调】），此外还有【仙腔】和【戏曲大歌】等；伴奏乐器有二胡、牛腿琴、侗琵琶、月琴、低胡、扬琴、竹笛和芦笙等；开台和人物上下场时用鼓、锣、钹和镲伴奏。侗戏表演比较朴实，服饰、道具都是本民族的日常用品。表演时一般由两人用侗语对唱，每唱完最后一句，表演者便在音乐过门中走"∞"字交换位置，然后接着唱下一句，如此反复直至一段唱词结束。侗戏没有严格的行当划分，唯丑角的表演有独特程式，无论从哪个方向出场，都只能向里跳，人称"跳丑脚"。《梅良玉》《毛洪玉英》《刘知远》《江女万良》《珠郎娘美》等是侗戏的传统剧目。侗戏民族特色鲜明，有深厚的群众基础，在侗族地区，多数村寨都有群众自己组织的业余侗戏班。侗族没有文字，过去戏师们全凭记忆把数出戏记于脑中，再传授给演员；有的则利用汉字记音，借用汉文字把传统的侗戏记录下来。①

---

① 《侗戏》，中国非物质文化遗产网，http://www.ihchina.cn/Article/Index/detail?id=13364，检索日期：2019年8月19日。

Item 4: Dong Opera

Item Serial Number: 227	Item ID Number: IV-83	Released Date: 2006 (Batch 1)	Category: Traditional Opera
Affiliated Province: Guizhou Province	Type: New Item	Application Province or Unit: Liping County, Guizhou Province	

Dong Opera was founded by Wu Wencai, a singer of the Dong nationality in Ladong Village of Liping County. It has a history of more than 150 years, mainly popular in the stockaded villages inhabited by the Dong nationality in Liping, Congjiang and Rongjiang counties of Guizhou Province.

The tunes of **Dong Opera** mainly include "the Flat Board" (also called "the Normal Board" or "Huqinban Board") and "the Plaintive Tune" (also called "the Crying Tune"). In addition, there are also "the Celestial Being's Tone", "the Operatic Big Songs", etc. The accompaniment instruments are Erhu (a two-stringed bowed instrument), Niutui Lute (a bow-and-string instrument of the Dong nationality, named for its slender body looking like cattle's thigh), Dong Pipa (a plucked string instrument with a fretted fingerboard), Yueqin (a four-stringed plucked musical instrument with a full-moon-shaped sound box), Bass Erhu (a two-stringed bowed instrument), dulcimers, bamboo flutes, Lusheng Musical Instruments, etc. When a theatrical performance begins and actors get on or off the stage, drums, gongs, cymbals and small cymbals are played to accompany them. The performance of **Dong Opera** is relatively simple, its costumes and props are all daily necessities of this ethnic group. When performing it, usually two actors sing it in antiphonal style in the Dong language. Whenever they finish singing the last sentence, the two performers will exchange their positions by moving in the shape of "∞", and then start to sing the next sentence. This process is repeated until the end of one passage of the librettos. **Dong Opera** has no strict division of role types, and only the performance of Chou Character (a clown) has a unique pattern, that is, from no matter which direction he appears, he can only jump inward, which is called "a jumping clown". Such plays as "Mei Liangyu", "Mao Hong and Yuying", "Liu Zhiyuan", "Jiang Nü and Wan Liang" as well as "Zhulang and Niangmei" are the traditional repertoire of **Dong Opera**. **Dong Opera** has distinctive ethnic characteristics and a solid foundation of the masses. In areas inhabited by the Dong nationality, the masses in most stockaded villages organize their own amateur theatrical troupes of **Dong Opera**. As the Dong nationality has no written language, in the past, the masters of **Dong Opera** performers had to memorize many plays and then imparted them to actors/actresses, and some even recorded the traditional **Dong Opera** by using Chinese characters.

布依戏表演
the Performance of Buyi Opera

第5项：布依戏

项目序号：228	项目编号：Ⅳ-84	公布时间：2006（第一批）	类别：传统戏剧
所属地区：贵州省	类型：新增项目	申报地区或单位：贵州省册亨县	

　　布依戏主要流传于贵州南部及西南部布依族聚居的册亨、安龙和兴义等县，是受汉、壮、苗族戏曲的影响，用布依语演唱布依族乐曲，在八音坐弹、板凳戏的基础上发展形成的。

　　其音乐曲调有【京调】、【起落调】、【翻演调】、【马倒铃】、【正调】、【长调】、【八谱调】、【反调】、【武打升官调】、【过场调】、【倒茶调】和【吃酒调】。伴奏乐器主要有尖子胡琴、朴子胡琴、笛、短箫、木叶、三弦、琵琶、月琴及大锣、大钹、鼓、木鱼、包包锣和小马锣等。其表演有固定程序，一般由祭祀、请祖师开箱、降三星、打加官、正戏、扫台和封箱组成，其中正戏是主体部分。正戏的剧目包括本民族剧目和移植剧目两类。本民族剧目以讲述布依族传说故事为主，有《三月三》《六月六》《罗细杏》《人财两空》等，唱、白均用布依语；移植剧目主要从汉族民间故事移植而来，包括《玉堂春》《蟒蛇记》《秦香莲》《祝英台》等，用"双语"表演。人物出场念"引子""定场诗""自报家门"时说汉语，演唱、对白、插科打诨时用布依语。布依戏中有生、旦、丑及大王、大将等分工，各角色的舞台调度都是三步或五步一转身，演唱过程中对面穿梭。布依戏主要由村寨的民间业余戏班加以传承。戏班一般有30多人，以自然村寨为基础，戏师为班头，各班每年春节期间都要为本寨或没有戏班的村寨演出，以禳灾祈福、驱鬼逐疫。①

---

① 《布依戏》，中国非物质文化遗产网，http://www.ihchina.cn/Article/Index/detail?id=13367，检索日期：2019年8月19日。

Item 5: Buyi Opera

Item Serial Number: 228	Item ID Number: IV-84	Released Date: 2006 (Batch 1)	Category: Traditional Opera
Affiliated Province: Guizhou Province	Type: New Item	Application Province or Unit: Ceheng County, Guizhou Province	

Buyi Opera is mainly spread in counties inhabited by the Buyi nationality, such as Ceheng, Anlong and Xingyi, in the southern and southwestern parts of Guizhou Province. It has been influenced by operas of the Han, Zhuang and Miao nationalities, and has been formed on the basis of Bayin Sitting and Playing and the Bench Opera, with Buyi melodies sung in the Buyi language.

Its music tunes include "Beijing Tune", "the Rising-and-falling Tune", "the Rolling-and-performance Tune", "Madaoling Tune", "the Positive Tune", "the Long Tune", "the Eight Music Score Tune", "the Inverted Tune", "the Promotion Tune of Martial Arts", "the Interlude Tune", "the Tea-pouring Tune" and "the Toasting Tune". The accompaniment instruments are mainly Jianzi Huqin Musical Instruments, Puzi Huqin Musical Instruments, flutes, Short Xiao (a vertical bamboo flute), Muye (leaves), Sanxian (a three-stringed plucked musical instrument), Pipa (a plucked string instrument with a fretted fingerboard), Yueqin (a four-stringed plucked musical instrument with a full-moon-shaped sound box), big gongs, big cymbals, drums, the Wooden Fish (a percussion instrument of a hollow wooden block, originally used by Buddhist priests to beat rhythm when chanting scriptures), Baobao Gong, Small Maluo (a kind of Chinese percussion instrument), etc. Its performance has a fixed procedure, which is generally composed of offering sacrifices to the god, inviting the grandmaster to open the box of costumes and stage props, the descending of three stars, congratulating on the promotion, formal performance, sweeping the stage and sealing the box of costumes and stage props. Among them, formal performance is the main body, the repertoire of which includes two types: the native one and the transplanted one. The native repertoire mainly focuses on telling legendary stories of the Buyi nationality, such as "The Double Third Festival", "The Double Sixth Festival", "Luo Xixing" and "The Losing of both Men and Money", and its singing and speaking parts are both performed in the Buyi language. The transplanted repertoire mostly comes from the folk tales of the Han nationality, including "Yu

·**贵州省**·国家级非物质文化遗产文献资料汇编（汉英对照）

The Documentary Compilation of the State-level Intangible Cultural Heritage of Guizhou Province (Chinese-English Versions)

Tangchun", "The Story of the Python", "Qin Xianglian" and "Zhu Yingtai", which are performed bilingually. When performers get on the stage to recite "the opening words", "Dingchang poem" and make "self-introduction", they use Chinese. When they perform the singing and speaking parts as well as gags, they use the Buyi language. In **Buyi Opera**, there are role divisions of Sheng Character (a male role in Chinese opera, usually referring to the role with a beard or a young man), Dan Character (a female role), Chou Character (a clown), the great king, the senior general, etc. On the stage, each role walks three or five steps, and then turns around once. During the singing process, he/she shuttles between the two ends of the stage. **Buyi Opera** is mainly inherited by folk amateur theatrical troupes in stockaded villages, each generally consisting of more than 30 people with natural stockaded villages as the basis and opera masters as the head. Each troupe performs for its own village or villages without troupes during the Spring Festival every year, praying for good fortune and expelling ghosts and pestilence.

撮泰吉表演
the Performance of Cuotaiji Opera

项目序号：229	项目编号：Ⅳ-85	公布时间：2006（第一批）	类别：传统戏剧
所属地区：贵州省	类型：新增项目	申报地区或单位：贵州省威宁彝族回族苗族自治县	

　　撮泰吉为彝文译音，意为"变人戏"，是仅存于贵州省威宁彝族回族苗族自治县板底乡裸嘎寨的一种古老的戏剧形态，于农历正月初三到十五演出。

　　撮泰吉表演形式十分独特，表演者用白色头帕将头缠成尖锥形，身体及四肢用布紧缠，象征裸体；部分人头戴面具，分别扮作彝族老人（1700 岁）、老妇人（1500 岁）、苗族老人（1200 岁）、汉族老人（1000 岁）及小孩。面具长约一尺，前额突出，鼻子直长，眼睛及嘴部挖出空洞，用锅烟涂为黑色，又以石灰及粉笔在额头和脸部勾出各种线条，黑白相间，极显粗犷、神秘、森严、古朴。表演中不戴面具者为山林老人或山神（2000 岁），是自然与智慧的化身。撮泰吉表演分为四部分：祭祀、耕作、喜庆和扫寨，耕作是全戏的核心，主要反映彝族迁徙、农耕和繁衍的历史。正月十五的扫寨，即"扫火星"活动，将整个撮泰吉演出推向高潮，表演者走村串寨，扫除灾难和瘟疫，祝愿人畜兴旺、五谷丰登。彝族撮泰吉具有民间信仰和祖先祭祀的功能，成为当地民众祭祀祖先，祈愿人畜兴旺、风调雨顺的重要方式。①

Item 6: Cuotaiji Opera of the Yi Nationality

Item Serial Number: 229	Item ID Number: Ⅳ-85	Released Date: 2006 (Batch 1)	Category: Traditional Opera

---

① 《彝族撮泰吉》，中国非物质文化遗产网，http://www.ihchina.cn/Article/Index/detail?id=13368，检索日期：2019 年 8 月 12 日。

贵州省 国家级非物质文化遗产文献资料汇编（汉英对照）

The Documentary Compilation of the State-level Intangible Cultural Heritage of Guizhou Province (Chinese-English Versions)

Affiliated Province: Guizhou Province	Type: New Item	Application Province or Unit: Weining Yi, Hui and Miao Autonomous County, Guizhou Province

Cuotaiji is the transliteration of the Yi language, meaning "the People-changing Opera". It is an ancient form of opera that only exists in Luoga Stockaded Village, Bandi Township, Weining Yi, Hui and Miao Autonomous County, Guizhou Province, which is performed from the 3rd to the 15th days of the first month of the lunar calendar.

The performance form of **Cuotaiji Opera** is very unique. The performers wrap their heads into the shape of pointed cones with white handkerchiefs, and bind up their bodies and four limbs tightly with cloth to symbolize nudity. Some of them wear masks to dress up as old men of the Yi nationality (1700 years old), old women (1500 years old), old men of the Miao nationality (1200 years old), old men of the Han nationality (1000 years old) and children. The masks are about one *chi* (a Chinese unit of length, with one *chi* roughly equal to 13 inches) in length, with protruding foreheads as well as long and straight noses, and the eyes and mouths are dug into holes. They are painted black by using pot smoke, and various black-and-white lines are drawn on the foreheads and faces by using lime and chalk, very rough, mysterious, solemn and quaint. During the performance, those who do not wear masks are mountain forest elders or mountain gods (2000 years old), the embodiment of nature and wisdom. The performance of **Cuotaiji Opera** is divided into four parts: offering sacrifices, farming, festivity and sweeping the stockaded village. Farming is the core of the whole opera, which mainly reflects the history of the Yi People's migration, farming and reproduction. The activity of "sweeping the stockaded village" on the 15th day of the first month of the lunar calendar, that is, the activity of "sweeping the sparks", pushes the performance of **Cuotaiji Opera** to a climax. The performers go from village to village to sweep away disasters and pestilence, praying for the prosperity of human and livestock as well as an abundant harvest of all crops. **Cuotaiji Opera of the Yi Nationality** has the functions of folk belief and ancestor worship, which has become an important way for local people to offer sacrifices to their ancestors, and to pray for the prosperity of human and livestock as well as timely wind and rain.

德江傩堂戏表演
the Performance of Dejiang Nuotang Opera

第7项：
傩戏（德江傩堂戏）

项目序号：233	项目编号：Ⅳ-89	公布时间：2006（第一批）	类别：传统戏剧
所属地区：贵州省	类型：新增项目	申报地区或单位：贵州省德江县	

　　傩戏是在民间祭祀仪式基础上吸取民间戏曲而形成的一种戏曲形式，流行于中国的多个省份。贵州傩戏吸收了花灯的艺术成分，用本地方言演唱，唱腔多采用本地群众熟悉的戏曲腔调，主要分为地戏、阳戏和傩堂戏三种。地戏是由明初"调北征南"留守在云南、贵州屯田戍边将士的后裔屯堡人为祭祀祖先演出的一种傩戏，都是反映历史故事的武打戏。阳戏以演出反映民间生活的小戏为主，所唱腔调多吸收自花鼓和花灯等民间小戏。

　　德江傩堂戏属于傩堂戏，是一种佩戴面具表演的宗教祭祀戏剧，也是一种古老的民族民间风俗文化活动，源于古时的傩仪，汉代以后，逐渐发展成为具有浓厚娱人色彩的礼仪祀典。德江傩堂戏包括傩戏演出和傩技表演：傩戏演出是主体部分，分正戏和插戏；傩技，土家人称"绝活"，其表演项目由主家与坛班约定。举行傩事活动前，土家族老师都要精心布置一个傩坛（傩堂），故傩堂戏又称傩坛戏。傩坛布置精致，集编扎、剪纸、染印、绘画、书法、建筑等艺术为一体。德江自古为土家族等少数民族聚居地，特殊的地理位置使德江傩堂戏源远流长，保存得十分原始和完整。①

---

① 《傩戏（德江傩堂戏）》，中国非物质文化遗产网，http://www.ihchina.cn/Article/Index/detail?id=13380，检索日期：2019 年 6 月 12 日。

Item 7: Nuo Opera (Dejiang Nuotang Opera)

Item Serial Number: 233	Item ID Number: IV-89	Released Date: 2006 (Batch 1)	Category: Traditional Opera
Affiliated Province: Guizhou Province	Type: New Item	Application Province or Unit: Dejiang County, Guizhou Province	

Nuo Opera is a kind of theatrical form which has been developed on the basis of the folk sacrificial ceremony and has absorbed folk operas, popular in many provinces of China. Guizhou Nuo Opera has absorbed the artistic elements of the Lantern Opera, sung in local dialect with the opera tones familiar to local people. It is mainly divided into three kinds: the Ground Opera, Yangxi Opera and Nuotang Opera. The Ground Opera is a kind of Nuo Opera performed by Tunbu people, the descendants of the soldiers who garrisoned the frontier, opened up wasteland and grew food grain in Yunnan and Guizhou provinces in the early Ming Dynasty, to offer sacrifices to ancestors. Its content is the martial arts operas reflecting historical stories. Yangxi Opera mainly focuses on the performance of the minor operas that reflect folk life, and its singing tunes have mostly absorbed minor folk operas, such as the Drum Opera and the Lantern Opera.

Dejiang Nuotang Opera belongs to Nuotang Opera. It is a religious sacrificial opera performed with masks, and is also an ancient ethnic folk custom and cultural activity. Originating from the ancient Nuo ceremony, it has gradually developed into a ritual ceremony with the strong color of entertaining people after the Han Dynasty. **Dejiang Nuotang Opera** includes Nuo Opera performance and Nuo technique show. Nuo Opera performance is the main body, divided into the main opera and the interposed opera. Nuo technique is called "the unique skill" by the Tujia people, and its performance items are discussed by hosts and altar troupes. Before the Nuo activity, Tujia seniors should elaborately arrange a Nuotan Altar (Nuotang Hall), so Nuotang Opera is also called Nuotan Opera. Nuotan Altar is exquisitely arranged, integrating the arts of weaving, paper cutting, dyeing, drawing and painting, calligraphy, architecture, etc. Dejiang has been a living place of Tujia and other ethnic minorities since ancient times, and its special geographical location has made **Dejiang Nuotang Opera** keep a long history and well preserved in the original form.

仡佬族傩戏表演
the Performance of Nuo Opera of the Gelao Nationality

第8项：
傩戏（仡佬族傩戏）

项目序号：233	项目编号：Ⅳ-89	公布时间：2008（第二批）	类别：传统戏剧
所属地区：贵州省	类型：扩展项目	申报地区或单位：贵州省道真仡佬族苗族自治县	

　　仡佬族傩戏由湘西傩戏发展而来，元明时期传入贵州省道真仡佬族苗族自治县，开始在当地流传。它以巫术为内核，与贵州地域文化和仡佬族文化合流，形成佛巫或道巫、清巫、儒巫合一的特殊坛门形式。目前在道真县从事傩仪活动的有 50 多个坛班、360 多人。

　　道真仡佬傩戏以祈福迎祥为目的，由民间称为"道士先生"的艺人组班表演，有冲傩、打保福、阳戏和梓潼戏等 130 余种表现形式，演出时以锣、鼓、钹和唢呐等乐器伴奏，有歌有舞，或说或唱，文武并重，演员扮演山王、秦童等角色进行表演时需戴上特制的傩面具。参与表演者一二人至十余人不等，时间一两个小时至几天几夜不等，内容因信众目的与坛门派别而异，整个演出过程呈现出娱神和娱人结合、祭祀与艺术交融的特征。目前道真仡佬族傩戏记录成文的约 800 多万字，据初步估计，将全部傩戏加以演示约需两个月。仡佬族傩戏是仡佬族文化与贵州巫傩文化的重要载体。①

---

① 《傩戏（仡佬族傩戏）》，中国非物质文化遗产网，http://www.ihchina.cn/Article/Index/detail?id=13384，检索日期：2019 年 8 月 19 日。

Item 8: Nuo Opera (Nuo Opera of the Gelao Nationality)

Item Serial Number: 233	Item ID Number: IV-89	Released Date: 2008 (Batch 2)	Category: Traditional Opera
Affiliated Province: Guizhou Province	Type: Extended Item	Application Province or Unit: Daozhen Gelao and Miao Autonomous County, Guizhou Province	

Nuo Opera of the Gelao Nationality developed from Nuo Opera of Western Hunan, was introduced into Daozhen Gelao and Miao Autonomous County in Guizhou Province in the Yuan and Ming dynasties, and began to spread in the local area. It takes witchcraft as its core, and combines with the regional culture and Gelao culture of Guizhou Province, forming special altar forms of integrating Buddhism and witchcraft, Taoism and witchcraft, Qing religion and witchcraft, as well as Confucianism and witchcraft. Up to now, there are more than 50 altar troupes and over 360 actors engaged in Nuo ceremonial activities in Daozhen County.

Nuo Opera of the Gelao Nationality in Daozhen aims at praying for blessings and auspiciousness, performed by folk artists called "Taoist priests" who form troupes. It has more than 130 forms of expression, such as Chongnuo activity, Dabaofu activity, Yangxi Opera and Zitong Opera. It is performed to the accompaniment of gongs, drums, cymbals, Suona Horn (a woodwind instrument) and other musical instruments, with singing and dancing, either talking or singing, and equal emphasis is laid on civil and martial arts. When acting the roles of the Mountain King, Qintong (a role of clown in Nuo Opera), etc., the performers need to wear special Nuo masks during the performance. The number of performers varies from one or two to over ten, and the performance time ranges from one or two hours to several days and nights. Its content varies with the purpose of believers and the sect of the altar. The whole performance shows the characteristics of the combination of amusing both the god and human beings, and the integration of sacrifice and art. Now, there are about more than 8 million words recorded in **Nuo Opera of the Gelao Nationality** in Daozhen. According to preliminary estimation, it takes about two months to finish performing all Nuo operas. **Nuo Opera of the Gelao Nationality** is an important carrier of the Gelao culture as well as the witchcraft and Nuo cultures of Guizhou Province.

荔波布依族傩戏
Libo Nuo Opera of the Buyi Nationality

第9项：傩戏（荔波布依族傩戏）

项目序号：233	项目编号：Ⅳ-89	公布时间：2011（第三批）	类别：传统戏剧
所属地区：贵州省	类型：扩展项目	申报地区或单位：贵州省荔波县	

　　荔波布依族傩戏源于宋元时期，由广西河池市思恩县傩戏坛祖玉氏传到荔波布依族地区。

　　荔波布依族傩戏面具有木刻面具、皮胎面具、笋壳面具和竹编纸糊面具等，每堂为 36 面，每面为一尊神，每一尊神有一本经书，叙述该神的形态特征、功能、神力和由来。每尊神都有布依语和汉语两种称谓，演出时主要用布依语。[①] 荔波布依族傩戏分文戏和武戏。戏目有十余种，布依人称"桥"，分为"大桥"和"小桥"。大桥演出七天以上，最多的十三天，有戏曲表演，戴面具。小桥演出三天，没有戏曲表演，不戴面具。[②] 荔波布依族傩戏以求子保子为内容，由一家一户将傩戏班子请到家举行七天七夜的活动。过去这种做法很普遍，布依族男性的一生中必须举行一次。后来部分地区衍变成婚后久不生育者才举行。其形式有"做桃"和"架桥"两种。前者请傩戏班子举行七天七夜的活动；后者只请魔公或坛师，带几个弟子举行三天三夜的活动。送花是"做桃"和"架桥"的中心内容，因为"花"在布依族人眼里是妇女受孕的因子。"做桃"和"架桥"的宗旨是主家求子，外家给女婿送花。[③]

---

① 柏果成、黎汝标，《贵州荔波县布依族傩戏》，载《中华艺术论丛》，2009 年第 1 期，第 262-276 页。

② 《傩戏（荔波布依族傩戏）》，中国非物质文化遗产网，http://www.ihchina.cn/Article/Index/detail?id=13388，检索日期：2019 年 8 月 17 日。

③ 柏果成、黎汝标，《贵州荔波县布依族傩戏》，载《中华艺术论丛》，2009 年第 1 期，第 262-276 页。

贵州省·国家级非物质文化遗产文献资料汇编（汉英对照）

The Documentary Compilation of the State-level Intangible Cultural Heritage of Guizhou Province (Chinese-English Versions)

Item 9: Nuo Opera (Libo Nuo Opera of the Buyi Nationality)

Item Serial Number: 233	Item ID Number: IV-89	Released Date: 2011 (Batch 3)	Category: Traditional Opera
Affiliated Province: Guizhou Province	Type: Extended Item	Application Province or Unit: Libo County, Guizhou Province	

Libo Nuo Opera of the Buyi Nationality originated from the Song and Yuan dynasties, introduced to areas inhabited by the Buyi nationality in Libo by the altar master of Nuo Opera with the surname of Yu from Si'en County, Hechi City, Guangxi Zhuang Autonomous Region.

The masks for performing **Libo Nuo Opera of the Buyi Nationality** include woodcut masks, leather masks, bamboo-shoot shell masks and bamboo-woven masks pasted with paper. Each opera needs 36 masks, each mask stands for one god and each god has a scripture, which describes the physique features, functions, divine power and the origin of the god. Each god has a Chinese name and a Buyi name, and the Buyi language is used mostly in performances. **Libo Nuo Opera of the Buyi Nationality** is divided into Wenxi (operas characterized by singing and acting) and Wuxi (operas characterized by acrobatic fighting), with more than ten kinds of repertoire. The Buyi people call these operas as "Qiao", which is divided into "Big Qiao" and "Small Qiao". The "Big Qiao" lasts more than 7 days, with a maximum of 13 days, which has opera performances with actors wearing masks. The "Small Qiao" lasts for three days without opera performances or wearing masks. The content of **Libo Nuo Opera of the Buyi Nationality** is to pray for a son and protect him. The Nuo Opera Troupe is invited by each household to perform it for seven days and nights at home. It used to be very common that a Buyi man must hold its performance once in his life. Later, it is held only by those who have no child for a long time after marriage in some areas. Its performance has two forms: "Zuotao (making the peach)" and "Jiaqiao (building the bridge)". The former is to invite a Nuo Opera Troupe to hold activities for seven days and nights; while the latter is to only invite the Demon Lord or the Altar Master, together with a few disciples, to hold activities for three days and nights. Sending flowers is the core of "Zuotao (making the peach)" and "Jiaqiao (building the bridge)", because "flowers" are one factor of women's pregnancy in the eyes of the Buyi people. The purpose of "Zuotao (making the peach)" and "Jiaqiao (building the bridge)" is that the family of the host prays for giving birth to a son, and the daughter-in-law's family sends flowers to the son-in-law.

第10项：
傩戏（庆坛）

金沙庆坛活动
Jinsha Qingtan Activity

项目序号：233	项目编号：Ⅳ-89	公布时间：2014（第四批）	类别：传统戏剧
所属地区：贵州省	类型：扩展项目	申报地区或单位：贵州省金沙县	

　　金沙傩戏在当地俗称"庆坛"，是流传于贵州省金沙县长坝乡一带的仪式性民间戏剧，又称为"端公戏"，已有260多年的历史。

　　在金沙县，无论是老人逝世还是修建房屋、搬家，都会进行庆坛仪式。庆坛至今延续着古代傩祭仪式的古朴形式：每坛的演出都有固定的剧目程式；各种坛分别由若干折子戏组成；不同的坛演出不同的折子。伴奏只有打击乐；唱腔、道白接近川剧但更古朴；角色全是男性（偶有女角也用男扮女装），有的佩戴面具。"庆坛"是一种能阴阳两度的戏剧仪式活动，与当地驱邪纳福、祈求平安的民间信仰密切相关，反映百姓对美好生活的追求；它既娱神又娱人，具有丰富的内涵和表现形式。庆坛分"文坛"和"武坛"。"文坛"是当地民间死人祭祀活动的重要组成部分，为亡人做道场，包括从人死到入葬的全部祭奠，为丧礼仪式和娱神活动；"武坛"是祈福仪式和娱人活动，类似跳端公，为许愿和寿诞所做。金沙庆坛表现了汉民族万物有灵、生命神圣、众生平等、人与自然共生共荣的哲学思想，体现了尊祖敬老、忠孝节义、除暴安良和济民普渡的民族共识。①

---

① 李朝举，《毕节之最｜国家级非物质文化遗产——金沙傩戏（庆坛）》，http://mini. eastday.com/mobile/170909030443782.html，检索日期：2019年8月9日。

Item 10: Nuo Opera (Qingtan)

Item Serial Number: 233	Item ID Number: IV–89	Released Date: 2014 (Batch 4)	Category: Traditional Opera
Affiliated Province: Guizhou Province	Type: Extended Item	Application Province or Unit: Jinsha County, Guizhou Province	

Jinsha Nuo Opera, commonly called "Qingtan" by local people, is a ceremonial folk opera that is spread in Changba Township, Jinsha County, Guizhou Province, which is also called "Duangong Opera", with a history of more than 260 years.

In Jinsha County, whether it is the passing away of an elderly person or the building of houses, and moving to a new house, people will hold the ceremony of Qingtan. Qingtan has retained the simple and unsophisticated form of the ancient Nuo ceremony up to now: the performance for each altar has a fixed repertoire procedure; each altar is composed of several Zhezi plays; and for different altars, different Zhezi plays are performed. The accompaniment is only percussion music. The singing tones and Daobai (spoken parts in an opera) are similar to those of Sichuan Opera, but more primitive. The roles are all male (occasionally, there are female roles, but they are dressed up by male actors), and some wear masks. "Qingtan" is a theatrical ritual activity that can be performed with the characteristics of Yin or Yang. It is closely related to the local folk beliefs of exorcising evil spirits, receiving blessings and praying for peace, and reflects the common people's pursuit of a better life. It amuses not only gods but also people with rich connotations and forms of expression. Qingtan is divided into "Civil Tan (altar)" and "Martial Arts Tan (altar)". "Civil Tan (altar)" is an important part of local folk sacrificial activities for the dead, which is to make a Daochang (a place where the Taoist or Buddhist rites are performed) for the dead, including all sacrificial ceremonies from death to burial. It is a funeral ceremony and an activity of entertaining gods. "Martial Arts Tan (altar)" is a ceremony of praying for blessings and an activity of entertaining people, similar to Duangong Dance, which is performed to make wishes and celebrate birthdays. **Jinsha Qingtan** reflects the philosophical thoughts of the Han nationality that all things have souls, that life is sacred, that all living creatures are equal, and that man and nature coexist and prosper together, which embodies the national consensus of respecting ancestors and the elderly, showing loyalty, filial piety, chastity and righteousness, eliminating the tyrant, pacifying the people, as well as aiding the masses.

第11项：
安顺地戏

安顺地戏表演
the Performance of Anshun Ground Opera

项目序号：234	项目编号：Ⅳ-90	公布时间：2006（第一批）	类别：传统戏剧
所属地区：贵州省	类型：新增项目	申报地区或单位：贵州省安顺市	

　　安顺地戏，俗称"跳神"，是明初留守在安顺屯田戍边将士的后裔屯堡人为祭祀祖先演出的一种傩戏，主要流行于贵州省安顺市。表演地戏大都在露天场所进行，无须舞台。跳地戏一是自娱，二是祭神、娱神，驱鬼逐邪，祈祷丰年，祝愿平安。

　　安顺地戏演出以村寨为单位，演员是地道的农民。一般一个村寨一堂戏，演员二三十人，由"神头"负责。演出在每年的新春佳节和农历七月稻谷扬花时举行，村民还会在建房求财、祈福求子的时候请地戏队中的"神灵"如关羽、佘太君等去进行"开财门""送太子"等活动。安顺地戏是一种古老的戏剧，其显著特点是演出者首蒙青巾，腰围战裙，戴假面于额前，手执戈矛刀戟，随口而唱，应声而舞。地戏的表演方式以说唱为主，伴以舞蹈。剧情发展以说白方式推动，人物间的矛盾冲突、人物感情的变化则通过唱的方式来传达。其演唱是七言和十言韵文的说唱，在一锣一鼓伴奏下，一人领唱众人伴和，其舞主要表现征战格斗的打杀。安顺地戏所演内容全部是金戈铁马的征战故事，以屯堡人喜爱的薛家将、杨家将、岳家将、狄家将、三国英雄和瓦岗好汉为主角，赞美忠义，颂扬报国。[①]

Item 11: Anshun Ground Opera

Item Serial Number: 234	Item ID Number: Ⅳ-90	Released Date: 2006 (Batch 1)	Category: Traditional Opera

---

① 《安顺地戏》，中国非物质文化遗产网，http://www.ihchina.cn/Article/Index/detail?id=13391，检索日期：2019年8月19日。

Affiliated Province:	Type:	Application Province or Unit:
Guizhou Province	New Item	Anshun City, Guizhou Province

Anshun Ground Opera, commonly known as "Tiaoshen (a sorcerer's dance in a trance)", is a kind of Nuo Opera performed to offer sacrifices to ancestors by the Tunbu people, the descendants of the soldiers who were garrisoned in Anshun in the early Ming Dynasty, opening up wasteland and defending the frontier. It is mainly popular in Anshun City, Guizhou Province. **Anshun Ground Opera** is mostly performed in the open air with no need of stage, the purposes of which are to amuse oneself, offer sacrifices to the god, amuse the god, expel ghosts and evil spirits, pray for a good harvest and wish for peace.

The performance of **Anshun Ground Opera** is based on a stockaded village as a unit, with actors being farmers. Generally, there is one troupe of Ground Opera in one stockaded village, with twenty to thirty actors/actresses and under the charge of "Shentou (the master of the troupe)". The performance is held at the Spring Festival and in the 7th month of the lunar calendar when rice is in full bloom every year. Villagers will also invite the "deity" in the Ground Opera team, such as Guan Yu and She Taijun, to carry on the activities of "opening the Door of Wealth", "sending the crown prince", etc. when they build houses, as well as pray for wealth, blessings and sons. **Anshun Ground Opera** is an ancient opera. Its remarkable features are that performers wear cyan scarves on their heads, battle skirts around their waists and masks on their foreheads, and hold dagger-axes, spears, sabers and halberds in hands, singing at will and dancing in response to the voice. Its performance way is mainly talking and singing, accompanied by dances. The development of the plot is promoted by Shuobai (spoken parts in an opera), while the conflicts between characters and the changes of characters' feelings are conveyed by means of singing. Its performance is the talking and singing of the seven- or ten-character verses to the accompaniment of one gong and one drum, with one singer leading the singing and others accompanying it in chorus. The dance mainly shows the fighting and killing in battles. The content performed by **Anshun Ground Opera** is all about the fierce fighting stories on the battle field. Its main characters are generals of the Xue family, generals of the Yang family, generals of the Yue family, generals of the Di family, heroes of the Three Kingdoms, brave men of Wagang Stockaded Village, etc., which are loved by the Tunbu people, praising loyalty and righteousness as well as serving the country worthily.

第12项：
木偶戏（石阡木偶戏）

石阡木偶戏
Shiqian Puppet Play

项目序号：236	项目编号：Ⅳ-92	公布时间：2006（第一批）	类别：传统戏剧
所属地区：贵州省	类型：新增项目	申报地区或单位：贵州省石阡县	

　　石阡木偶戏是流传于贵州省石阡县各民族中的一种民间傀儡戏曲剧种，其远祖可追溯到汉魏"刻木人像"的"傀儡"。据传，约200年前自湖南辰溪传入，至今已有七代传人。至20世纪四五十年代发展为鼎盛时期，拥有太平班、兴隆班、天福班、杨本家班、泰洪班等。

　　石阡木偶戏基本要素包括唱腔、锣鼓牌子、"头子"、戏装、道具和表演六方面：唱腔，包括高腔和平弹两种；锣鼓牌子，主要有"大出场""小出场"等十余个牌子；"头子"，分为生、旦、净、丑四个行当；戏装，包括盔头、方巾、蟒袍、拷子、折子和披挂等部件；道具，包括各种兵器、"肚腹""踩脚""手柄""冉须"等部件；表演，包括表演手法和身段等。[1] 根据不同的标准，石阡木偶戏可分为很多类：以唱腔分，分为"高腔戏"和"平弹戏"；以剧目内容分，分为"撰本戏"和"小本子戏"；以表演场合和社会功用分，分为"庙会戏"和"愿戏与众戏"；以伦理道德准则分，分为"忠戏""孝戏""节戏""义戏"。石阡木偶戏有着独特的民族性、地域性及多样性的社会功能。[2]

---

[1] 《石阡木偶戏的基本要素》，多彩贵州网，http://culture.gog.cn/system/2016/10/31/015193604.shtml，检索日期：2019年8月19日。

[2] 《贵州非物质文化遗产——石阡木偶戏》，多彩贵州网，http://www.sqxw.gov.cn/html/2016/1109/minsuzongjiaowenhua7905.html，检索日期：2019年8月10日。

Item 12: the Puppet Play (Shiqian Puppet Play)

Item Serial Number: 236	Item ID Number: IV-92	Released Date: 2006 (Batch 1)	Category: Traditional Opera
Affiliated Province: Guizhou Province	Type: New Item	Application Province or Unit: Shiqian County, Guizhou Province	

Shiqian Puppet Play is a kind of folk puppet show spread among all ethnic groups in Shiqian County, Guizhou Province. Its origin can be traced back to the "puppet" of "the carved wooden figure" in the Han-Wei Period. It's said that it was introduced from Chenxi County of Hunan Province about 200 years ago, which has been handed down for seven generations. It has reached its peak in the 1940s and 1950s, having Taiping Troupe, Xinglong Troupe, Tianfu Troupe, Yangbenjia Troupe, Taihong Troupe, etc.

The basic elements of **Shiqian Puppet Play** include six aspects: singing tones, Gong-and-drum Paizi, "Touzi (role types)", costumes, props and performance. Singing tones are divided into two kinds: high tone and Pingtan; Gong-and-drum Paizi mainly includes more than ten kinds of Paizi (also called Qupai, meaning the tune name of a melody), such as "grand appearance on the stage" and "petty appearance on the stage"; "Touzi (role types)" is divided into four types of roles: Sheng Character (a male role in Chinese opera, usually referring to the role with a beard or a young man), Dan Character (a female role), Jing Character (a male role in Chinese opera, usually with rough and bold personalities) and Chou Character (a clown); costumes include Kuitou (caps worn by actors), kerchiefs, the Python Robe (official robe), handcuffs, Zhezi and suits of armors; props include a variety of weapons, "belly parts", "foot supports", "handles", "moustache" and other parts; and performance includes performance techniques and postures. According to different standards, **Shiqian Puppet Play** can be divided into many categories: based on singing tones, it is divided into "High Tone Play" and "Pingtan Play"; based on content, it is divided into "the Compiled Benxi Play" and "the Short Benzi Play"; based on performing occasions and social functions, it is divided into "the Temple-fair Play" and "the Vow-fulfilling Play and the Masses Play"; based on ethical and moral standards, it is divided into "Play of Loyalty", "Play of Filial Piety", "Play of Chastity" and "Play of Righteousness". **Shiqian Puppet Play** has unique ethnical and regional nature, as well as diverse social functions.

第13项：**黔剧**

黔剧《奢香夫人》
Guizhou Opera of "Madame Shexiang"

项目序号：732	项目编号：Ⅳ-131	公布时间：2008（第二批）	类别：传统戏剧
所属地区：贵州省	类型：新增项目	申报地区或单位：贵州省黔剧团	

　　黔剧是在贵州扬琴基础上发展起来的一个新兴地方戏曲剧种，又名"文琴""贵州弹词"，1960年2月正式定名为"黔剧"。清康熙年间，贵州扬琴开始在贵州境内流传，至今已有约300年的历史。

　　黔剧用贵州方言演唱，以贵阳官话及黔西话为代表，属于北方语系、西南官话，其声、韵、调都个性鲜明。其唱腔音乐属板腔体，有"清板""二板""扬调""苦禀""二流""二簧"等基本曲调。伴奏乐器除扬琴外，还有瓮琴、月琴、小京胡、二胡、琵琶、三弦、箫和笛。黔剧唱词以七言和十言为主，按照尾字平仄偶句押脚韵的规律，形成严格的上下句式，沿用了讲唱文学"三三四"或"二二三"的句式，语言质朴，唱腔婉转。黔剧的角色行当主要有生、旦、净、末、丑等，其中生行分为小生、正生、老生等；旦行分为正旦、小旦、贴旦、花旦、老旦等。黔剧现存传统剧目四百多种，主要是由古典小说、戏曲改编而成。多年来黔剧又创作、移植了大量剧目，其中改编自侗剧的《秦娘美》被拍摄成舞台艺术片，创作的彝族历史故事剧《奢香夫人》荣获文化部颁发的演出一等奖、创作一等奖。在音乐唱腔、乐器配备、表演程式和舞台美术等方面，黔剧也进行了革新，艺术上进一步发展成熟。[①]

---

① 《黔剧》，中国非物质文化遗产网，http://www.ihchina.cn/Article/Index/detail?id=13543，检索日期：2019年8月19日。

Item 13: Guizhou Opera

Item Serial Number: 732	Item ID Number: IV–131	Released Date: 2008 (Batch 2)	Category: Traditional Opera
Affiliated Province: Guizhou Province	Type: New Item	Application Province or Unit: Guizhou Opera Troupe of Guizhou Province	

Guizhou Opera is a new type of local opera developed on the basis of Guizhou Dulcimer Art, also called "Wenqin" and "Guizhou Tanci (a talking-and-singing art with roles performing it while sitting to the accompaniment of a dulcimer)", and was officially named "**Guizhou Opera**" in February 1960. During the reign of Emperor Kangxi of the Qing Dynasty, Guizhou Dulcimer Art began to spread in Guizhou, with a history of about three hundred years up to now.

Guizhou Opera is performed in Guizhou dialect, which is represented by Guiyang mandarin and the dialect spoken in the western region of Guizhou, belonging to the northern language family and the southwestern mandarin with distinctive sound, rhyme and tone. Its singing tone music belongs to Banqiang style, including the basic tunes of "Qingban", "Erban", "Yangdiao", "Kubing", "Erliu" and "Erhuang". In addition to dulcimers, the accompaniment instruments are Wengqin Musical Instrument, Yueqin (a four-stringed plucked musical instrument with a full-moon-shaped sound box), Small Jinghu (a traditional Chinese stringed instrument, also called Huqin Musical Instrument), Erhu (a two-stringed bowed instrument), Pipa (a plucked string instrument with a fretted fingerboard), Sanxian (a three-stringed plucked musical instrument), Xiao (a vertical bamboo flute) and flutes. The librettos of **Guizhou Opera** are mostly seven- and ten-character in each line. In accordance with the rule of the level and oblique tones of end words as well as the rule of the rhyming of even sentences, they form a strict up-and-down sentence pattern, which adopts the sentence pattern of the talking-and-singing literature, namely, "three-, three- and four-character" or "two-, two- and three-character" in each line. Its language is simple and unadorned, and singing tones are tactful. The role types of **Guizhou Opera** are mainly Sheng Character (a male role in Chinese opera, usually referring to the role with a beard or a young man), Dan Character (a female role), Jing Character (a male role in Chinese opera, usually with rough and bold personalities), Mo Character (a middle-aged male role in Chinese opera), Chou Character (a clown), etc. Among them, the role type of Sheng is divided into Xiaosheng (the young male role in Chinese opera), Zhengsheng (the main male role in Chinese opera), Laosheng (a male role of middle age and above in Chinese opera), etc.; and the role type of Dan is divided into Zhengdan (the main female role in Chinese opera), Xiaodan (a young female role in Chinese opera), Tiedan (a minor female role in Chinese opera), Huadan (a young or middle-aged female role in Chinese opera often with lively or boisterous personality and a hint of comedy), Laodan (an old female role in Chinese opera), etc. There are more than 400 kinds of traditional repertoire in **Guizhou Opera** currently, which are mainly adapted from classical novels and operas. Over the years, a large number of plays have also been created and transplanted in **Guizhou Opera**. Among them, "Qin Niangmei" adapted from Dong Opera has been shot into a stage art film; and "Madame Shexiang", the historical story opera of the Yi nationality, has won the first prize both in performance and in creation respectively awarded by the Ministry of Culture. In the aspects of the singing tones of music, accompaniment instruments, performing patterns, stage art, etc., **Guizhou Opera** has also been innovated, becoming mature in art further.

第五章
曲艺

Chapter Five

Quyi (a general term for all Chinese talking-and-singing art forms)

第 1 项:
布依族八音坐唱

布依族八音坐唱表演
the Performance of Bayin Sitting-and-singing of the Buyi Nationality

项目序号：282	项目编号：V-46	公布时间：2006（第一批）	类别：曲艺
所属地区：贵州省	类型：新增项目	申报地区或单位：贵州省兴义市	

　　布依族八音坐唱又叫"布依八音"，是布依族世代相传的一种民间曲艺说唱形式，主要在南盘江流域的村寨中流传。据传其原型是宫廷雅乐，以吹打为主。元明以后，逐渐发展为以丝竹乐器为主伴奏表演的曲艺形式，常在布依族的传统节日，或婚嫁、建房、祝寿等场合演奏。

　　八音坐唱的表演形式为八人分持牛骨胡（牛角胡）、葫芦琴（葫芦胡）、月琴、刺鼓（竹鼓）、箫筒、钗、包包锣和小马锣等八种乐器，围成圈轮递说唱。表演以第一人称的"跳入"唱叙故事，以第三人称的"跳出"解说故事，也有加入勒朗、勒尤和木叶等布依族乐器伴奏的情形。男艺人多采用高八度演唱，女子则在原调上演唱，从而产生强烈的音高和音色对比。八音坐唱的唱腔曲调主要为"正调"，其他曲调统称为"闲调"。代表性传统节目有《布依婚俗》《贺喜堂》《迎客调》《唱王玉莲传》《敬酒歌》《梁山伯与祝英台》等。八音坐唱是布依族人民在长期的生产与生活中逐步创造形成的，深深扎根于布依族群众之中，具有鲜明的布依族特色和广泛的群众基础。①

Item 1 Bayin Sitting-and-singing of the Buyi Nationality

Item Serial Number: 282	Item ID Number: V-46	Released Date: 2006 (Batch 1)	Category: Quyi (a general term for all Chinese talking-and-singing art forms)
Affiliated Province: Guizhou Province	Type: New Item	Application Province or Unit: Xingyi City, Guizhou Province	

Bayin Sitting-and-singing of the Buyi Nationality, also called "Buyi Bayin", is a kind of talking-and-singing form of folk Quyi (a general term for all Chinese talking-and-singing art forms) handed down from generation to generation by the Buyi people, mainly spread in the stockaded villages in the Nanpanjiang River Basin. It's said that its prototype is court music, which is mainly produced through blowing and beating. After the Yuan and Ming dynasties, it gradually developed into a form of Quyi (a general term for all Chinese talking-and-singing art forms) performed mainly to the accompaniment of traditional Chinese stringed instruments and bamboo wind instruments. It is often performed at traditional festivals, or on the occasions of weddings, house building, birthday celebration, etc. of the Buyi nationality.

The performance form of **Bayin Sitting-and-singing** is that eight people take turns to talk and sing while sitting, holding eight musical instruments respectively, namely Niuguhu Musical Instrument (Niujiaohu Musical Instrument), Huluqin Musical Instrument (Huluhu Musical Instrument), Yueqin (a four-stringed plucked musical instrument with a full-moon-shaped sound box), Cigu Drum (the Bamboo

---

① 《布依族八音坐唱》，中国非物质文化遗产网，http://www. ihchina. cn/Article/Index/detail?id=13668，检索日期：2019 年 8 月 7 日。

Drum), Xiaotong flute, small cymbal, Baobao Gong and Small Maluo (a kind of Chinese percussion instrument). The performer "jumps in" to sing and narrate the story in the first person, and "jumps out" to comment on the story in the third person. Sometimes, musical instruments of the Buyi nationality, such as Lelang (a wind instrument of the Buyi nationality made of bamboo), Leyou Musical Instrument and Muye (leaves), are added to accompany the performance. When singing, male performers mostly adopt a higher octave, while females sing in the original tone, resulting in strong contrasts in pitch and timbres. The tune for the singing tones of **Bayin Sitting-and-singing** is mainly "the formal tune", and other tunes are collectively referred to as "the casual tune". Representative traditional plays are "Marriage Customs of the Buyi nationality", "Hexi Hall", "The Tune of Welcoming Visitors", "The Biography of Yulian, the King of Singing", "Toasting Songs", "Liang Shanbo and Zhu Yingtai", etc. **Bayin Sitting-and-singing** has been created and gradually formed by the Buyi people in the long-term production and life, deeply rooted among the masses of the Buyi nationality, with distinct Buyi characteristics and extensive mass base.

第六章
传统体育、游艺与杂技

Chapter Six
Traditional Sports,
Recreations and Acrobatics

第1项：
赛龙舟

铜仁赛龙舟
the Dragon-boat Racing of Tongren

项目序号：1148	项目编号：VI-65	公布时间：2011（第三批）	类别：传统体育、游艺与杂技
所属地区：贵州省	类型：新增项目	申报地区或单位：贵州省铜仁市、镇远县	

  铜仁赛龙舟是铜仁多民族参与的传统游艺体育活动。铜仁是苗族、土家族、侗族、仡佬族和满族等多民族聚居地区。自古以来，象征着团结精神与竞争意志的赛龙舟，便是铜仁最具特色的民间传统习俗。每年四五月间，各村寨的村民便将搁置一年的龙船"油"上桐油，画上"龙纹"，安上龙头，下水操

练。待到端阳，便会聚在城南双江汇流处的铜岩下参加赛龙舟比赛。届时，铜仁男女老少齐聚江岸边观看比赛。水上岸上热闹非凡，鞭炮声、呐喊声、加油声此起彼伏，呈现出这方热土人水交融、民族交融的欢乐景象。赛龙舟在铜仁历史悠久，通过祭龙船、点龙睛、龙船下水、龙舟竞技、抢鸭子和垂钓等一系列传统习俗，形成了多民族共同造就的人文祥和与安宁的龙舟水文化。[1]

镇远赛龙舟是流传于贵州省镇远县的传统游艺体育活动。每年端阳之际，镇远县举办以划龙舟比赛为主，包括集传统的祭龙仪式、舞龙舞狮游街、彩船游江、水中抢鸭子、放河灯、燃礼花和文艺表演为一体的赛龙舟活动。自古镇远民间便有以赛龙舟纪念爱国诗人屈原的习俗，早在明代，镇远就有"龙舟之乡"的美誉。20 世纪 80 年代以来，镇远县的赛龙舟活动更为活跃，90 年代中期，"镇远端阳龙舟节"正式命名。[2]

 **Item 1: the Dragon-boat Racing**

Item Serial Number: 1148	Item ID Number: VI-65	Released Date: 2011 (Batch 3)	Category: Traditional Sports, Recreations and Acrobatics
Affiliated Province: Guizhou Province	Type: New Item	Application Province or Unit: Tongren City and Zhenyuan County of Guizhou Province	

The Dragon-boat Racing of Tongren is a traditional recreational sports activity participated by many ethnic groups in Tongren City. Tongren is an area inhabited by the ethnic groups of Miao, Tujia, Dong, Gelao, Man, etc. Since ancient times, **the Dragon-boat Racing** that symbolizes the spirit of unity and the awareness of competition is the most distinctive traditional folk custom in Tongren City. In April and May every year, villagers in all stockaded villages paint the dragon boats laid aside for one year with Tung oil, draw "dragon patterns" and install dragon heads on them, and then enter the water to practice. When the Dragon Boat Festival comes, they gather under Tongyan Rock at the confluence of two rivers in the south of the

---

① 《赛龙舟》，中国非物质文化遗产网，http://www.ihchina.cn/Article/Index/detail?id= 138 79，检索日期：2019 年 8 月 16 日。

② 《赛龙舟》，中国非物质文化遗产网，http://www.ihchina.cn/Article/Index/detail?id= 138 80，检索日期：2019 年 8 月 18 日。

city to participate in **the Dragon-boat Racing**. At that time, people of all ages and both sexes in Tongren City gather on the bank of the river to watch the match. There is a lot of excitement on both banks and on the water, the sounds of firecrackers, shouts and cheers rising one after another, presenting a joyful scene of the fusion of people and water as well as the national integration on this hot land. **The Dragon-boat Racing** has a long history in Tongren. Through a series of traditional customs, such as offering sacrifices to the dragon boats, drawing the pupils in dragons' eyes, the dragon boat entering the water, the dragon boat competition, snatching ducks and fishing, it has formed a humanistic, harmonious and peaceful dragon-boat water culture created by multi-ethnic groups.

The Dragon-boat Racing of Zhenyuan is a traditional recreational sports activity spread in Zhenyuan County, Guizhou Province. On the Dragon Boat Festival every year, in Zhenyuan County, people will hold the activities of **the Dragon-boat Racing**, with the competition of rowing the Dragon Boat as the main one, including the traditional ceremony of offering sacrifices to the dragon, performing the Dragon-lion Dance to parade along the street, colorful boats touring the river, snatching ducks in the water, floating River Lanterns, setting off fireworks and theatrical performances. Since ancient times among the people in Zhenyuan County, there is a custom to commemorate the patriotic poet, Qu Yuan, by racing the dragon boats. As early as the Ming Dynasty, Zhenyuan has been acclaimed as "the hometown of dragon boats". Since the 1980s, **the Dragon-boat Racing** in Zhenyuan County has been more active, and in the mid-1990s, "Duanyang Dragon Boat Festival of Zhenyuan County" was officially named.

第七章
传统美术

Chapter Seven

Traditional Fine Arts

第 1 项：
苗绣（雷山苗绣）

雷山苗绣
Leishan Miao Embroidery

项目序号：321	项目编号：Ⅶ-22	公布时间：2006（第一批）	类别：传统美术
所属地区：贵州省	类型：新增项目	申报地区或单位：贵州省雷山县	

  雷山苗绣是指流传于贵州省雷山县的苗族刺绣技艺，历史悠久。

  雷山苗绣是雷山苗族服饰的重要组成部分。雷山苗族的服饰至今仍保留着原汁原味的传统风格，精美绝伦的刺绣技艺和璀璨夺目的银饰让人赞叹不已。雷山苗族服饰按结构和风格划分，主要有长裙、中裙、短裙和超短裙四种，分别称为西江型、也蒙型、公统型和大塘型。雷山苗族服饰制作工艺独特，形制很有代表性，有些是雷山独有，有些他处亦有却主要分布在雷山县境内。与形制相关的刺绣工艺亦有其独特性，如双针锁绣、绉绣、辫绣、丝絮贴绣等；尽管别处也有，但就技巧而言，雷山苗绣更具特色，且技法多样。雷山苗绣的图案在形制和造型方面，大量运用各种变形和夸张手法，并大胆使用多维立体造型和型中型的复合手段及比喻、暗喻、借喻、象征等的表达技巧，体现出别具民族风格的审美情趣。[1]

Item 1: Miao Embroidery (Leishan Miao Embroidery)

Item Serial Number: 321	Item ID Number: VII−22	Released Date: 2006 (Batch 1)	Category: Traditional Fine Arts
Affiliated Province: Guizhou Province	Type: New Item	Application Province or Unit: Leishan County, Guizhou Province	

Leishan Miao Embroidery refers to the Miao people's embroidery skills popular in Leishan County, Guizhou Province, which has a long history.

Leishan Miao Embroidery is an important part of the Costumes of the Miao Nationality in Leishan. The latter still retains the original traditional style up to now, and its exquisite embroidery skills and dazzling silver ornaments are amazing. According to the structure and style, the Costumes of the Miao Nationality in Leishan are divided into four types: long skirts, medium skirts, short skirts and miniskirts, which are also called Xijiang type, Yemeng type, Gongtong type and Datang type respectively. The craft of making the Costumes of the Miao Nationality in Leishan is distinctive, with their designing quite representative. Some are unique to Leishan, while some can also be found in other places, but are mainly distributed in Leishan County. The embroidery craft related to designing also has its uniqueness, such as double-needle locking embroidery, crepe embroidery, braid embroidery and silk-wadding patching embroidery. Although there are some in other places, in terms of skills, **Leishan Miao Embroidery** is more distinctive and has diverse techniques. In the aspects of designing and modelling, patterns of **Leishan Miao Embroidery** massively adopt various kinds of deformation and exaggeration, and boldly use multi-dimensional modelling, pattern-within-pattern composite means, as well as the expression skills of analogies, metaphors, metonymy, symbolism, etc., which reflect the aesthetic taste with unique

---

[1] 《苗绣（雷山苗绣）》，中国非物质文化遗产网，http://www. ihchina. cn/Article/Index/detail?id=13989，检索日期：2019 年 8 月 18 日。

花溪苗绣
Huaxi Miao Embroidery

第2项：
苗绣（花溪苗绣）

ethnic style.

贵州省·国家级非物质文化遗产文献资料汇编（汉英对照）

The Documentary Compilation of the State-level Intangible Cultural Heritage of Guizhou Province (Chinese-English Versions)

项目序号：321	项目编号：Ⅶ-22	公布时间：2006（第一批）	类别：传统美术
所属地区：贵州省	类型：新增项目	申报地区或单位：贵州省贵阳市	

　　流传于贵阳市花溪苗族中的挑花技艺在贵州苗族刺绣技艺中具有一定的代表性。常见挑花图案有猪蹄杈、牛蹄杈、牛头、羊头、狗头、冰雪花、刺藜花、浮萍、荷花、稻穗、荞子花、铜鼓、灯笼、银杈、铜钱、太阳、青蛙、螃蟹、燕子、楼阁、田园、桥梁和河流等。

　　花溪苗族挑花技艺具有追念先祖、记录历史、表达爱情和美化自身等功用，同时又有很强的装饰性。以十字绣为基本针法，不用底稿，用反面挑正面看的特殊技法，使整件挑花作品更加美观精巧。花溪苗族挑花的艺术风格分早、中、晚三个时期：早期，1900 年以前，挑花底布为自织青色麻布，色彩单纯雅致，以银色调为主，白色中点缀有小面积的彩色，构图严谨，图案有几何化、程式化的特征；中期，1900 年至 1966 年，挑花底布仍多为青色麻布，也有少量青色土棉布，色彩热烈华丽，多以红色为主，配以黄、绿、白等色丝线，构图更活泼，图案更丰富；晚期，1967 年以后，挑花底布色彩和质地都呈多样化趋势，增加了红、蓝、黄、白、黑等机织布，甚至使用塑料窗纱和粗麻袋布做底布，挑绣用的彩线除了蚕丝线又增加了十字线和毛线，构图更自由，图案更多样化。花溪苗族挑花成为本民族历史和传说的载体，在花溪苗族的日常生活、节日庆典及择偶、婚丧、宗教等仪式中得到广泛运用。[①]

Item 2: Miao Embroidery (Huaxi Miao Embroidery)

Item Serial Number: 321	Item ID Number: Ⅶ-22	Released Date: 2006 (Batch 1)	Category: Traditional Fine Arts
Affiliated Province: Guizhou Province	Type: New Item	Application Province or Unit: Guiyang City, Guizhou Province	

　　The craft of Cross Stitch, popular in the Miao nationality in Huaxi District, Guiyang City, has certain representativeness in the embroidery craft of the Miao nationality in Guizhou. Common patterns of Cross Stitch include pig hoof tines, cattle hoof tines, cattle heads, sheep heads, dog heads, frozen snowflakes, prickly

---

[①] 《苗绣（花溪苗绣）》，中国非物质文化遗产网，http：//www. ihchina. cn/Article/Index/ detail?id=13987，检索日期：2019 年 9 月 7 日。

pear flowers, duckweed, lotus flowers, ears of rice, buckwheat flowers, the Bronze Drum, lanterns, silver forks, copper coins, the sun, frogs, crabs, swallows, pavilions, fields and gardens, bridges and rivers.

The craft of Cross Stitch of the Miao nationality in Huaxi has the functions of remembering ancestors, recording history, expressing love, self-beautification, etc. At the same time, it also has a strong decorative property. The special technique of adopting cross stitch as the basic stitch without using a draft, embroidering on the back side and producing the embroidery work that needs to be looked from the front side has made the whole cross-stitch work more beautiful and exquisite. The artistic style of the Cross Stitch of the Miao nationality in Huaxi is divided into three periods: early, middle and late. The early period was before 1900, when the bottom cloth for Cross Stitch was self-woven cyan linen. Its colors were simple and elegant, with silver as the main tone, and small areas of color interspersed in white. Its composition was rigorous, and its patterns had geometric and stylized characteristics. The middle period referred to the years from 1900 to 1966, when the bottom cloth for Cross Stitch was still mostly cyan linen, with a small amount of homespun cyan cotton cloth. Its colors were lively and gorgeous, mostly in red, paired with yellow, green, white and other colored silk threads. Its composition was livelier and its patterns were richer. The late period is after the year of 1967. During this period, the color and texture of the bottom cloth for Cross Stitch show a trend of diversification, with machine-woven cloth of red, blue, yellow, white, black, etc. added, and even plastic window gauze and coarse sackcloth used as bottom cloth. Besides silk threads, cross-stitch threads and wool threads have been added for Cross Stitch. The composition is more liberal and the patterns are more diversified. The Cross Stitch of the Miao nationality in Huaxi has become the carrier of the history and legends of this ethnic group, and is widely used in the daily life, festival celebrations, as well as the rituals of spouse selection, weddings, funerals, religion, etc. of the Miao nationality in Huaxi.

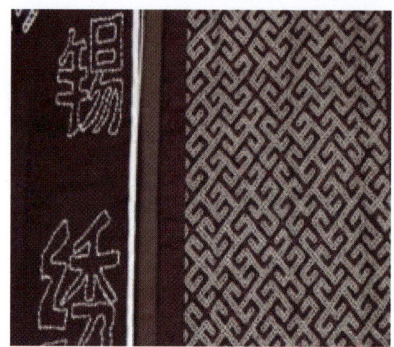

第 3 项：
苗绣（剑河苗绣）

苗族锡绣
Tin Embroidery of the Miao Nationality

项目序号：321	项目编号：Ⅶ-22	公布时间：2006（第一批）	类别：传统美术
所属地区：贵州省	类型：新增项目	申报地区或单位：贵州省剑河县	

  剑河苗绣是流传于贵州省剑河县的苗族刺绣，以苗族锡绣最具代表性，主要分布于贵州省剑河县境内的南寨、敏洞和观么等乡镇。

  苗族锡绣以藏青色棉织布为载体，先用棉纺线按传统图案在布上穿线挑花，然后将金属锡丝条绣缀于图案中，再用黑、红、蓝、绿四色蚕丝线在图案空隙处绣出彩色的花朵。银白色的锡丝绣在藏青色布料上，对比鲜明，明亮耀眼，光泽度好，使布料看上去酷似银质，与银帽、银耳环、银项圈、银锁链和银手镯相配，华丽高贵。苗族锡绣工艺独特，手工精细，图案清晰，做工复杂，用料特殊，具有极高的鉴赏和收藏价值。苗族锡绣与其他民族刺绣的不同之处在于，它不是用蚕丝线，而是用金属锡丝条在藏青棉布挑花图案上刺绣而成，其核心图案犹如一座迷宫，变化莫测，寓意深刻，充满强烈的神秘意味。[1]

Item 3: Miao Embroidery (Jianhe Miao Embroidery)

Item Serial Number: 321	Item ID Number: Ⅶ-22	Released Date: 2006 (Batch 1)	Category: Traditional Fine Arts
Affiliated Province: Guizhou Province	Type: New Item	Application Province or Unit: Jianhe County, Guizhou Province	

---

[1]《苗绣（剑河苗绣）》，中国非物质文化遗产网，http://www.ihchina.cn/Article/Index/detail?id=13988，检索日期：2019 年 9 月 7 日。

Jianhe Miao Embroidery is the embroidery of the Miao nationality spread in Jianhe County, Guizhou Province, with Tin Embroidery of the Miao Nationality as the most representative one. It is mainly distributed in Nanzhai, Mindong, Guanmo and other townships in Jianhe County, Guizhou Province.

Tin Embroidery of the Miao Nationality takes navy blue cotton-woven fabrics as the carrier. First, cotton-spun threads are used to embroider cross-stitch patterns on cloth according to traditional patterns. Next, tin wires are embroidered and interspersed within the patterns. Then, black, red, blue and green silk threads are used to embroider colorful flowers within gaps between patterns. The silvery white tin wires are embroidered on navy blue cloth, which is in a sharp contrast, bright and dazzling, having good glossiness. This makes the cloth look like silver. Matched with silver hats, silver earrings, silver collars, silver chains and silver bracelets, it is gorgeous and dignifying. The craft of Tin Embroidery of the Miao Nationality is unique, with fine handwork, clear patterns, complex workmanship and special materials, which has high value of appreciation and collection. The difference between Tin Embroidery of the Miao Nationality and the embroidery of other ethnic groups lies in that tin wires instead of silk threads are used to embroider patterns within the cross-stitch patterns on navy blue cotton cloth. Its core pattern is like a maze, unpredictable, profound and full of strong mysterious implication.

凯里苗绣：端午节划龙舟
Kaili Miao Embroidery: Dragon-boat Rowing at the Dragon Boat Festival

第4项：
苗绣

项目序号：321	项目编号：Ⅶ-22	公布时间：2008（第二批）	类别：传统美术
所属地区：贵州省	类型：扩展项目	申报地区或单位：贵州省凯里市	

　　凯里苗绣主要流传于贵州省黔东南苗族侗族自治州凯里市，尤以舟溪镇曼洞村的苗绣最具代表性，这里被誉为"刺绣之乡"。

　　凯里苗绣的工序十分复杂。先在布上画出花样，然后将绣布用绷架绷紧，用针线捆缝一圈，接着根据纹样的内容及装饰对象，结合配色设计，精心搭配好不同颜色和粗细的绣线，之后开始刺绣。凯里苗绣的技法主要有平绣、绉绣、破丝绣、数纱绣、堆花绣和补花辫绣等，其图案设计自由，刺绣者天马行空、不拘一格，全凭想象和情感自由发挥。不过，在看似繁复的图案中又有着整体的和谐统一。凯里苗绣的色彩艳丽浓烈，多以红、绿为主，辅以其他颜色，花纹稠密。用色大胆，大红大绿，鲜亮夺目，是凯里苗绣的主要特点。凯里苗绣艺人不照搬物象的固有色彩，而是凭直觉观察事物，把生活中获得的色彩印象按照自己的意愿设计。她们喜欢将色彩用得浓重而艳丽，用活了红、绿、蓝"三原色"，讲究色彩的冷暖对比，并注重在强烈的对比中取得协调，形成一种既古朴又绚丽多彩的效果。凯里苗绣蕴藏着凯里苗族先民朴素的原始宗教和审美意识，记录着其发展变化和南迁的记忆片段。[①]

---

① 雷安平，《凯里苗族刺绣：华美多彩的明艳》，凯里市人民政府网，http://www.kaili.gov.cn/zjkl/lswh/201703/t20170316_20492719.html，检索日期：2020年8月21日。

Item 4: Miao Embroidery

Item Serial Number: 321	Item ID Number: VII-22	Released Date: 2008 (Batch 2)	Category: Traditional Fine Arts
Affiliated Province: Guizhou Province	Type: Extended Item	Application Province or Unit: Kaili City, Guizhou Province	

Kaili Miao Embroidery is mainly spread in Kaili City, Qiandongnan Miao and Dong Autonomous Prefecture of Guizhou Province. Especially, **Miao Embroidery** in Mandong Village of Zhouxi Township is the most representative one. This place has been acclaimed as "the Hometown of Embroidery".

The process of **Kaili Miao Embroidery** is very complicated. First, patterns are drawn on a piece of cloth. Then, the embroidery cloth is tightened with a tension frame and fixed around by using a needle and thread. Next, the embroidery threads with different colors and thickness are selected carefully and matched properly in accordance with the pattern content and the object to be decorated; and finally, artisans start to embroider. The techniques of **Kaili Miao Embroidery** mainly include flat embroidery, crepe embroidery, silk-split embroidery, yarn-counting embroidery, flower-piling embroidery, and patching-and-braiding embroidery. Its pattern design is free, and embroiderers give free rein to their minds, without any restraints, solely relying on imaginations and emotions to express themselves freely. However, within the seemingly complex patterns, there is an overall harmonious unity. The colors of **Kaili Miao Embroidery** are gorgeous and strong, mainly red and green, supplemented by other colors, and its patterns are dense. The main features of **Kaili Miao Embroidery** are applying colors boldly, gaudy and showy, bright and eye-catching. The artisans of **Kaili Miao Embroidery** do not copy the inherent colors of objects, but observe things by intuition, and design the color impressions obtained in life according to their own wishes. They like to use strong and bright colors, creatively apply "the three primary colors" of red, green and blue, pay attention to the contrast of cold and warm colors, and focus on achieving coordination in sharp contrasts, thus forming a kind of effect with both primitive simplicity and gorgeousness. **Kaili Miao Embroidery** contains the simple primitive religion and aesthetic consciousness of the Miao ancestors in Kaili, and records the fragmented memories of their development, changes and southward migration.

台江苗绣
Taijiang Miao Embroidery

第5项：
苗绣

项目序号：321	项目编号：Ⅶ-22	公布时间：2011（第三批）	类别：传统美术
所属地区：贵州省	类型：扩展项目	申报地区或单位：贵州省台江县	

　　台江苗绣是苗族刺绣中最具典型意义的民间艺术品之一，主要分布在贵州省黔东南苗族侗族自治州台江县的施洞镇。

　　台江苗绣是台江苗族服饰的重要组成部分，其图案纹饰所蕴含的文化内涵折射出苗族屡经迁徙的历史变迁过程。根据内容和样式，台江苗族服饰分为方你型、方纠型、方南型、方翁型、方白型、方秀型、方黎型、翁芒型和后哨型等九种，堪称"无字史"，是族群识别的标志和符号。服饰的精美造型、精湛工艺和色彩搭配是衡量苗族妇女聪明才智的标准。苗族姑娘未出嫁前，都要亲手绣一套嫁妆，从开始到完成要3～5年，只有心灵手巧的苗族姑娘才能博得人们的赞许、爱慕和追求。台江苗绣的画面丰富，常见题材有造型独特的飞禽走兽、花鸟鱼虫等，以龙、鱼、蝴蝶、蜈蚣和蝙蝠等图案使用最为广泛。所采用的针法有平绣、皱绣、缠绣、叠绣、锁绣、堆绣、辫绣、锡绣、数纱绣、破线绣、打籽绣、马尾绣和钉线绣等。台江苗绣用色和谐文静，行针平均熨帖，具有色彩艳丽、形象逼真、层次分明的特点。[①]

---

① 《苗绣》，中国非物质文化遗产网，http://www.ihchina.cn/Article/Index/detail?id=13991，检索日期：2019 年 8 月 20 日。

Item 5: Miao Embroidery

Item Serial Number: 321	Item ID Number: VII–22	Released Date: 2011 (Batch 3)	Category: Traditional Fine Arts
Affiliated Province: Guizhou Province	Type: Extended Item	Application Province or Unit: Taijiang County, Guizhou Province	

Taijiang Miao Embroidery is one of the most typical folk artistic works in Miao Embroidery, mainly distributed in Shidong Township, Taijiang County, Qiandongnan Miao and Dong Autonomous Prefecture, Guizhou Province.

Taijiang Miao Embroidery is an important part of the Costumes of the Miao Nationality in Taijiang. The cultural connotation implied in its patterns reflects the process of historical changes of the Miao people's frequent migration. According to content and styles, the Costumes of the Miao Nationality in Taijiang are divided into nine types: Fangni type, Fangjiu type, Fangnan type, Fangweng type, Fangbai type, Fangxiu type, Fangli type, Wengmang type and Houshao type, which can be called "the history without words" and are the signs and symbols of ethnic identification. The elegant modelling, exquisite workmanship and color matching of costumes are considered as the standards to measure the intelligence and talents of the women of the Miao nationality. Before marriage, all Miao girls will embroider a set of dowries with their own hands, which takes 3-5 years from the beginning to the completion. Only those who are clever in mind and skillful in hand can win people's praise, admiration and pursuit. **Taijiang Miao Embroidery** is rich in images, and its common themes include fowls and animals, flowers, birds, fish and insects that are unique in modelling, among which patterns of dragons, fish, butterflies, centipedes, bats, etc. are used most widely. The embroidery methods used include flat embroidery, wrinkling embroidery, twining embroidery, folding embroidery, locking embroidery, piling embroidery, braiding embroidery, tin embroidery, yarn-counting embroidery, thread-split embroidery, seed-knitted embroidery, horsetail embroidery and thread-fixed embroidery. **Taijiang Miao Embroidery** is harmonious and gentle in color, and its stitches are neat and balanced, showing the characteristics of bright colors, vivid images and distinct layers.

马尾绣背带
a Horsetail-embroidered Back Strap

第6项： 水族马尾绣

项目序号：322	项目编号：Ⅶ–23	公布时间：2006（第一批）	类别：传统美术
所属地区：贵州省	类型：新增项目	申报地区或单位：贵州省三都水族自治县	

　　水族马尾绣是水族妇女世代传承的，以马尾为重要原料的一种特殊刺绣技艺，流传于全国唯一的水族自治县——贵州省三都县境内的水族村寨。[①]

　　马尾绣的制作主要有四个步骤，即制作原材料、固定图案、添饰和填心等。首先，用纺车纺好白色丝线，取马尾3～5根作芯，用手工将白色丝线紧密地缠绕在马尾上，使之成为类似低音琴弦的马尾白色预制绣花线；然后，按照传统刺绣纹样或剪纸纹样，将这种马尾白色绣线盘绣于花纹的轮廓上；接着，用七根彩色丝线编织成扁形彩线，添绣在盘绣花纹的轮廓中间部位；最后，其余部分则按通常的结绣、平绣、挑花、乱针和跳针等刺绣工艺进行装饰。[②]马尾绣工艺复杂，采用这种工艺制作的绣品具有浅浮雕感，造型抽象夸张，主要用于制作背小孩的背带、翘尖绣花鞋、女性的围腰和胸牌、童帽、荷包和刀鞘护套等。马尾绣背带是通体绣花的完整艺术品，有三部分：上半部为主体图案，由二十多块大小不同的马尾绣片组成，周围边框在彩色缎料底上用大红或墨绿色丝线绣出几何图案；上部两侧为马尾绣背带手；下半部为背带

---

① 《水族马尾绣》，中国非物质文化遗产网，http://www.ihchina.cn/Article/Index/detail?id=13992，检索日期：2019年8月9日。

② 《水族马尾绣绣品》，贵州省非物质文化遗产保护中心官网，http://www.gzfwz.org.cn/fycp/201806/t20180612_3159580.html，检索日期：2019年8月12日。

尾，有精美的马尾绣图案与主体部位相呼应。[1] 水族马尾绣以历史悠久、针法古朴而著称。

Item 6: the Horsetail Embroidery of the Shui Nationality

Item Serial Number: 322	Item ID Number: Ⅶ–23	Released Date: 2006 (Batch 1)	Category: Traditional Fine Arts
Affiliated Province: Guizhou Province	Type: New Item	Application Province or Unit: Sandu Shui Autonomous County, Guizhou Province	

The Horsetail Embroidery of the Shui Nationality is a special embroidery craft with horsetail as an important material inherited by women of the Shui nationality from generation to generation. It is spread in stockaded villages inhabited by the Shui nationality in Sandu County of Guizhou Province, the only Shui Autonomous County in China.

The making of **the Horsetail Embroidery** involves four steps: making raw materials, fixing patterns, adding decorations and filling the core. First, white silk threads are spun by using a spinning wheel, 3-5 pieces of horsetail are taken as the core, and then the white silk threads are winded around the horsetail tightly by hand to make them into white horsetail pre-embroidery threads that are similar to bass strings. Second, the white horsetail pre-embroidery threads are coiled and embroidered on the outline of the pattern according to the traditional embroidery pattern or paper-cut pattern. Third, flat colored threads are woven by using seven pieces of colored silk threads, and then embroidered in the middle part of the outline of the pattern that is coiled and embroidered. Finally, the rest parts are decorated by using usual embroidery techniques, such as knotting embroidery, flat embroidery, cross stitch, random stitch embroidery and skipping stitch. The craft of **the Horsetail Embroidery** is complex, and the embroidered products made by using this craft has a sense of bas-relief, abstract and exaggerated in modelling. It is mainly used to make back straps that are used to carry kids on the back, tip-upturned embroidered shoes, women's aprons as well as chest tags, children's hats, pouches, scabbards, etc.

---

① 《水族马尾绣》，中国非物质文化遗产网，http://www. ihchina. cn/Article/Index/detail? id=13992，检索日期：2019 年 8 月 9 日。

A horsetail-embroidered back strap is a complete artistic work that is embroidered wholly, consisting of three parts. The upper part is the main pattern, which is composed of more than twenty horsetail-embroidered pieces in different sizes. The surrounding frame is embroidered by using bright red or dark green silk threads to produce geometric patterns on the colored satin base. The two sides of the upper part are the two hands of a horsetail-embroidered back strap. The lower part is the tail of the back strap, which has exquisite horsetail-embroidered patterns to correspond to the main part. **The Horsetail Embroidery of the Shui Nationality** is famous for its long history and primitive needling.

苗族剪纸吹芦笙
Paper Cutting of the Miao Nationality: Playing Lusheng Musical Instruments

第 7 项：
苗族剪纸

项目序号：315	项目编号：Ⅶ-16	公布时间：2008（第二批）	类别：传统美术
所属地区：贵州省	类型：扩展项目	申报地区或单位：贵州省剑河县	

　　苗族剪纸俗称"苗族花纸""剪花""绣花纸"。贵州省剑河县流传的苗族剪纸分为革东型与新民、新合型两类，风格各不相同。

　　革东型剪纸构图饱满，画面内容丰富，纹样多为动物、花卉和人物，其中不乏神话传说中的形象；新民、新合型剪纸构图上相对灵动，纹样多为自然界中的花卉、鸟蝶等，造型生动。苗族剪纸的手法主要采用剪、刻、扎等方式，一般都是用刀口很尖细的小剪刀剪，纸层稍厚一点或多几层时，便在纸下垫一块木板，改用刻刀刻。无论剪或刻，都需要先把图案在表层纸上画好。多层纸叠合剪刻时，苗族剪纸艺人习惯用白皮纸捻或缝衣线将纸穿钉成册，一幅图案视大小固定数个点，以保证剪刻中各层不错移。苗族剪纸历史悠久，是研究剑河县境内清水江上游地区苗族历史和生活风习的珍贵形象资料，其中较多出现的双头龙、双头鸟、双头蛇、双身共头龙等共头共身的描述，实际是苗族"吃牯脏"仪式中一种巫仪的延伸。剑河苗族剪纸是革东、新民和新合等地苗族刺绣的底样和蓝本，经过第二次加工后，其艺术性在刺绣中得到丰富和延伸。[①]

---

① 《剪纸（苗族剪纸）》，中国非物质文化遗产网，http://www.ihchina.cn/Article/Index/detail?id=13964，检索日期：2019 年 8 月 9 日。

Item 7: Paper Cutting of the Miao Nationality

Item Serial Number: 315	Item ID Number: VII−16	Released Date: 2008 (Batch 2)	Category: Traditional Fine Arts
Affiliated Province: Guizhou Province	Type: Extended Item	Application Province or Unit: Jianhe County, Guizhou Province	

Paper Cutting of the Miao Nationality is commonly known as "Miao Flower Paper", "Flower Clipping" and "Embroidery Paper". The **Paper Cutting of the Miao Nationality** spread in Jianhe County of Guizhou Province is divided into two types: Gedong type and Xinmin-Xinhe type, each with different styles.

The composition of Gedong-type Paper Cutting is full, its content is rich, and its patterns are mostly animals, flowers and humans, many of which are images in myths and legends. Xinmin-Xinhe-type Paper Cutting is relatively flexible in composition, and its patterns are mostly flowers, birds, butterflies, etc. in nature, with vivid shapes. The techniques of **Paper Cutting of the Miao Nationality** are mainly clipping, carving, binding, etc. Generally, small scissors with very pointed tips are used to clip, and a graver is used when the paper is a little thicker or has more layers, with a board placed under the paper. Whether clipping or carving is adopted, one needs to draw the pattern on the surface paper first. When clipping and carving multi-layer paper, artisans of **Paper Cutting of the Miao Nationality** are accustomed to using white Zhinian (paper rolled into slim strips) or sewing threads to bind the paper into a book. They fix several points on the book according to the size of the pattern so as to ensure that all layers don't move in the process of clipping and carving. **Paper Cutting of the Miao Nationality** has a long history, and it is a valuable and vivid material for studying the history and living habits and customs of the Miao people in the upper reaches of the Qingshui River in Jianhe County. The commonly appeared double-headed dragons, double-headed birds, double-headed snakes, as well as the dragons that have one head and two bodies, etc. are actually an extension of the witchcraft ritual, "Chiguzang (also called the Drum Worship Festival, with cattle as sacrifices)", of the Miao nationality. **Paper Cutting of the Miao Nationality** in Jianhe County is the original pattern and chief source of Miao Embroidery in Gedong Township, Xinmin Village, Xinhe Village, etc. After the second processing, its artistry has been enriched and extended in embroidery.

第 8 项：
剪纸（水族剪纸）

水族剪纸
Paper Cutting of the Shui Nationality

项目序号：315	项目编号：Ⅶ-16	公布时间：2014（第四批）	类别：传统美术
所属地区：贵州省	类型：扩展项目	申报地区或单位：贵州省黔南布依族苗族自治州	

水族剪纸流传于贵州省黔南布依族苗族自治州三都水族自治县的水族村寨，剪纸内容主要是自然界中的花、鸟、雀、虫及各种装饰性图案。其图案选择标准是能赐福于人或具有吉祥美满的寓意以及具有图腾崇拜性质。[①]

根据不同功能，水族剪纸分为三种：（1）民间祭祀型剪纸。水族地区祭祀活动频繁，特殊形制的剪纸被大量运用，如祭拜"娘娘神"中的手拉手人形图、祭稻田使用的纸马、祭祖使用的经幡和丧葬时使用的"灵房花"等。这类剪纸具有神性光环，规范着水族人的思想和行为，成为水族文化的重要标志。（2）实用型剪纸。主要有装饰居室表达喜庆的剪纸，过年过节张贴的窗花剪纸，纯粹点缀居室的吉祥图案剪纸，用于雕刻、制陶、花边的剪纸以及用于刺绣艺术图样蓝本的剪纸等。实用型剪纸以寓意吉祥、福禄、安康、避邪、长寿、爱恋、繁衍的花草和动物等形象为主。（3）装饰型剪纸。形象以人物为主，内容涉及神话传说、民族迁徙和现实生活场景。特点是：题材关注生活，突出生活情趣；不具备传统的实用性意义，呈现纯视觉的欣赏性；关注艺术性与装饰性。[②]

---

① 杨先模，《水族民间剪纸艺术浅析》，载《贵州民族学院学报（哲学社会科学版）》，2000 年第 1 期，第 49-50 页。

② 《水族剪纸：跃然纸上的水族历史文化》，中华网，https://culture.china.com/heritage/11171062/20171019/31584311.html，检索日期：2019 年 10 月 23 日。

贵州省·国家级非物质文化遗产文献资料汇编（汉英对照）

The Documentary Compilation of the State-level Intangible Cultural Heritage of Guizhou Province (Chinese-English Versions)

Item 8: Paper Cutting (Paper Cutting of the Shui Nationality)

Item Serial Number: 315	Item ID Number: VII-16	Released Date: 2014 (Batch 4)	Category: Traditional Fine Arts
Affiliated Province: Guizhou Province	Type: Extended Item	Application Province or Unit: Qiannan Buyi and Miao Autonomous Prefecture, Guizhou Province	

Paper Cutting of the Shui Nationality is spread in stockaded villages inhabited by the Shui nationality in Sandu Shui Autonomous County, Qiannan Buyi and Miao Autonomous Prefecture, Guizhou Province. Its main content is flowers, birds, sparrows, insects in nature as well as various decorative patterns. The selection criteria for its patterns are to be able to bestow blessings on people, to have the implications of auspiciousness and happiness and to have the property of totemic worship.

Paper Cutting of the Shui Nationality is divided into three kinds according to different functions. (1) Folk Sacrificial Paper Cutting. In areas inhabited by the Shui people, sacrificial activities are held frequently, so paper-cuts with special shapes are widely used, such as the hand-in-hand figure patterns in the worship of "the Deity of Empress", the paper horses used in the worship of paddy fields, the prayer flags used in ancestor worship, and "Lingfang Flowers (wreaths for the deceased)" used at the funeral. This kind of paper-cuts has the aura of divinity, which regulates the thinking and behavior of the Shui people and becomes an important symbol of the culture of the Shui nationality. (2) Practical Paper Cutting. It mainly includes paper-cuts for decorating rooms to express festivity, window-decoration paper-cuts posted at the Spring Festival and other festivals, paper-cuts of auspicious patterns purely embellishing rooms, paper-cuts for carving, pottery making and lace making, as well as paper-cuts for embroidering artistic patterns. Practical Paper Cutting mainly focuses on the images of flowers, plants and animals that have the implied meanings of auspiciousness, happiness and richness, well-being, avoiding evil spirits, longevity, loving and breeding. (3) Decorative Paper Cutting. Its images focus on human figures, and its content involves myths and legends, ethnic migration and real-life scenes. The characteristics are: with the theme focusing on life and highlighting the delight of life, it has no traditional practical significance, but shows pure visual appreciativeness, emphasizing artistry and decoration.

苗族泥哨
Clay Whistles of the Miao Nationality

第9项：
泥塑（苗族泥哨）

项目序号：346	项目编号：Ⅶ-47	公布时间：2008（第二批）	类别：传统美术
所属地区：贵州省	类型：扩展项目	申报地区或单位：贵州省黄平县	

　　苗族泥哨是贵州省黄平县旧州镇寨勇村苗族老艺人吴国清在传统陶俑、泥俑基础上创造发展出来的一种泥捏儿童玩具，哨体下部留有回气孔，能吹出清脆的响声，深受儿童喜爱。吴国清授徒百余人，工艺传承已80余年。

　　泥哨制作主要是手工将黏土捏制成形，而后低温烘烧，再施以彩绘，罩以清漆，做出成品。黄平苗族泥哨以塑造动物见长，动物造型400余种。另有组合式的"十二生肖""斗牛"等作品，借助各种动物的有趣神态来反映生活，艺术水准极高。泥哨艺人以山川河流、民俗风情为创作灵感，吸收苗地挑花刺绣和女性服饰的特点，先用柴火将泥哨熏烧成漆黑的底色，而后着以红、黄、蓝、白、绿、紫等颜色，使哨体鲜明醒目又不失厚重感，显得古朴大方、自然明快，具有浓厚的生活气息。黄平苗族泥哨艺人在造型时不拘泥于物象的客观外形，善于捕捉和提炼其神态及内在情感，大胆采用夸张、变形、写意的手法，重点表现所塑对象的特殊部位以突出其特征，使每一个泥哨作品都形神兼备。①

Item 9: Clay Sculpture (Clay Whistles of the Miao Nationality)

Item Serial Number: 346	Item ID Number: Ⅶ-47	Released Date: 2008 (Batch 2)	Category: Traditional Fine Arts

① 《泥塑（苗族泥哨）》，中国非物质文化遗产网，http://www.ihchina.cn/Article/Index/detail?id=14049，检索日期：2019年9月8日。

贵州省·国家级非物质文化遗产文献资料汇编（汉英对照）

The Documentary Compilation of the State-level Intangible Cultural Heritage of Guizhou Province (Chinese-English Versions)

Affiliated Province:	Type:	Application Province or Unit:
Guizhou Province	Extended Item	Huangping County, Guizhou Province

Clay Whistles of the Miao Nationality are a kind of clay-kneaded children's toys created and developed by Wu Guoqing, an old artisan of the Miao nationality in Zhaiyong Village, Jiuzhou Township, Huangping County, Guizhou Province, based on traditional pottery figurines and clay figurines. There are air holes in the lower parts of the whistles, through which crisp sounds can be blown out. They are deeply loved by children. Wu Guoqing has taught more than one hundred apprentices, and his craft has been passed down for over eighty years.

The making of clay whistles mainly goes: kneading clay into the shape of a whistle by hand, baking it at low temperature, applying colors to it, and then varnishing it to produce a finished product. **Clay Whistles of the Miao Nationality** in Huangping are known for modelling animals, with over four hundred animal shapes. In addition, there are combined clay whistles, such as "the Twelve Chinese Zodiac Signs" and "Bullfighting", which reflect life through the interesting expressions of various animals, with a high artistic level. Artisans of clay whistles take mountains, rivers and folk customs as creative inspiration, and absorb the characteristics of the Cross-stitch Embroidery and women's clothing in areas inhabited by the Miao nationality. They first fumigate and burn clay whistles into pitch-black color by using firewood, and then paint them red, yellow, blue, white, green, purple, etc., which make whistles brightly-colored and eye-catching without losing a sense of thickness, quaint and elegant, natural and lively, with a strong flavor of life. Artisans of **Clay Whistles of the Miao Nationality** in Huangping are not confined to the external forms of the objects in modelling, but are good at capturing and refining their expressions and intrinsic emotions. They boldly adopt the techniques of exaggeration, deformation and freehand brushwork, focusing on the special parts of the molded objects to highlight their characteristics, so that every clay whistle is a unity of form and spirit.

第10项：
侗族刺绣

侗族刺绣
the Embroidery of the Dong Nationality

项目序号：1164	项目编号：Ⅶ-107	公布时间：2011（第三批）	类别：传统美术
所属地区：贵州省	类型：新增项目	申报地区或单位：贵州省锦屏县	

　　侗族刺绣中最具代表性的是"盘轴滚边绣"，以出自贵州省黔东南苗族侗族自治州锦屏县平秋镇及周边地区侗族妇女之手的绣作最为有名。

　　"盘轴滚边绣"的基本绣法由"盘轴绣"和"滚边绣"两种刺绣方法组合而成。"盘轴绣"是取一根彩色丝线作为"引线"，即"轴线"；再取两根彩色丝线将其紧密缠绕在一起，使之成为较粗的二合一的预制绣线，也称"盘线"。绣制时，将"引线"从纹样底面向上绣、拉直；用"盘线"在"引线"根部绕一圈，拉紧；将此过程反复进行，绣出花纹的轮廓，为"盘轴绣"。"滚边绣"是取一根白纱线作"引线"，再取两根白纱线将其紧密地缠绕在一起，然后将这根二合一的白纱线紧密地缠绕在"引线"上，使之成为一条较粗的三合一的绣线，将其在"盘轴绣"的花纹图案轮廓周围绣（滚）上一道边，为"滚边绣"。一般的绣品是由三道"盘轴绣"和一道"滚边绣"构成，在花纹的轮廓中间以同样的手法用色线填绣。余者通常采用平绣、挑花、乱针和跳针等手法绣制。侗族的"盘轴滚边绣"具有浅浮雕感，是侗族刺绣中的精品。[1]

① 《侗族刺绣》，中国非物质文化遗产网，http://www.ihchina.cn/Article/Index/detail?id=14241，检索日期：2019年8月20日。

·贵州省·国家级非物质文化遗产文献资料汇编（汉英对照）

The Documentary Compilation of the State-level Intangible Cultural Heritage of Guizhou Province (Chinese-English Versions)

Item 10: the Embroidery of the Dong Nationality

Item Serial Number: 1164	Item ID Number: Ⅶ-107	Released Date: 2011 (Batch 3)	Category: Traditional Fine Arts
Affiliated Province: Guizhou Province	Type: New Item	Application Province or Unit: Jinping County, Guizhou Province	

The most representative **Embroidery of the Dong Nationality** is "the Axis-coiled and Edge-rolled Embroidery", and the embroidered products made by the Dong women in Pingqiu Township and the surrounding areas in Jinping County, Qiandongnan Miao and Dong Autonomous Prefecture, Guizhou Province are the most famous.

The basic embroidery craft of "the Axis-coiled and Edge-rolled Embroidery" consists of two embroidery methods: "the Axis-coiled Embroidery" and "the Edge-rolled Embroidery". The former is to take out a colored silk thread to serve as "the main thread", that is the "axis". Then, two other colored silk threads are taken out and winded together tightly to be made into a thicker two-in-one prefabricated embroidery thread, which is also called "the coiled thread". When embroidering patterns, artisans embroider and straighten "the main threads" from the bottom of the patterns. Then, they wind "the coiled threads" around the roots of "the main threads" and tighten them. They repeat this process constantly to finish embroidering the outlines of the patterns, which is called "the Axis-coiled Embroidery". "The Edge-rolled Embroidery" is to take out one white yarn as "the main thread", then take out another two pieces of white yarn, wind them together closely, and then wind the two-in-one white yarn around "the main thread" tightly to make them into a thicker three-in-one embroidery thread, and later embroider (roll) it into an edge around the pattern contour of "the Axis-coiled Embroidery". Ordinary embroidery products are made through three times of "the Axis-coiled Embroidery" and one time of "the Edge-rolled Embroidery", while in the middle of the pattern contour, colored threads are used to fill the embroidery by adopting the same technique. The rest parts are usually embroidered by using the methods of flat embroidery, cross stitch, random stitch embroidery, skipping stitch, etc. "The Axis-coiled and Edge-rolled Embroidery" of the Dong nationality has a sense of bas-relief, which is the best of **the Embroidery of the Dong Nationality**.

第八章

传统技艺

Chapter Eight

Traditional Craft

第 1 项：

苗族蜡染技艺

蜡刀
Wax Knives

项目序号：375	项目编号：Ⅷ-25	公布时间：2006（第一批）	类别：传统技艺
所属地区：贵州省	类型：新增项目	申报地区或单位：贵州省丹寨县	

　　蜡染是贵州省丹寨县、安顺县和织金县苗族世代传承的传统技艺，古称"蜡缬"，苗语称"务图"，意为"蜡染服"。

　　苗族蜡染有点蜡和画蜡两种技艺。制作工具有铜刀（蜡笔）、瓷碗、水盆、大针、骨针、谷草和染缸等。制作时，先用草木灰滤水浸泡土布，脱去纤维中的脂质，使之易于点蜡和上色。然后把适量黄蜡放在小瓷碗里，置于热木灰上，黄蜡受热熔化成液体后即可往布上点画。点好蜡花的布用温水浸湿，放入蓝靛染缸，反复浸泡，确认布料已经染好，即可拿到河边漂洗，冲去浮色，再放进锅里加水煮沸，使黄蜡熔化浮在水面上，回收后以备再用。之后，再将蜡染反复漂洗，使残留的黄蜡脱净，即算完工。丹寨蜡染在这之后还要拼涂红色和黄色，涂红一般用茜草根，涂黄则用栀子。为避免褪色，待蜡染品制成后才能着色。除上述步骤外，蜡染还有制作蓝靛和发染缸等工序，各道工序前后连接，构成一套完整成熟的操作流程。苗族蜡染产品主要为生活用品，包括女性服装、床单、被面、包袱布、包头巾、背包、提包、背带、丧事用的葬单等。其图案有几何纹和自然纹两大类。^①

Item 1: the Batik Craft of the Miao Nationality

Item Serial Number: 375	Item ID Number: Ⅷ-25	Released Date: 2006 (Batch 1)	Category: Traditional Craft
Affiliated Province: Guizhou Province	Type: New Item	Application Province or Unit: Danzhai County, Guizhou Province	

Batik is a traditional craft handed down from generation to generation by the Miao people in Danzhai, Anshun and Zhijin counties of Guizhou Province. It was called "batik" in ancient times and "Wutu" in the Miao language, meaning "batik clothes".

The Batik of the Miao Nationality involves two crafts: dot waxing and painting with wax. The making tools include copper knives (crayons), enamel bowls, water basins, big needles, bone needles, straw and dyeing vats. When it is made, at first, the handwoven cloth will be soaked in water filtered through plant ash to remove the lipid in the fiber, which can make it easy for the handwoven cloth to be waxed and colored. Then, a proper amount of beeswax is put in a small enamel bowl and placed on the hot wood ash. When it is melted into liquid by heating, the melted wax can be stippled on the cloth. Next, the cloth with wax flowers is wetted by using warm water,

---

① 《苗族蜡染技艺》，中国非物质文化遗产网，http://www.ihchina.cn/Article/Index/detail?id=14300，检索日期：2019年7月30日。

then put into the indigo vat and soaked repeatedly. After making sure that the cloth is dyed, it can be taken to the river to be rinsed, with the floating color washed off. Then, it is put into the pot with water to get boiled, which can make the beeswax melt and float on water surface to be recycled for later use. After that, the batik cloth is rinsed repeatedly to remove the residual beeswax completely. Then, the final product is finished. The batik products in Danzhai County will be painted red and yellow after that. Generally, madder roots are used to dye them red, and gardenias are used to dye them yellow. In order to avoid fading, only after the batik products are made, can they be colored. In addition to the above steps, the batik craft also involves the procedures of making indigo and preparing dyeing vats. All procedures are connected, forming a complete and mature operation process. The batik products of the Miao nationality are primarily daily necessities, including women's clothing, bed sheets, quilt covers, cloth wrappers, turbans, backpacks, handbags, shoulder straps and burial sheets for funeral affairs. Their patterns are divided into two categories: geometric pattern and natural pattern.

安顺蜡染制品
a Batik Product of Ansthun County

第2项：蜡染技艺

项目序号：375	项目编号：VIII-25	公布时间：2008（第二批）	类别：传统技艺
所属地区：贵州省	类型：扩展项目	申报地区或单位：贵州省安顺市	

　　贵州省安顺市的蜡染技艺历史悠久，早在春秋战国时期，这里的居民已掌握了蜡染制作工艺。1987年，在安顺市平坝县苗族洞葬群棺墓中发掘出宋代蜡染衣裙，色彩艳丽，图案严谨，充分展示了安顺蜡染的高超技艺。

　　安顺蜡染主要分为苗族蜡染和布依族蜡染两种。苗族蜡染在安顺38个苗族支系中均有分布，所染图案丰富多彩，包括古老传说和原始认知等内容，集中反映了古代先民的自然崇拜和图腾崇拜意识。布依族蜡染主要分布在镇宁、关岭和黄果树等县区，染出的成品构图巧妙，变化多端，纹样多为写实的花鸟鱼虫或抽象的螺旋、水波、菱形、云雷等几何图形，表现了人们对宇宙的认知、对自然山川的崇敬和对美好生活的向往。安顺苗族蜡染和布依族蜡染除图案有所差异外，制作工具、原料及工艺流程基本相同，均以铜制蜡刀蘸蜡液后在白布上勾勒图案，经过浸染等工序制成蜡染品。安顺蜡染行业中不乏画蜡技艺高超的民间工艺大师，她们曾远赴欧美表演蜡染技艺，所到之处赢得一片赞誉。①

---

① 《蜡染技艺》，中国非物质文化遗产网，http://www.ihchina.cn/Article/Index/detail?id=14301，检索日期：2019年8月9日。

 ## Item 2: the Batik Craft

Item Serial Number: 375	Item ID Number: Ⅷ-25	Released Date: 2008 (Batch 2)	Category: Traditional Craft
Affiliated Province: Guizhou Province	Type: Extended Item	Application Province or Unit: Anshun City, Guizhou Province	

The batik craft of Anshun City in Guizhou Province has a long history. As early as the Spring and Autumn Period and the Warring States Period, the residents here have mastered this craft. In 1987, the batik clothes and skirts of the Song Dynasty were excavated from the Cave-burial Group-coffin Tomb of the Miao nationality in Pingba County, Anshun City, beautiful in colors and rigorous in patterns, which fully demonstrate the superb craftsmanship of Anshun Batik.

Anshun Batik is mainly divided into two kinds: the Batik of the Miao Nationality and the Batik of the Buyi Nationality. The Batik of the Miao Nationality is distributed throughout the 38 branches of the Miao nationality in Anshun City. Its patterns are rich and colorful, including ancient legends and primitive cognition, which reflect the Miao ancestors' consciousness of worshiping nature and totems. The Batik of the Buyi Nationality is mainly distributed in Zhenning County, Guanling County, Huangguoshu Township, etc. Their batik products are ingenious and varied in composition. Their patterns are mostly realistic flowers, birds, fish and insects or abstract geometric figures of spirals, water waves, rhombuses, cloud, thunder, etc., showing people's cognition of the universe, their respect for nature, mountains and rivers, as well as their yearning for a better life. Apart from the differences in patterns between the Batik of the Miao Nationality and the Batik of the Buyi Nationality in Anshun County, their production tools, raw materials and technological processes are basically the same. They both use copper wax knives dipped in wax liquid to sketch patterns on white cloth, and then make the batik products through dip dyeing and other procedures. There are many folk craftsmen with excellent batik crafts in the batik industry of Anshun City. They have been to Europe and America to display their batik crafts, and have won a lot of praise wherever they have gone.

黄平蜡染制品
a Huangping Batik Product

第3项：
蜡染技艺（黄平蜡染技艺）

项目序号：375	项目编号：Ⅷ-25	公布时间：2011（第三批）	类别：传统技艺
所属地区：贵州省	类型：扩展项目	申报地区或单位：贵州省黄平县	

　　黄平蜡染技艺是黄平革家妇女在长期的生产劳动和生活中创造的一种民族民间艺术，是贵州高原最古老的民族传统蜡染艺术之一，具有独特的艺术特色，主要流传于贵州省黄平县的革家族群中。

　　黄平蜡染技艺主要有点蜡和浸染两个步骤。点蜡：先把白布平铺在一块平面光滑的正（长）方形木板上，再把盛有蜂蜡的土陶碗放在火盆旁使蜡熔化，然后用蜡刀蘸蜡作画，俗称点蜡花。浸染：把画好的蜡片放进蓝靛染缸染三天左右，连续技术处理十多次后，煮沸水洗，脱蜡现图。黄平蜡染作品在色彩表现上只是蓝、白两色或黑、白两色，蓝或黑色为底色，花纹图案为白色。其图案线条洁白无瑕，无鬓纹和断痕，黑白分明，干净利索，这是区别于其他民族蜡染作品的重要特征。黄平革家蜡染构图独特，图案具有丰富的寓意和哲理，主要以太阳为构图中心点。革家认为太阳是宇宙的中心，所有的物体都围绕太阳转动，为此革家妇女们对蜡染作品图案的创作大都以太阳为中心，充分表现人与自然和谐共生的意境和艺术美感，完整地体现了革家人爱美、爱生活、爱劳动的思想感情。①

----

① 《蜡染技艺（黄平蜡染技艺）》，中国非物质文化遗产网，http://www.ihchina.cn/Article/Index/detail?id=14303，检索日期：2019 年 8 月 93 日。

 ## Item 3: the Batik Craft (Huangping Batik Craft)

Item Serial Number: 375	Item ID Number: VIII-25	Released Date: 2011 (Batch 3)	Category: Traditional Craft
Affiliated Province: Guizhou Province	Type: Extended Item	Application Province or Unit: Huangping County, Guizhou Province	

Huangping Batik Craft is a kind of ethnic folk art created by the Gejia women in Huangping County in their long-term laboring and life. It is one of the oldest traditional ethnic batik arts on the Guizhou Plateau, having unique artistic characteristics and mainly spread among the Gejia people in Huangping County, Guizhou Province.

Huangping Batik Craft mainly includes two steps: waxing and dip dyeing. Waxing: First, a piece of white cloth is spread on a square (rectangular) board with smooth surface. Next, an earthenware bowl containing beeswax is put beside the brazier to melt the wax. Then, craftsmen draw patterns on the cloth by using wax knives dipped in the wax, which is commonly known as drawing wax flowers. Dip dyeing: First, the cloth on which wax flowers have been drawn is put into the indigo vat for about three days. Then, after continuous technical treatment for more than ten times, it is put in the boiling water to be washed and dewaxed until the patterns appear. Huangping batik works are only blue and white or black and white in colors. Blue and black are background colors and the patterns are white. Their pattern lines are pure and white, without sideburns grain or broken marks, clear black and white, clean and neat, which is an important feature different from other ethnic batik products. The batik of the Gejia people in Huangping is unique in composition, and its patterns have abundant implied meanings and philosophic theories, mainly centered on the sun in composition. The Gejia people think that the sun is the center of the universe, with all objects revolving around it. Consequently, patterns created on batik works by the Gejia women are mostly centered on the sun, which fully shows the artistic conception and artistic beauty of the harmony between man and nature, and fully reflects the Gejia people's love for beauty, life and labor.

贵州省 国家级非物质文化遗产文献资料汇编（汉英对照）

The Documentary Compilation of the State-level Intangible Cultural Heritage of Guizhou Province (Chinese-English Versions)

第4项：
苗寨吊脚楼营造技艺

苗寨吊脚楼
Diaojiao Buildings (pile dwellings) of Miao Stockaded Villages

项目序号：381	项目编号：Ⅷ-31	公布时间：2006（第一批）	类别：传统技艺
所属地区：贵州省	类型：新增项目	申报地区或单位：贵州省雷山县	

　　西江千户苗寨位于贵州省雷山县西江镇境内，包括平寨、东引、羊排和南贵四个行政村、十个自然寨。这里的居民建筑系木质结构，不用一钉一铆，房子框架由榫卯连接，依山势而成，形成独特的苗寨吊脚楼景观。

　　西江千户苗寨吊脚楼的营造技艺远承七千年前河姆渡文化中"南人巢居"的干栏式建筑，在历史沿革中又结合居住环境的要求进行了变化。西江的造房匠师根据地形和主人的需要确定相应的建房方案，使用斧凿锯刨和墨斗、墨线，在 30～70 度的斜坡陡坎上搭建吊脚楼。这种建筑以穿斗式木构架为主，因前檐柱吊脚，故而得名。吊脚楼一般有三层，四榀三间、五榀四间、六榀五间成座，依山错落，鳞次栉比。吊脚楼具有简洁、稳固和防潮的优点，还能节省耕地和建材。西江千户苗寨吊脚楼连同相关营造习俗形成了苗族吊脚楼建筑文化，它对于西江苗族社会文明进程和建筑科学的研究具有珍贵的价值。①

Item 4: the Craft of Constructing Diaojiao Buildings (pile dwellings) of Miao Stockaded Villages

Item Serial Number: 381	Item ID Number: Ⅷ-31	Released Date: 2006 (Batch 1)	Category: Traditional Craft

---

① 《苗寨吊脚楼营造技艺》，中国非物质文化遗产网，http://www.ihchina.cn/Article/Index/detail?id=14316，检索日期：2019 年 8 月 10 日。

Affiliated Province: Guizhou Province	Type: New Item	Application Province or Unit: Leishan County, Guizhou Province

Xijiang Qianhu Miao Stockaded Village is located in Xijiang Township, Leishan County, Guizhou Province, including four administrative villages of Pingzhai, Dongyin, Yangpai and Nangui, and ten natural stockaded villages. The residential buildings here are wooden structures, with no nail or rivet. The frame of the house is connected by mortises and tenons, and built in accordance with the mountain shape, forming a unique landscape of Diaojiao Buildings (pile dwellings) of Miao Stockaded Villages.

The craft of constructing Diaojiao Buildings (pile dwellings) of Xijiang Qianhu Miao Stockaded Village derived from the pile dwelling architecture of "southerners' nest residence" in the Hemudu culture 7,000 years ago, but has been changed in combination with the requirements of the living environment in the historical evolution. The building artisans in Xijiang design corresponding building scheme according to the terrain and the needs of the owner. By using axes, chisels, saws, planers, carpenter's ink markers and ink lines, they put up Diaojiao Buildings (pile dwellings) on the slopes and scarps of 30-70 degrees. The main structure of this kind of building is Chuandou-style timber frame, and it gets its name because the front-eave pillars hang in the air. Generally, Diaojiao Buildings (pile dwellings) have three floors, with three rooms within four *pin* (a measurement unit, referring to a house frame), four rooms within five *pin* (a measurement unit, referring to a house frame) and five rooms within six *pin* (a measurement unit, referring to a house frame). They are strewn at random along the mountain, row upon row. Diaojiao Buildings (pile dwellings) have the advantages of simplicity, stability and moisture-proof, and can save arable land and building materials. The Diaojiao Buildings (pile dwellings) of Xijiang Qianhu Miao Stockaded Village, together with the related construction custom, have formed the architectural culture of Diaojiao Buildings (pile dwellings) of the Miao nationality, which have precious value for the research of the process of the social civilization and the architectural science of the Miao nationality in Xijiang Township.

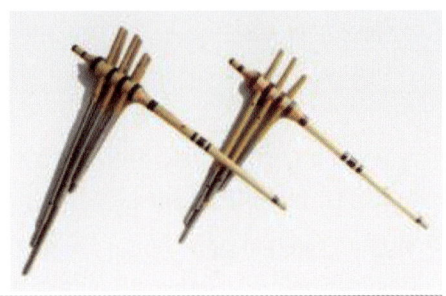

第5项：
苗族芦笙制作技艺

苗族芦笙
Lusheng Musical Instruments of the Miao Nationality

项目序号：383	项目编号：Ⅷ-33	公布时间：2006（第一批）	类别：传统技艺
所属地区：贵州省	类型：新增项目	申报地区或单位：贵州省雷山县	

　　贵州省雷山县苗族居住区村村有芦笙，是芦笙的重要产地。芦笙制作工匠居住在雷山县丹江镇的排卡村、方祥乡的平祥村和雀鸟村、桃江乡的桃梁村和年写村，这些村寨都位于大山之中，交通极不方便。

　　芦笙主要由笙管、笙斗、簧片和共鸣管组成。苗族芦笙的制作材料主要有铜（做簧片）、竹（做发音管）和木（做气箱）。主要工艺流程有选料、烤料、打磨簧片、制作竹木部件、装簧片和定音等，其中打磨簧片和定音最为关健，簧片缝隙的宽度和簧片的音色决定了芦笙质量的好坏。制作芦笙，除要懂得一定的乐理知识外，还要具备物理知识，了解力学原理。苗族传承芦笙制作技艺的师傅只用风箱、锤子、黄铜、斧子、凿子、锯子、钻子、苦竹、桐油和石灰（或乳胶）就能制作出精美实用的各式芦笙。雷山地区制作的芦笙音质纯正，外表光洁美观，极负盛名。芦笙是苗族文化的一种象征，苗族芦笙在表演吹奏上把词、曲、舞三者融为一体，保持了苗族历史文化艺术的原始性、古朴性。芦笙制作技艺历来都由师傅亲手教授，无文字资料留存，且技艺考究，传承比较困难。①

---

① 《苗族芦笙制作技艺》，中国非物质文化遗产网，http://www.ihchina.cn/Article/Index/detail?id=14318，检索日期：2019年8月9日。

Item 5: the Craft of Making Lusheng Musical Instruments of the Miao Nationality

Item Serial Number: 383	Item ID Number: VIII–33	Released Date: 2006 (Batch 1)	Category: Traditional Craft
Affiliated Province: Guizhou Province	Type: New Item	Application Province or Unit: Leishan County, Guizhou Province	

There are Lusheng Musical Instruments in every village inhabited by the Miao nationality in Leishan County of Guizhou Province, which is the important producing area of Lusheng Musical Instruments. The craftsmen who make Lusheng Musical Instruments live in Paika Village of Danjiang Township, Pingxiang Village and Queniao Village of Fangxiang Township, as well as Taoliang Village and Nianxie Village of Taojiang Township in Leishan County. These villages are located in big mountains, so their transportation conditions are extremely inconvenient.

Lusheng Musical Instruments are composed of vocal tubes, Shengdou (a container in Lusheng Musical Instruments where the air is retained and the reed is caused to vibrate), the reeds and resonance tubes. The materials for making Lusheng Musical Instruments of the Miao Nationality are mainly copper (used to make the reeds), bamboo (used to make vocal tubes) and wood (used to make air boxes). The main technological processes are material selection, material baking, reed polishing, bamboo-and-wood parts making, reed fixing and tone tuning, among which reed polishing and tone tuning are the most critical. The width of the reed gap and the timbre of the reed determine the quality of Lusheng Musical Instruments. To make them, besides certain knowledge about music theory, craftsmen should also have physical knowledge and understand mechanical principles. The Miao craftsmen who inherit this craft can make all kinds of exquisite and practical Lusheng Musical Instruments only by using air boxes, hammers, brass, axes, chisels, saws, drills, bitter bamboo, tung oil and lime (or latex). Lusheng Musical Instruments made in Leishan County are famous for their pure tone quality and beautiful appearance. Lusheng Musical Instruments are a symbol of the culture of the Miao nationality. The performance of Lusheng Musical Instruments of the Miao nationality integrates lyrics, music and dance together, and maintains the primitive and simple nature of the history, culture and art of the Miao nationality. The craft of making Lusheng Musical Instruments has always been taught by masters, without written material, which is sophisticated, so it is difficult to inherit.

第6项：民族乐器制作技艺
（苗族芦笙制作技艺）

凯里新光村苗族芦笙制作技艺
国家级非遗传承人潘柔达

Pan Rouda, the State-level Intangible Cultural Heritage Inheritor of the Craft of Making
Lusheng Musical Instruments of the Miao Nationality in Xinguang Village, Kaili City

项目序号：907	项目编号：Ⅷ-124	公布时间：2011（第三批）	类别：传统技艺
所属地区：贵州省	类型：扩展项目	申报地区或单位：贵州省凯里市	

芦笙是深受苗族群众喜爱的多簧气鸣乐器，不仅用于民间娱乐，也是和木鼓、铜鼓一样的圣器。民间认为，吹奏芦笙能带来风调雨顺、五谷丰登，还能与神灵沟通，与先祖交流。

在贵州省凯里市舟溪镇新光村，居住着128户潘姓苗族居民，现今还有38户芦笙工匠。据新光现存的家谱记载，这一支人到新光定居已经有19代，历史有500多年。工匠们祖祖辈辈制作芦笙，使用简单的工具、本地出产的竹木和采购来的响铜，制作出造型优美、音质优良的芦笙。新光是远近闻名的"芦笙村"，也是国内唯一的制作可手持演奏的特大芦笙的地方，被贵州省文化厅命名为"芦笙制作艺术之乡"。凯里新光制作的苗族传统芦笙为六管芦笙，沿用中国传统的五声音阶。响铜簧片气鸣发音，其音准的高低，全凭制作工匠特有的辨音能力来确定，他们手工制作的簧片，能够使所有的主奏芦笙的音准绝对相同；每组5～7支芦笙合奏，也符合和声学原理。新光苗族芦笙制作技艺的诀窍和绝技，父传子、子传孙，学习者只能在实践中靠自身的悟性，不断积累经验。[①]

---

① 《民族乐器制作技艺（苗族芦笙制作技艺）》，中国非物质文化遗产网，http://www. ihchina. cn/Article/Index/detail?id=14538，检索日期：2019年8月10日。

Item 6: the Craft of Making National Musical Instruments (the Craft of Making Lusheng Musical Instruments of the Miao Nationality)

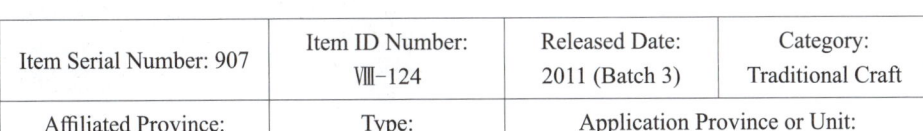

Item Serial Number: 907	Item ID Number: Ⅷ-124	Released Date: 2011 (Batch 3)	Category: Traditional Craft
Affiliated Province: Guizhou Province	Type: Extended Item	Application Province or Unit: Kaili City, Guizhou Province	

Lusheng Musical Instruments are a kind of multi-reed wind instrument deeply loved by the Miao people, not only used in folk entertainments, but also used as sacred instruments like the Wooden Drum and the Bronze Drum. The Miao people believe that playing Lusheng Musical Instruments can bring timely wind and rain as well as a bumper grain harvest, and can communicate with gods and ancestors.

In Xinguang Village, Zhouxi Township, Kaili City, Guizhou Province, there are 128 families of the Miao nationality who have the surname of Pan. Up to now, 38 of them are craftsmen who make Lusheng Musical Instruments. According to the existing genealogy of Xinguang Village, this clan has settled down here for 19 generations, with more than 500 years. Craftsmen have made Lusheng Musical Instruments for generations. By using simple tools, locally-produced bamboo and purchased brass alloy, they can make Lusheng Musical Instruments with beautiful shapes and excellent tone qualities. Xinguang is "a village of Lusheng Musical Instruments" well-known far and near. It is also the only place in China where the giant hand-held Lusheng Musical Instruments can be produced, named as "the hometown of Lusheng-making art" by the Department of Culture of Guizhou Province. The traditional Lusheng Musical Instruments of the Miao nationality made in Xinguang Village of Kaili City has six pipes, using the traditional Chinese pentatonic scale. The brass-alloy reeds produce sounds by blowing, and the high or low degree of intonation depends on craftsmen's unique sound recognition ability. Their hand-made reeds can make the intonation of all the main Lusheng Musical Instruments identical. In each group, 5-7 Lusheng Musical Instruments are played together, which also conforms to the principle of harmonics. The craft of making Lusheng Musical Instruments of the Miao nationality in Xinguang Village is handed down from father to son and from son to grandson. Learners can only rely on their own understanding in practice to accumulate experience constantly.

第 7 项：玉屏箫笛制作技艺

制作玉屏箫笛
Making Yuping Xiao and Flutes

项目序号：384	项目编号：Ⅷ-34	公布时间：2006（第一批）	类别：传统技艺
所属地区：贵州省	类型：新增项目	申报地区或单位：贵州省玉屏侗族自治县	

　　玉屏箫笛是我国著名的传统竹管乐器，以音色清越优美、雕刻精致而著称，因用贵州玉屏侗族自治县出产的竹子制成而得名。玉屏箫笛也称"平箫玉笛"，因箫笛上多有雕刻精美的龙凤图案，又称"龙箫凤笛"。其中，平箫由明代万历年间的郑维藩所创，玉笛则始创于清雍正五年。平箫玉笛与茅台酒、漆器一起被誉为"贵州三宝"。[①]

　　玉屏箫笛的制作原料为水竹。其制作工艺流程主要有取材、制坯、雕刻和成品等。具体的制作工序十分繁复，从伐竹到制成共 24 道工序，调音笛有 38 道工序，最后还要在箫笛表面刻以诗画。首先在立冬后两个月内砍伐生长在阴山溪旁三年以上、如拇指般粗细的水竹；然后经过下料、烘烤校直、检验入库环节完成取材工艺流程。制坯工艺主要包括刨外节、刮竹、通内节、再次烘烤加热校直（精校）、刨二道节（精刨）、弹中线、滚墨线、打音孔、水磨和修眼等工序。雕刻工艺分为刻字、刻图两种，主要有脱墨磨字、粘贴图样、雕刻和水磨纸屑等工序。刻字用单刀，传统雕刻刀法有搠、戮、划、剔、凿、挑、剜、拓八种。刻图初用单刀，运刃须滑回，速度较慢，后改用双刀刻图。成品工艺主要有烘烤上锅水，水磨洗涤，填色，揩去颜色和上漆等工序。玉屏箫笛的成品式样优美，雌雄成对，常被人们当作礼品赠送或收藏。

---

① 《玉屏箫笛制作技艺》，中国非物质文化遗产网，http://www.ihchina.cn/Article/Index/detail?id=14320，检索日期：2019 年 8 月 8 日。

Item 7: the Craft of Making Yuping Xiao and Flutes

Item Serial Number: 384	Item ID Number: VⅢ–34	Released Date: 2006 (Batch 1)	Category: Traditional Craft
Affiliated Province: Guizhou Province	Type: New Item	Application Province or Unit: Yuping Dong Autonomous County, Guizhou Province	

Yuping Xiao and Flutes are well-known traditional bamboo wind instruments in China, famous for their beautiful timbre and exquisite carving. They are named so because they are made of the bamboo from Yuping Dong Autonomous County, Guizhou Province. Yuping Xiao and Flutes are also known as "Pingxiao and Jade Flutes", or "Dragon Xiao and Phoenix Flutes" because exquisite dragon and phoenix patterns are usually engraved on them. Among them, Pingxiao was created by Zheng Weifan during the reign of Emperor Wanli of the Ming Dynasty, while Jade Flutes were initiated in the fifth year of Emperor Yongzheng's reign of the Qing Dynasty. Pingxiao and Jade Flutes, Maotai Liquor and lacquerware are acclaimed as "the Three Treasures of Guizhou Province".

The raw materials for making Yuping Xiao and Flutes are fishscale bamboo, and the technological process mainly includes selecting materials, making Pitai (a product that already has the required shape but still needs processing), carving and making final products. The specific production procedures are very complicated, involving 24 ones from cutting bamboo to making final products. There are 38 procedures of tuning up flutes. At last, the surfaces of Xiao and Flutes will be engraved with poems and paintings. First, within two months after the beginning of winter, fishscale bamboo, as thick as a thumb and grown by streams on the shady side of a mountain for over three years, is cut down. Then, after undergoing the steps of cutting the bamboo into sections, baking and straightening the bamboo, passing the quality inspection and putting it into a warehouse, the technological process of selecting materials is finished. The procedure of making Pitai (a product that already has the required shape but still needs processing) mainly involves planing outer bamboo joints, scraping bamboo, unblocking inner bamboo joints, second baking and heating for straightening (precise), second planing of bamboo joints (precise planing), drawing central lines, rolling ink lines, drilling sound holes, polishing by using

贵州省 国家级非物质文化遗产文献资料汇编（汉英对照）

The Documentary Compilation of the State-level Intangible Cultural Heritage of Guizhou Province (Chinese-English Versions)

waterproof abrasive paper, truing sound holes, etc. Engraving is divided into two kinds: engraving Chinese characters and engraving patterns. Its procedures mainly include deinking and polishing fonts, pasting patterns, engraving, and polishing by using waterproof abrasive paper. A single knife is used to engrave Chinese characters, and there are eight traditional engraving methods: pricking, chopping, scratching, scraping, chiseling, picking, gouging out and rubbing. At the beginning of engraving patterns, a single knife is used, with its blade slid back and forth at a slower speed. Later, two knives are used to engrave patterns. The procedure of making final products mainly includes baking with strong acid, polishing by using waterproof abrasive paper, rinsing, filling colors, wiping off colors and lacquering. The final products of Yuping Xiao and Flutes are beautiful in styles, with Dragon and Phoenix flutes in pairs, so they are often presented as gifts or collected.

银冠
a Silver Crest

第 8-9 项：苗族银饰锻制技艺

项目序号：390	项目编号：Ⅷ-40	公布时间：2006（第一批）	类别：传统技艺
所属地区：贵州省	类型：新增项目	申报地区或单位：贵州省雷山县	

项目序号：390	项目编号：Ⅷ-40	公布时间：2011（第三批）	类别：传统技艺
所属地区：贵州省	类型：扩展项目	申报地区或单位：贵州省剑河县、台江县	

贵州省的苗族银饰精致美观，以雷山县的制品为代表，该县银匠主要集中在西江镇的控拜村、麻料村和乌高村。剑河苗族银饰根据造型不同分为三个片区：革东片区、南寨片区和久仰片区。革东片区的项圈为链状绞花式；南寨片区的项圈为板圈式；久仰片区为横板头式。台江苗族银饰分为施洞型、巴拉河型和黄平型。

苗族银饰锻制技艺有 30 道工序，形成熔炼、铸造、捶打、制花、编结焊接、洗涤等一整套手工工艺流程。一套银饰需要几百个银花焊接而成，不能有焊接的痕迹。根据不同的需要，将银捶打为方条、圆条和片状等，用于压花、切花和拉丝。然后通过编、錾、刻、洗亮等工序制造上百种银花，通过焊接组合做成图案丰富的银饰品。① 苗族银饰的加工，以家庭作坊手工操作完成。银饰是苗族最喜爱的传统饰物，主要用于妇女的装饰，有头饰、面饰、颈饰、肩饰、胸饰、腰饰、臂饰、手饰和脚饰等。银凤冠和银花帽是头饰中的主要饰

---

① 《银饰锻制技艺（苗族银饰锻制技艺）》，中国非物质文化遗产网，http://www.ihchina.cn/Article/Index/detail?id=14335，检索日期：2019 年 8 月 10 日。

·贵州省·国家级非物质文化遗产文献资料汇编（汉英对照）

The Documentary Compilation of the State-level Intangible Cultural Heritage of Guizhou Province (Chinese-English Versions)

品，其制作较复杂，使用的小件饰品少则 150 余件，多则达 200 余件，价值昂贵。苗族银饰锻制技艺体现了苗族人民聪明能干、智慧机巧的民族性格。[①]

Items 8-9: the Craft of Making Silver Ornaments of the Miao Nationality

Item Serial Number: 390	Item ID Number: VIII-40	Released Date: 2006 (Batch 1)	Category: Traditional Craft
Affiliated Province: Guizhou Province	Type: New Item	Application Province or Unit: Leishan County, Guizhou Province	

Item Serial Number: 390	Item ID Number: VIII-40	Released Date: 2011 (Batch 3)	Category: Traditional Craft
Affiliated Province: Guizhou Province	Type: Extended Item	Application Province or Unit: Jianhe County and Taijiang County of Guizhou Province	

The silver ornaments of the Miao nationality in Guizhou Province are exquisite and beautiful, represented by the products of Leishan County. The silversmiths in Leishan County mainly live in Kongbai, Maliao and Wugao villages of Xijiang Township. According to different shapes, the silver ornaments of the Miao nationality in Jianhe County are distributed in three areas: Gedong area, Nanzhai area and Jiuyang area. The necklaces in Gedong area are chain-shaped cross hawse type, the necklaces in Nanzhai area are plate-ring type, and the necklaces in Jiuyang area are horizontal plate-head type. The silver ornaments of the Miao nationality in Taijiang County are divided into Shidong type, Balahe type and Huangping type.

The Craft of Making Silver Ornaments of the Miao Nationality involves thirty procedures, forming a complete set of manual technological process, such as smelting, casting, hammering, flower making, knitting, welding and rinsing. A set of silver ornament need to be welded by using hundreds of silver flowers, which can't have any welding mark. According to different needs, silver is hammered into square bars, circular bars and sheets for embossing, cutting flowers and drawing wires. After

---

① 《苗族银饰锻制技艺》，中国非物质文化遗产网，http://www. ihchina. cn/Article/Index/detail?id=14331，检索日期：2019 年 8 月 10 日。

that, over one hundred kinds of silver flowers are made through weaving, chiseling, engraving, polishing and other procedures, and then silver ornaments with rich patterns are made by welding these silver flowers together. The making of the silver ornaments of the Miao nationality is usually completed by hand in family workshops. Silver ornaments are the favorite traditional ornaments of the Miao people, mainly used for women's decoration, including headdresses, facial ornaments, neck ornaments, shoulder ornaments, chest ornaments, waist ornaments, arm ornaments, hand ornaments and foot ornaments. Silver crests and silver flower caps are the major ornaments in headdresses. Their production is rather complicated, and the small ornaments used are as few as over 150 pieces and as many as over 200 pieces, making them very expensive. **The Craft of Making Silver Ornaments of the Miao Nationality** embodies the Miao people's national characters of smartness, capability, intelligence and ingenuity.

贵州省·国家级非物质文化遗产文献资料汇编（汉英对照）

The Documentary Compilation of the State-level Intangible Cultural Heritage of Guizhou Province (Chinese-English Versions)

制曲

the Making of Qu (yeast)

第10项： 茅台酒酿制技艺

项目序号：407	项目编号：Ⅷ-57	公布时间：2006（第一批）	类别：传统技艺
所属地区：贵州省	类型：新增项目	申报地区或单位：贵州省	

茅台酒酿制技艺主要流传于贵州省仁怀市茅台镇的贵州茅台酒厂，这里独特的水质、土质及气候环境为茅台酒酿制提供了最佳的天然条件。

茅台酒是大曲酱香型白酒，生产工艺有制曲、制酒、贮存、勾兑、检验和包装六个环节。整个生产周期为一年，端午踩曲，重阳投料，酿造期间九次蒸煮，八次发酵，七次取酒，经分型贮放、勾兑贮放，五年后包装出厂。茅台酒的酿制有两次投料、固态发酵、高温制曲、高温堆积、高温摘酒等特点，由此形成独特的酿造风格。白酒界专家称"贵州茅台酒技术是最独特的大曲酱香型酿酒工艺，是人类将微生物应用于酿造领域的典范"。茅台酒是中国大曲酱香型的代表和鼻祖，历史悠久。距今两千多年前的汉武帝时期，茅台当地就已经开始酿酒。明末清初，以大曲参与糖化、发酵、蒸馏取酒的工艺日趋成熟。数百年来，茅台酒酿制技艺在继承和发展中不断完善，至今仍完整延用。①

 Item 10: the Craft of Making Maotai Liquor

Item Serial Number: 407	Item ID Number: Ⅷ-57	Released Date: 2006 (Batch 1)	Category: Traditional Craft
Affiliated Province: Guizhou Province	Type: New Item	Application Province or Unit: Guizhou Province	

---

① 《茅台酒酿制技艺》，中国非物质文化遗产网，http://www.ihchina.cn/Article/Index/detail?id=14365，检索日期：2019 年 8 月 9 日。

The Craft of Making Maotai Liquor is mainly spread in Guizhou Maotai Distillery in Maotai Township, Renhuai City, Guizhou Province. The unique water quality, soil property and climate environment here provide the best natural conditions for making Maotai Liquor.

Maotai Liquor is a kind of Daqu (yeast)-fermented alcohol with sauce flavor. Its production process consists of six procedures: Qu (yeast) making, liquor making, storage, blending, inspection and packaging, with one year as a production cycle. Qu (yeast) should be made at the Dragon Boat Festival, and the materials should be added at the Double Ninth Festival. During the period of making Maotai Liquor, the materials should be steamed nine times and fermented eight times, with liquor collected seven times. After that, the liquor is stored according to liquor types, then blended, and packed to be sold from the factory five years later. The making of Maotai Liquor has the characteristics of adding materials twice, solid-state fermentation, making Qu (yeast) at high temperature, piling up at high temperature, collecting liquor at high temperature, etc., thus forming a unique style of making liquor. Experts in liquor industry have claimed that "the technique of making Guizhou Maotai Liquor is the most unique craft for making Daqu (yeast)-fermented liquor with sauce flavor, and a model for human beings to apply microorganisms to the field of liquor making". Maotai Liquor is the representative and originator of Daqu (yeast)-fermented liquor with sauce flavor in China, which has a long history. During the reign of Emperor Wu of the Han Dynasty more than 2000 years ago, liquor has been made in Maotai Township locally. At the end of the Ming Dynasty and the beginning of the Qing Dynasty, the craft of saccharification, fermentation and distillation by using Daqu (yeast) has become more and more mature. For hundreds of years, **the Craft of Making Maotai Liquor** has been constantly improved in the process of inheritance and development, and is still fully used today.

第11项：
皮纸制作技艺

丹寨石桥造纸
Papermaking in Shiqiao Village of Danzhai County

项目序号：417	项目编号：Ⅷ-67	公布时间：2006（第一批）	类别：传统技艺
所属地区：贵州省	类型：新增项目	申报地区或单位：贵州省贵阳市、贞丰县、丹寨县	

　　造纸术是中国古代四大发明之一，用竹和楮树皮制作的竹纸和皮纸是传统手工纸的两个重要品种。贵州的许多地区仍保留着传统竹纸和皮纸制作的古老技艺，尤以贵阳市香纸沟（布依族）、贞丰县小屯镇和丹寨县石桥村（苗族）的制作技艺最为杰出。

　　贵阳市香纸沟竹纸制作始于明代洪武年间，整套操作工艺有伐竹、破竹、沤竹、蒸煮、碾篾、提浆、抄纸、压榨和烘晾等72道工序。其成品既绵且韧，有隐形竹纹，散发出淡淡香气。贞丰县小屯镇所产白绵纸始于清咸丰年间，直至20世纪末全乡仍有千余户从事抄纸生产。所产纸以构皮为原料，整套操作也经72道工序，成品绵韧，平整润柔。丹寨县石桥村所产白皮纸以构皮和杉根为原料，另外还生产彩色纸，包括云龙纸、皱褶纸、凹凸纸、压平纸、花草纸和麻纸六个品种。制作过程一般有十多道环节，生产时将棉絮状纸浆兑水，加入"滑药"搅匀，经抄、压、晒、揭、包装而成品，纸质绵韧、光润，耐水性好。以上手工纸品对原料、水质、工艺均有严格要求，技艺的传承全靠口传心授。与制造相伴，产生了丰富的纸业习俗，每年都要祭祀造纸宗师蔡伦。由此可见，相关的竹纸、皮纸制造技艺已成为文化多样性和民族认同的重要证物。①

---

① 《皮纸制作技艺》，中国非物质文化遗产网，http://www.ihchina.cn/Article/Index/detail?id=14378，检索日期：2019年8月9日。

Item 11: the Craft of Making Bark Paper

Item Serial Number: 417	Item ID Number: Ⅷ-67	Released Date: 2006 (Batch 1)	Category: Traditional Craft
Affiliated Province: Guizhou Province	Type: New Item	Application Province or Unit: Guiyang City, Zhenfeng County and Danzhai County of Guizhou Province	

Papermaking is one of the four great ancient inventions in China. Bamboo paper and bark paper, made from bamboo and paper mulberry bark, are two important varieties of traditional handmade paper. In many areas of Guizhou Province, the ancient craft of making bamboo paper and bark paper is still preserved. Especially in Xiangzhi Valley (the Buyi nationality) of Guiyang City, Xiaotun Township of Zhenfeng County and Shiqiao Village (the Miao nationality) of Danzhai County, the making craft is the most outstanding.

The making of bamboo paper in Xiangzhi Valley of Guiyang City began in Hongwu Period of the Ming Dynasty. The whole set of operation process consists of 72 procedures, including felling bamboo, cutting bamboo into pieces, retting bamboo, steaming and boiling, rolling thin bamboo strips, extracting paper pulp, papermaking, pressing, drying and airing, etc. The finished products are soft and tough with invisible bamboo grain, emitting a faint aroma. The white tissue paper made in Xiaotun Township of Zhenfeng County began during the reign of Emperor Xianfeng of the Qing Dynasty. Until the end of the 20th century, there had still been more than 1000 households engaged in papermaking in the whole Township. The paper produced here is made from paper mulberry bark, which also undergoes 72 procedures in the whole process. The finished products are soft and tough, flat and smooth. The white bark paper produced in Shiqiao Village of Danzhai County takes paper mulberry bark and Chinese fir root as raw materials. Besides, colored paper is also produced here, including six varieties of cloud-dragon paper, pleated paper, embossed paper, flattened paper, flower-grass paper and jute paper. Its making process generally consists of more than ten steps. In the process of making paper, the batt-shaped pulp is mixed with water and added with "lubricant" to mix well. After being scooped out, pressed, dried, torn off and packaged, the pulp is made into finished products. This kind of paper is soft, tough and smooth, having good water

贵州省·国家级非物质文化遗产文献资料汇编（汉英对照）

The Documentary Compilation of the State-level Intangible Cultural Heritage of Guizhou Province (Chinese-English Versions)

resistance. The above handmade paper products have strict requirements for raw materials, water quality and workmanship. The inheritance of the craft relies entirely on oral transmission and heart-to-heart instruction. Together with papermaking, rich customs in paper industry have emerged. Every year, paper craftsmen will worship Cai Lun, the paper master. Thus, it can be seen that the related craft of making bamboo paper and bark paper has become an important evidence of cultural diversity and national identity.

牙舟陶器
Yazhou Pottery

第12项：
陶器烧制技艺
（牙舟陶器烧制技艺）

项目序号：881	项目编号：Ⅷ-98	公布时间：2008（第二批）	类别：传统技艺
所属地区：贵州省	类型：新增项目	申报地区或单位：贵州省平塘县	

　　牙舟陶器产于贵州省平塘县牙舟镇，始于明代洪武年间，距今已有600多年的历史。

　　牙舟陶制作原料有黄泥、白泥和青色泥三种，在制作陶坯时多数采用快轮成形及手工捏法。牙舟陶的釉料就地取材。釉色以玻璃为基础，以黄白、褐色为基调色，几色相互调配可以形成光泽莹润的色调。艺人们在陶坯上绘制花草、鸟兽等，融书、画、刻为一体。烧制牙舟陶使用的窑子叫阶梯窑，或爬坡窑、梭坡窑，依山而建。将半成品堆放在窑子的泥板架上，泥板架共七层，每层可放十件。根据釉和泥土质量，将耐火差一点的先放进窑子，耐火强的后放（靠近火口），然后密封洞口，点火烧制，温度达到1000℃，20～24个小时后，冷却出窑。牙舟陶产品多为生活用具、陈设品、动物玩具和祭祀器皿，其特点是造型自然古朴，线条简洁明快，色调淡雅和谐，具有浓重的出土文物神韵和浓厚的民族特色。[①] 牙舟陶器烧制现仍保持原始古老的手工制作方式，以古朴淳厚著称，尤其是陶器的玻璃釉能自然流淌，在烧制过程中随着温度的变化而产生各种纹理（俗称"窑变"），令人叹为观止。[②]

---

① 《平塘牙舟陶：穿越了600余年的国家级非物质文化遗产》，贵州省非物质文化遗产保护中心官网，http://www.gzfwz.org.cn/xwdt/201804/t20180416_3122601.html，检索日期：2019年9月7日。

② 《陶器烧制技艺（牙舟陶器烧制技艺）》，中国非物质文化遗产网，http://www.ihchina.cn/Article/Index/detail?id=14457，检索日期：2019年9月7日。

Item 12: the Craft of Firing Pottery (the Craft of Firing Yazhou Pottery)

Item Serial Number: 881	Item ID Number: Ⅷ-98	Released Date: 2008 (Batch 2)	Category: Traditional Craft
Affiliated Province: Guizhou Province	Type: New Item	Application Province or Unit: Pingtang County, Guizhou Province	

Yazhou Pottery is produced in Yazhou Township, Pingtang County, Guizhou Province. Starting from the reign of Emperor Hongwu of the Ming Dynasty, it has a history of more than six hundred years.

The raw materials for making Yazhou Pottery are divided into three kinds: yellow clay, white clay and cyan clay. The making of greenware mostly adopts the methods of forming via a fast turning wheel and manual kneading. The glazes of Yazhou Pottery are made from local materials. The glaze color is based on glass, with yellow, white and brown as basic colors. The combination of several colors can form a lustrous hue. Artisans paint flowers, plants, birds, animals, etc. on the greenware, integrating calligraphy, painting and carving. The kilns used for firing Yazhou Pottery are called ladder kilns, or slope kilns and Suopo kilns, built against the mountain. The semi-finished products are stacked on the mud rack in the kiln. Each mud rack has seven layers, and each layer can hold ten pieces. According to the quality of the glaze and clay, the semi-finished products with poor fire resistance are put into the kiln first, and the ones with strong fire resistance are put later (close to the fire). Then, the kiln is sealed and the fire is ignited to fire the pottery, with the temperature reaching 1000 °C. 20-24 hours later, the pottery is cooled and taken out from the kiln. The products of Yazhou Pottery are mostly living goods, furnishing articles, animal toys and worshipping vessels, which are characterized by natural and simple shapes, concise and bright lines, and elegant and harmonious colors. They have a strong charm of unearthed cultural relics and ethnical characteristics. The firing of Yazhou Pottery still maintains the primitive and ancient hand-made method, which is famous for primitive simplicity. In particular, the glass glaze of the pottery can flow naturally. The most amazing is that in the process of firing, various veins (commonly known as "kiln change") are produced with the change of the temperature.

苗族织锦技艺传承人潘英织锦图
the Picture of Weaving Brocade of Pan Ying , the Inheritor of the Craft
of Making Brocade of the Miao Nationality

第13项：
苗族织锦技艺

项目序号：888	项目编号：Ⅷ-105	公布时间：2008（第二批）	类别：传统技艺
所属地区：贵州省	类型：新增项目	申报地区或单位：贵州省麻江县、雷山县	

　　贵州的苗族织锦技艺已有 700 余年的历史，流传于贵州省的苗族聚居区，主要以母传女的方式世代相传。

　　流传于麻江县的苗族织锦主要有锦布和花带两种。锦布一般宽一尺余；花带根据用途宽窄不一，宽者 5～6 厘米，窄者仅 2～3 厘米，长度根据需要确定。苗族织锦所用丝纱分素、彩两种，彩纱有五色。织锦图案多源于生产生活，以自由灵活的装饰纹样为主，主体是几何图形，以大菱形为框架，各种图案花纹连接在一起，布满画面，整体图案规整紧凑，饱满对称。

　　流传于雷山县的苗族织锦有手织和机织两种，以手织为主。手织指将织锦带的一端系于固定的树干，一端系在织者的腰带上，然后用综线在织锦带上挑织经线纬线。织平布的综线只要两综，一般用黑线和白线即可织成；织锦则至少要五综以上，经纬交织，显出立体感较强的图案。苗锦大都反面织线，正面现图，交替使用红与绿、黑与白等彩线以造成颜色的交错。苗锦是苗族人民生活中不可或缺的物品，多用做衣服、围腰、背带、背包和腰带等的面料。织锦本身构图精美，图案灵活多变、协调对称、立体感强，美学价值极高。[①]

---

① 《苗族织锦技艺》，中国非物质文化遗产网，http://www.ihchina.cn/Article/Index/detail?id=14492，检索日期：2019 年 8 月 11 日。

·贵州省·国家级非物质文化遗产文献资料汇编（汉英对照）

The Documentary Compilation of the State-level Intangible Cultural Heritage of Guizhou Province (Chinese-English Versions)

Item 13: the Craft of Making Brocade of the Miao Nationality

Item Serial Number: 888	Item ID Number: VIII−105	Released Date: 2008 (Batch 2)	Category: Traditional Craft
Affiliated Province: Guizhou Province	Type: New Item	Application Province or Unit: Majiang County and Leishan County of Guizhou Province	

The Craft of Making Brocade of the Miao Nationality in Guizhou Province has a history of more than seven hundred years, spread in areas inhabited by the Miao nationality in Guizhou, which has been mainly passed on from generation to generation through mother to daughter.

The brocade of the Miao nationality spread in Majiang County is divided into brocade cloth and flower belt. Brocade cloth is generally more than one *chi* (a Chinese unit of length, with one *chi* roughly equal to 13 inches) wide. The widths of flower belts vary from 2-3 cm to 5-6 cm according to uses, and their lengths are determined according to the need. There are two kinds of silk yarn used in the brocade of the Miao nationality: plain yarn and colored yarn. The latter has five different colors. Brocade patterns mostly come from production and life. They are mainly free and flexible decorative patterns. Their principal parts are geometric figures, with large rhombuses as the frame. All kinds of patterns are connected together, covering the whole brocade, which makes the overall pattern neat and compact, full and symmetrical.

The brocade of the Miao nationality spread in Leishan County includes two kinds: being hand-woven and being machine-woven, with the former as the main one. Being hand-woven means to tie one end of the brocade belt on to a fixed tree trunk and the other end on to the weaver's waist, and then weave patterns by picking and weaving the warp and weft threads on the brocade belt with Zong threads. The Zong threads for weaving plain cloth only needs two pieces, generally black and white threads; while weaving brocade requires at least five Zong threads, with the warp and weft threads interwoven, showing strong three-dimensional patterns. Miao brocade is mostly woven on the reverse side to make the pattern show on the front side. Red and green, black and white and other colored threads are used alternately to create the interlacing of colors. Miao brocade is an indispensable item in the Miao people's daily life, mostly used as fabric to make clothes, aprons, straps, backpacks, belts, etc. The brocade itself has an exquisite composition, flexible and changeable patterns, a harmonious symmetry and a strong three-dimensional sense, which has a high aesthetic value.

苗族织锦技艺

凯里苗族织锦技艺展示
the Exhibition of the Craft of Making Brocade of the Miao Nationality in Kaili City

项目序号：888	项目编号：Ⅷ-105	公布时间：2011（第三批）	类别：传统技艺
所属地区：贵州省	类型：扩展项目	申报地区或单位：贵州省台江县、凯里市	

苗族织锦技艺是指苗族女性用染好颜色的彩色经纬线经提花、织造等工艺织出图案织物的技艺，主要流传于苗族聚居地区。

流传于贵州台江县的苗族织锦分机织和编织：机织的为宽锦，流行于清水江两岸和巴拉河一带；编织的是锦带，流行于雷公山区。机织是苗族妇女采用传统"通经回纬"技艺和平纹木机，利用当地所产的蚕丝、苎麻和木棉等纤维染彩织就的提花织物。台江苗锦纹饰题材有飞禽走兽、花草鱼虫、山川日月。其艺术手法简洁，巧妙运用点、线、面的疏密虚实、粗细大小、斜直长短等进行变化与组合，总体布局结构严谨，规整中有变化，展现了明快活泼而又朴实的艺术情趣。台江苗锦多作头帕、裹腿、围腰、衣袖、背饰、肩饰和床上用品。[①]

流传于贵州凯里市的苗族织锦分素锦和彩锦。素锦主要分布在舟溪镇、万潮镇；彩锦分布在凯棠乡、湾水镇。素锦用蚕丝织造，采用通经通纬法，蓝底起白色图案，其中技艺最精湛者是舟溪"中裙苗"的背带细丝锦。其用丝每平方厘米达到60经、90纬的高精密度，手感轻柔润滑，纹样精妙绝伦。彩锦用彩色丝线织造，采用通经断纬法。凯里苗族织锦工艺复杂，织工需要面对数千根细丝线，数纱挑经、露纬起花或断纬起花，即使是熟练织工，一天也只能织寸许。[②]

---

① 《苗族织锦技艺》，中国非物质文化遗产网，http://www. ihchina. cn/Article/Index/detail?id=14494，检索日期：2019 年 8 月 12 日。

② 《苗族织锦技艺》，中国非物质文化遗产网，http://www. ihchina. cn/Article/Index/detail?id=14493，检索日期：2019 年 8 月 13 日。

# Item 14: the Craft of Making Brocade of the Miao Nationality

Item Serial Number: 888	Item ID Number: VIII-105	Released Date: 2011 (Batch 3)	Category: Traditional Craft
Affiliated Province: Guizhou Province	Type: Extended Item	Application Province or Unit: Taijiang County and Kaili City of Guizhou Province	

The Craft of Making Brocade of the Miao Nationality refers to the Miao women's craft of weaving patterned fabrics by using colored warp and weft threads through the procedures of jacquard, weaving, etc. It is mainly spread in areas inhabited by the Miao nationality.

The brocade of the Miao nationality spread in Taijiang County of Guizhou Province is divided into hand-woven brocade and machine-woven brocade. The machine-woven brocade is wide brocade, popular along both sides of the Qingshui River and the Bala River. The hand-woven brocade is brocade belts, prevalent in the Leigong Mountain. The machine-woven brocade is the jacquard fabric made by the Miao women who use the traditional "warp and weft returning" technique and the plain weave wooden loom, and make use of the local silk, ramie, kapok and other fibers that have been dyed to weave. The patterns on Miao brocade in Taijiang County include birds, animals, flowers, plants, fish, insects, mountains, rivers, the sun and the moon. Its artistic technique is simple, skillfully using the density of points, lines and surfaces, as well as their thickness, bigness and smallness, slant and straightness, and length and shortness to make changes and combination. The overall layout is rigorous in structure, changing in regularity, which shows a bright, lively and plain artistic taste. Miao brocade in Taijiang County is mainly used for kerchiefs, leggings, aprons, sleeves, back ornaments, shoulder ornaments and bedding.

The brocade of the Miao nationality spread in Kaili City of Guizhou Province is divided into plain brocade and colored brocade. Plain brocade is mainly distributed in Zhouxi Township and Wanchao Township, while colored brocade is mainly distributed in Kaitang Township and Wanshui Township. Plain brocade is made of silk by using the method of connecting warp and weft threads. Blue color is used as the background with white patterns woven on it. The brocade that has the most excellent craftsmanship is the fine-silk brocade strap of "Zhongqun Miao (the

Miao nationality wearing medium-length skirts)" in Zhouxi Township. It has a high precision of 60 warp threads and 90 weft threads per square centimeter, feeling soft and smooth, with extremely exquisite patterns. Colored brocade is woven with colored silk threads by using the method of connecting warp threads and breaking weft threads. **The Craft of Making Brocade of the Miao Nationality** in Kaili City is complex, and weavers need to face thousands of fine threads, counting the yarn, picking up warp threads, exposing weft threads to weave flowers or breaking weft threads to weave flowers. Even for a skillful weaver, she can only weave about one *cun* (a Chinese unit of length, with one *cun* roughly equal to 1.3 inches) in one day.

第15项：

枫香印染技艺

枫香印染制品
a Product of Fengxiang Dip Dyeing

项目序号：891	项目编号：Ⅷ-108	公布时间：2008（第二批）	类别：传统技艺
所属地区：贵州省	类型：新增项目	申报地区或单位：贵州省惠水县、麻江县	

　　枫香印染是一种独特的民间手工技艺。贵州省枫香印染主要集中在贵州省麻江县和惠水县。麻江县瑶族枫香印染技艺主要流传于以麻江县龙山乡河坝村为主的 18 个自然村寨，在邻近的干桥、秧塘村的部分村寨也有流传。惠水县枫香印染技艺流传于惠水县城东南部。

　　枫香印染的工艺流程是先在老枫香树脂中加入适量牛油，用文火煎熬后过滤形成枫香油，然后用毛笔蘸上即时溶化的枫香油，在自织的白布上描绘图案，再用蓝靛浸染，沸水脱去油脂，清水漂洗，晒干，碾平。麻江县瑶族枫香印染的技艺和用料自成一体，所用材料均取自天然枫香树油和牛油，用配制的油料在布上绘图点花，风干后质地柔软，图案清晰，色彩对比强烈。产品主要用于服装、背带和被面等。惠水县枫香印染技艺的传承以布依族民众为主，已有 150 余年的历史。印染成品主要用以裁制床单、被面、帐沿和服饰等。惠水县枫香印染图案清新明快，纹样寓意吉祥，其青、蓝、白色的图案蕴蓄着深厚的民族文化内涵。[①]枫香印染技艺靠口传心授得以传承，印染的图案承载了相关民族的历史变迁、生活状况和民俗风情等信息。

Item 15: the Craft of Fengxiang Dip Dyeing

Item Serial Number: 891	Item ID Number: Ⅷ-108	Released Date: 2008 (Batch 2)	Category: Traditional Craft

---

① 《枫香印染技艺》，中国非物质文化遗产网，http://www.ihchina.cn/Article/Index/detail?id=14498，检索日期：2019 年 8 月 9 日。

Affiliated Province: Guizhou Province	Type: New Item	Application Province or Unit: Huishui County and Majiang County of Guizhou Province

Fengxiang Dip Dyeing is a unique folk craft. Fengxiang Dip Dyeing of Guizhou Province is mainly distributed in Majiang County and Huishui County of Guizhou Province. **The Craft of Fengxiang Dip Dyeing** of the Yao nationality in Majiang County is mainly spread in the 18 natural stockaded villages in Longshan Township of Majiang County, with Heba Village as the main one, as well as in some neighboring stockaded villages, such as Ganqiao and Yangtang. **The Craft of Fengxiang Dip Dyeing** in Huishui County is spread in the southeast of this county.

The technological process of Fengxiang Dip Dyeing is as follows: First, proper amount of beef tallow is added to the resin of old Chinese sweet gum trees, boiled over a gentle heat, and then filtered to form the resin oil. Next, the artisan dips a Chinese brush into the instantly-melted resin oil and draws patterns on the self-woven white cloth. Then, the cloth is soaked in the indigo to be dyed. After that, it is put into boiling water to remove the grease on it, then rinsed by using clean water, dried in the sun, and then flattened. The craft and materials of Fengxiang Dip Dyeing of the Yao nationality in Majiang County are self-contained. All materials are the natural resin of Chinese sweet gum trees as well as beef tallow. After mixing them together to make the oil material, artisans draw patterns and flowers on the cloth with the mixture. After getting dried in the air, the finished products have soft textures, clear patterns and sharp color contrasts. The products are mainly used for clothes, straps, quilt covers, etc. The inheritance of **the Craft of Fengxiang Dip Dyeing** in Huishui County is mainly among the Buyi people, which has a history of more than 150 years. Its final products are mostly used to make bed sheets, quilt covers, curtain edges, clothes, etc. The patterns of Fengxiang Dip Dyeing in Huishui County are fresh and bright with auspiciousness. The cyan, blue and white patterns contain profound national culture connotations. **The Craft of Fengxiang Dip Dyeing** has been inherited by oral instruction, and the dip-dyed patterns carry the information about the historical changes, living conditions, folk customs, etc. of relevant ethnic groups.

彝族漆器制品
Lacquerware Products of the Yi Nationality

第16项：
彝族漆器髹饰技艺

项目序号：911	项目编号：Ⅷ-128	公布时间：2008（第二批）	类别：传统技艺
所属地区：贵州省	类型：新增项目	申报地区或单位：贵州省大方县	

　　彝族漆器髹饰技艺主要流传于贵州省大方县，有600多年的历史，以大方县优质生漆涂髹物品，以木、皮、角、蹄和布为坯胎，用色调漆涂髹，制成优质漆器用具。

　　大方彝族漆器以工序细腻，工艺精湛名扬四海，其制作主要有制漆、胎坯、灰地、漆地和装饰五大工艺，工序有50多道，髹饰环节有82道。[①] 依照传统的彝族制漆做法，从原木的砍伐、坯胎制作、大漆的收集、生漆的晾晒、漆色的形成，到漆物、打磨、推光等程序，制作过程少则10个月，多则3～5年。上品彝族漆器的主体以皮质和木头为主，皮质要以优质的牛羊皮或其他兽皮，木质则要以杜鹃木和桦槁树等优质木材为原材料，经过深埋之后做成坯胎，将坯胎进行干燥、粗坯、干燥、细坯、干磨、吃青、补灰三次、水磨三次、验收、打底、细磨、小补、塞孔、磨孔、点敏、磨敏、验收、清洗、吹尘、盖面、阴干、磨花、除尘、盖面、阴干、验收、磨花、圈地、阴干、验收、清洁和包装等50多道工序。[②] 彝族漆器纹饰源于自然，来自生活，图案多以日月星辰、山河树木、花鸟蛇虫、飞禽走兽及生活用具为素材，以抽象化、艺术化、规则化的手法在胎体上再现大自然及人类的生产生活场景。彝族漆器具有无毒、无异味、耐酸碱、耐高温、不变形、不易裂和不脱漆的性能。

---

① 马锦卫、吉伍依作，《彝族漆器企业发展情况调查与研究》，载《民族学刊》，2018年第5期，第78-83页。

② 任小宇，《贵州大方彝族漆器髹饰工艺的传承困境及对策》，载《安顺学院学报》，2017年第2期，第107-110页。

·贵州省· 国家级非物质文化遗产文献资料汇编（汉英对照）

The Documentary Compilation of the State-level Intangible Cultural Heritage of Guizhou Province (Chinese-English Versions)

Item 16: the Craft of Painting Lacquerware of the Yi Nationality

Item Serial Number: 911	Item ID Number: Ⅷ-128	Released Date: 2008 (Batch 2)	Category: Traditional Craft
Affiliated Province: Guizhou Province	Type: New Item	Application Province or Unit: Dafang County, Guizhou Province	

The Craft of Painting Lacquerware of the Yi Nationality is mainly spread in Dafang County, Guizhou Province, with a history of more than six hundred years. Using wood, leather, horns, hooves and cloth, artisans make Pitai (a product that already has the required shape but still needs processing), and paint it with high-quality raw lacquer of Dafang County and colored lacquer, making it into top-grade lacquerware.

The lacquerware of the Yi Nationality in Dafang County is famous for its fine production process and excellent workmanship. Its production mainly involves five crafts: making lacquer, making Pitai (a product that already has the required shape but still needs processing), plastering, painting and decoration, with more than 50 procedures. For painting and decoration, there are 82 procedures. According to the traditional lacquer making practice of the Yi nationality, the whole process lasts as few as ten months and as many as 3-5 years, involving the procedures of cutting logs, making Pitai (a product that already has the required shape but still needs processing), collecting lacquer, drying raw lacquer, forming lacquer color, lacquering, polishing, finishing, etc. The main body of the top-quality lacquerware of the Yi nationality is mostly leather and wood. The material of leather should be high-quality cowhide, sheep skin or other animal hides, while the material of wood should be high-grade wood, such as azalea wood and white birch tree. After deeply buried, these raw materials are made into Pitai (a product that already has the required shape but still needs processing). Then, they are processed through more than 50 procedures, such as drying, making rough Pitai (a product that already has the required shape but still needs processing), second drying, making fine Pitai (a product that already has the required shape but still needs processing), dry grinding, Chiqing, applying putty three times, grinding with water three times, acceptance check, priming, fine grinding, minor filling, filling holes, grinding holes, Dianmin, Momin, second acceptance check, washing, blowing dust, covering, drying in the shade, grinding to make flowers, removing dust, second covering, second drying in the shade, third acceptance check, second grinding to make flowers, enclosure, third drying in the shade, fourth acceptance check, cleaning and packaging. The lacquerware patterns of the Yi nationality come from nature and life, mostly the sun, the moon, stars, mountains, rivers, trees, flowers, birds, snakes, insects, fowls, beasts and household goods. They represent the scenes of nature and human production and life on the lacquerware by means of abstraction, artistry and regularization. The lacquerware of the Yi nationality has the properties of being non-toxic, odorlessness, acid resistance, alkali resistance, high-temperature resistance, no deformation, no cracking or no depainting.

第17项：
侗族木构建筑营造技艺

侗族鼓楼和花桥
the Drum Tower and the Flower Bridge of the Dong Nationality

项目序号：380	项目编号：Ⅷ-30	公布时间：2008（第二批）	类别：传统技艺
所属地区：贵州省	类型：扩展项目	申报地区或单位：贵州省黎平县、从江县	

　　贵州省侗族的鼓楼和花桥是侗人在长期生活实践中创造出来的具有独特风格的木构建筑样式。鼓楼由简单的干阑式卡房发展而来，采用上下串穿的穿云式整体框架和木构体系，是侗寨的象征。侗族花桥结构巧妙，运用杠杆原理，大小柱子、枋、檩和栏杆全部以贵州当地杉木凿孔穿榫制成，结构严谨，工艺精湛，展示了侗族木构建筑营造技艺的独特风格。

　　黎平县侗族鼓楼集塔、阁、亭等建筑形式于一体。鼓楼在侗寨中属高层建筑，高3～5丈，底部宽度为7～10米，楼檐层叠，上覆青瓦，饰以各种彩塑。有的围以栏杆，有的空敞而中置火塘，四周有长凳供人休息。从江县侗族鼓楼营造技艺已有300余年，侗族群众用当地杉木建造了108座侗族鼓楼，其中增冲鼓楼被列为全国重点文物保护单位，成为从江侗族鼓楼的代表。侗族鼓楼和花桥融多种建筑形式于一体，富于少数民族地方特色。侗人在建造鼓楼和花桥时采用竹条制成的"匠杆"竹尺和自成体系的设计施工符号，形成了独特的侗族木构建筑营造技艺体系，成为中国民族建筑文化的重要组成部分。侗族工匠采用以师带徒、言传身授的方式，将这一宝贵技艺完整地留存至今。①

---

① 《侗族木构建筑营造技艺》，中国非物质文化遗产网，http://www.ihchina.cn/Article/Index/detail?id=14314，检索日期：2019年9月8日。

Item 17: the Craft of Constructing Wooden Structures of the Dong Nationality

Item Serial Number: 380	Item ID Number: VIII−30	Released Date: 2008 (Batch 2)	Category: Traditional Craft
Affiliated Province: Guizhou Province	Type: Extended Item	Application Province or Unit: Liping County and Congjiang County of Guizhou Province	

The Drum Tower and the Flower Bridge of the Dong nationality in Guizhou Province are the wooden structures with unique styles created by the Dong people in their long-term life practice. The Drum Tower is a symbol of Dong Stockaded Villages, which has been developed from simple pile-dwelling house, adopting the cloud-piercing integral frame and the wooden structure system. The Flower Bridge of the Dong nationality has an ingenious structure. By using lever principle, big and small pillars, square columns, purlins and railings are all made of the local Chinese fir wood that has been mortised and tenoned. It has a strict structure and an exquisite workmanship, showing the unique style of **the Craft of Constructing Wooden Structures of the Dong Nationality**.

The Drum Tower of the Dong nationality in Liping County is the integration of the tower, the pavilion and other architectural forms. The Drum Tower is a high-rise building in Dong Stockaded Villages, with a height of 3-5 *zhang* (a Chinese unit of length, with one *zhang* roughly equal to 131 inches) and a bottom width of 7-10 meters. The eaves are stacked tier upon tier, covered with grey tiles and decorated with various colored sculptures. Some are surrounded by railings, and some are acant, with the Fire Pit in the middle and benches around for people to rest. The craft of constructing the Drum Tower of the Dong nationality in Congjiang County has a history of more than three hundred years. The Dong people have built 108 Drum Towers by using local Chinese fir wood, among which Zengchong Drum Tower has been listed as a national key cultural relic protection unit, becoming the representative of the Drum Tower of the Dong nationality in Congjiang County. The Drum Tower and the Flower Bridge of the Dong nationality integrate various architectural forms, rich in local characteristics of ethnic minorities. When building them, the Dong people use the bamboo ruler called "craftsman's pole" which is made

贵州省 国家级非物质文化遗产文献资料汇编（汉英对照）

The Documentary Compilation of the State-level Intangible Cultural Heritage of Guizhou Province (Chinese-English Versions)

of bamboo strips, as well as the self-contained designing and construction symbols, and have formed a unique system about **the Craft of Constructing Wooden Structures of the Dong Nationality**, which has become an important part of Chinese national architectural culture. The artisans of the Dong nationality have preserved this precious craft completely by masters' oral instruction of apprentices with words and deeds.

第18项：
银饰制作技艺（苗族银饰制作技艺）

黄平苗族银饰
the Silver Ornaments of the Miao Nationality in Huangping County

项目序号：390	项目编号：VIII-40	公布时间：2008（第二批）	类别：传统技艺
所属地区：贵州省	类型：扩展项目	申报地区或单位：贵州省黄平县	

　　贵州省黄平县苗族银饰制作技艺十分发达，制品主要包括妇女佩戴的银冠、耳环、项圈、项链、手圈、银腰带等，其中以银冠、响铃板、银项链和银腰带最为精美。

　　黄平苗族银饰的加工以家庭作坊手工操作完成。主要制作工具有火炉、风箱、坩埚（俗称"银窝"）、铁锤、铁砧、冲具、刻具、拉丝眼板、铜锅、钳子、镊子、油灯吹管、铅坯模具和松脂板等。其制作工艺流程十分复杂，一件银饰要经过一二十道工序才能完成，其中主要有铸炼、锤打、拉丝、搓丝、掐丝、焊接、编结、雕镂和洗涤等工序。银匠先把熔炼过的白银制成薄片、银条或银丝，利用压、刻、搂等工艺，制出精美纹样，再经过焊接、编结、雕镂和洗涤（俗称"洗银"）等工序，即制成洁白光亮的银饰。黄平苗族银饰图纹题材丰富，昆虫、花草、鸟雀、龙鱼等均可作为表现对象，这些图纹多来自黄平苗族祖辈生存的自然环境，体现着苗族社会人与自然和谐相处的生态状况。银饰常出现于苗族的喜庆场合，蕴涵有避邪趋正、纳福迎祥的寓意，生动地反映了苗族人民的生存状况、精神面貌和审美心理。①

---

① 《银饰制作技艺（苗族银饰制作技艺）》，中国非物质文化遗产网，http://www.ihchina. cn/Article/Index/detail?id=14333，检索日期：2019 年 9 月 8 日。

贵州省·国家级非物质文化遗产文献资料汇编（汉英对照）

The Documentary Compilation of the State-level Intangible Cultural Heritage of Guizhou Province (Chinese-English Versions)

Item 18: the Craft of Making Silver Ornaments (the Craft of Making Silver Ornaments of the Miao Nationality)

Item Serial Number: 390	Item ID Number: Ⅷ–40	Released Date: 2008 (Batch 2)	Category: Traditional Craft
Affiliated Province: Guizhou Province	Type: Extended Item	Application Province or Unit: Huangping County, Guizhou Province	

The Craft of Making Silver Ornaments of the Miao Nationality in Huangping County, Guizhou Province is well-developed. Its products mainly include silver crowns, earrings, neck rings, necklaces, hand rings and silver belts that are worn by women. Among them, silver crowns, ringing boards, silver necklaces and silver belts are the most exquisite.

The processing of the silver ornaments of the Miao nationality in Huangping County is generally done by hand in family workshops. The main tools for making silver ornaments are stoves, bellows, crucibles (commonly known as "silver nest"), iron hammers, anvils, punching tools, carving tools, wire-drawing plates, copper pots, pliers, tweezers, oil lamps and blowing tubes, lead molds, pine resin boards, etc. The technological process for making is very complex, and one silver ornament can only be completed after going through about twenty procedures, mainly including casting, hammering, wire drawing, wire rubbing, wire inlay, welding, weaving and knotting, chasing and washing. First, silversmiths make melted silver into thin pieces, silver bars or silver wires. Next, they make exquisite patterns by using the crafts of pressing, engraving, raking, etc. Then, they can produce white and bright silver ornaments after going through the procedures of welding, weaving and knotting, chasing, washing (commonly known as "silver washing"), etc. The patterns of the silver ornaments of the Miao nationality in Huangping County are rich and diverse. Insects, flowers, plants, birds, dragons, fish, etc. all can be designed as ornaments. These patterns mostly come from the natural environment where the Miao ancestors in Huangping County have lived, reflecting the ecological situation of the Miao people living in harmony with nature. The Miao people wear silver ornaments on festive occasions, which contains the implied meanings of exorcising evil spirits, pursuing justice, and embracing blessings and auspiciousness, vividly reflecting their living conditions, mental outlook and aesthetic psychology.

第19项：

绿茶制作技艺

（都匀毛尖茶制作技艺）

高温杀青
Heating Green Tea leaves at High Temperature

项目序号：931	项目编号：Ⅷ-148	公布时间：2014（第四批）	类别：传统技艺
所属地区：贵州省	类型：扩展项目	申报地区或单位：贵州省都匀市	

　　都匀毛尖茶又名"鱼钩茶""雀舌茶"，是贵州三大名茶之一，中国十大名茶之一。产于贵州黔南布衣族苗族自治州都匀市，其形可与太湖碧螺春并提，其质能同信阳毛尖媲美。

　　都匀毛尖茶以主产区团山乡的哨脚村、哨上村、黄河村、黑沟村和钱家坡村所产品质最佳。这里气候温和，适宜毛尖茶的生长。芽叶茸毛多、肥厚柔嫩、发芽早、持嫩性强，其鲜叶内含物丰富，为创造优质的都匀毛尖奠定基础。毛尖茶清明前后开采，采摘标准为一芽一叶初展，长度不超过两厘米，俗称"瓜米茶"或"雅雀嘴"的茶青，用手工炒制而成。通常炒制500克高级毛尖茶约需5.3～5.6万个芽头。都匀毛尖茶的制作工艺有四道工序，即高温杀青、低温揉捻、搓团提毫和及时焙干。都匀毛尖茶具有"三绿透三黄"的特点：干茶色泽绿中带黄，汤色绿中透黄，叶底绿中显黄。成品都匀毛尖色泽翠绿、外形匀整、白毫显露、条索卷曲、香气清嫩、回味甘甜、汤色清澈、芽头肥壮。[①] 都匀毛尖茶具有生津解渴、清心明目、提神醒脑、去腻消食、抑制动脉粥样硬化、降脂减肥以及防癌、防治坏血病和护御放射性元素等多种功效，被誉为"茶中极品，保健首品"。[②]

---

① 郭邱磊，《都匀毛尖不亚龙井碧螺春》，http://culture. gog. cn/system/2015/05/28/014338534. shtml，检索日期：2019年8月13日。

② 郭邱磊，《2014年都匀毛尖入选第四批国家级非物质文化遗产名录》，http://culture. gog. cn/system/2015/05/25/014328293. shtml，检索日期：2019年8月12日。

贵州省·国家级非物质文化遗产文献资料汇编（汉英对照）

The Documentary Compilation of the State-level Intangible Cultural Heritage of Guizhou Province (Chinese-English Versions)

Item 19: the Craft of Making Green Tea (the Craft of Making Duyun Maojian Tea)

Item Serial Number: 931	Item ID Number: VIII–148	Released Date: 2014 (Batch 4)	Category: Traditional Craft
Affiliated Province: Guizhou Province	Type: Extended Item	Application Province or Unit: Duyun City, Guizhou Province	

Duyun Maojian Tea, also called "Fishhook Tea" and "Sparrow-Tongue tea", is one of the three famous varieties of tea in Guizhou Province and one of the top ten famous varieties of tea in China. It is produced in Duyun City, Qiannan Buyi and Miao Autonomous Prefecture, Guizhou Province. Its shape can be compared with that of Taihu Biluochun Tea, and its quality can be comparable to that of Xinyang Maojian Tea.

Duyun Maojian Tea which is produced in Shaojiao Village, Shaoshang Village, Huanghe Village, Heigou Village and Qianjiapo Village of Tuanshan Township, the main tea producing area, has the best quality. The climate here is mild and suitable for the growth of Maojian Tea. The buds and leaves are hairy, thick and tender. The tea germinates early, and its tenderness lasts long. Its fresh leaves are rich in content, which lays the foundation for producing high-quality Duyun Maojian Tea. Maojian Tea is picked before and after the Tomb Sweeping Day. Its picking standard is the first sprout with a bud and a leaf no more than two cm long, which is commonly known as "Guami Tea" or "Yaquezui Tea", fried by hand. Generally, to make 500g high-grade Maojian Tea needs about 53,000-56,000 buds. The making of Duyun Maojian Tea involves four procedures: heating green tea leaves at high temperature, kneading tea leaves at low temperature, rubbing tea leaves to make their hairs erect and drying timely. It has the characteristics of "having three green colors and three yellow colors": the dry tea looks both green and yellow, the tea liquid seems both green and yellow, and the bottom of the tea leaf is both green and yellow. Its finished products are green in color and neat in shape, with visible white hairs, curly shapes, clear and tender aromas, sweet aftertaste, limpid tea liquid colors and plump bud heads. Duyun Maojian Tea is acclaimed as "the best tea and the first health care product" for it has various functions, such as promoting the secretion of saliva and relieving thirst, clearing heart and improving eyesight, refreshing brain, degreasing, helping digestion, inhibiting atherosclerosis, reducing fat and weight, preventing cancer and scurvy, and protecting against radioactive elements.

第九章 传统医药

Chapter Nine
Traditional Medicine

同济堂商标
the Brand of TONGJI TANG

第 1 项：传统中医药文化

（同济堂传统中药文化）

项目序号：971	项目编号：Ⅸ-11	公布时间：2008（第二批）	类别：传统医药
所属地区：贵州省	类型：新增项目	申报地区或单位：贵州省同济堂制药有限公司	

同济堂是贵州中药行业闻名遐迩的老字号，建于清光绪十四年（1888），由唐炯（曾任清朝矿务大臣，云贵总督）和于德楷（曾任清朝知县）合资开办。1994 年，被中华人民共和国国内贸易部评为“中华老字号”。目前变更为“贵州同济堂制药有限公司”，但其一以贯之地秉承百余年来形成的同济堂传统中药文化，制良心之药。[①]

① 《同济堂（1888 年）》，国医小镇网，http://www.tcm360.com/culture/lzhyg/75130.html，检索日期：2020 年 7 月 10 日。

同济堂传统中药文化体现在五方面：（1）"同心协力、济世为民"的价值观；（2）"购药须出地道，制作必须精细，配售必依法度"的质量观；（3）"货真价实""童叟无欺"的经营理念；（4）"济世活人，急人之急，质量取胜，济世取信"的职业道德；（5）"遵古炮制"的中药炮制技术。[1]同济堂以生产新特药为主，如仙灵骨葆胶囊（片）、枣仁安神胶囊、补肾益脑胶囊、润燥止痒胶囊、心脑康胶囊和胶体果胶铋胶囊等，其中有 5 个为专利产品。其生产剂型有胶囊剂、片剂、颗粒剂、锭剂、糖浆剂、酊剂、口服溶液剂和膏剂等。同济堂主要生产普药，有 140 多个中西药品种，如复方牙痛酊、滇白珠糖浆、诺氟沙星和复方甘草口服溶液等，其产品药材好，价钱公道，不得二价。[2]

Item 1: Traditional Chinese Medicine Culture (the Traditional Chinese Medicine Culture of TONGJI TANG)

Item Serial Number: 971	Item ID Number: IX-11	Released Date: 2008 (Batch 2)	Category: Traditional Medicine
Affiliated Province: Guizhou Province	Type: New Item	Application Province or Unit: TONGJI TANG Pharmaceutical Co., Ltd, Guizhou Province	

TONGJI TANG is a famous time-honored brand in the traditional Chinese medicine industry of Guizhou Province, jointly founded by Tang Jiong (a former minister of Mining Affairs of the Qing Dynasty and governor of Yunnan and Guizhou) and Yu Dekai (a former magistrate of the Qing Dynasty) in the 14th year during the reign of Emperor Guangxu of the Qing Dynasty (1888). In 1994, it was rated as "time-honored brand of China" by the Ministry of Internal Trade of the People's Republic of China. At present, its name has been changed into "Guizhou TONGJI TANG Pharmaceutical Co., Ltd.". It adheres to **the Traditional Chinese Medicine Culture of TONGJI TANG** that has been formed for more than one hundred years, and makes medicines of conscience.

---

[1] 《传统中医药文化（同济堂传统中药文化）》，中国非物质文化遗产网，http://www.ihchina.cn/Article/Index/detail?id=14875，检索日期：2019 年 9 月 7 日。

[2] 《同济堂（1888 年）》，国医小镇网，http://www.tcm360.com/culture/lzhyg/75130.html，检索日期：2020 年 7 月 10 日。

The Traditional Chinese Medicine Culture of TONGJI TANG is reflected in the following five aspects: (1) the values of "working together to help the world and the people"; (2) the quality views of "purchasing authentic medicinal herbs, manufacturing with fine workmanship, and dispensing and selling in accordance with the law"; (3) the business philosophies of "genuine goods at a fair price" and "cheating neither the old nor the young"; (4) the professional ethics of "helping the common people cure their illness, enthusiastically helping others overcome difficulties, winning by quality, benefitting the masses and winning their trust"; (5) the technology of "processing traditional Chinese medicine by using ancient ways". TONGJI TANG focuses on the production of new and specific drugs, such as Xianling Bone-protecting Capsules (Tablets), Zaoren (kernels of wild jujubes) Tranquilizing Capsules, Capsules of Tonifying Kidneys and Benefiting Brains, Capsules of Moistening Dryness and Relieving Itching, Heart-and-Brain Recovery Capsules and Colloidal Bismuth Pectin Capsules. Among them, five are patented products. The dosage forms of its products include capsules, tablets, granules, pastilles, syrup, tinctures, oral solutions and ointments. TONGJI TANG mainly produces generic drugs, with more than 140 varieties of Chinese and Western medicines, such as Compound Toothache Tincture, Syrup of Dianbaizhu (*Gaultheria leucocarpa var. yunnanensis* in Latin), Norfloxacin and Compound Glycyrrhiza Oral Solution. Its products are made from high-quality medicinal materials and sold at a fair price, with each at only one price.

贵州省 国家级非物质文化遗产文献资料汇编（汉英对照）

The Documentary Compilation of the State-level Intangible Cultural Heritage of Guizhou Province (Chinese-English Versions)

第2项：
瑶族医药（药浴疗法）

瑶族药浴黄桶
the Barrel for the Therapy of Medicated Bath of the Yao Nationality

项目序号：974	项目编号：IX-14	公布时间：2008（第二批）	类别：传统医药
所属地区：贵州省	类型：新增项目	申报地区或单位：贵州省从江县	

　　瑶族药浴疗法是贵州省从江县高坡瑶寨瑶民以药物洗浴来强身健体、抵御风寒、消除疲劳、防治疾病的传统养生治疗方法，是瑶族祖先独创的传内不传外的保健良方。[①]

　　瑶族药浴疗法主要是将多种植物药，经过高温烧煮成药水，倒入杉木桶，人坐于桶内薰浴浸泡，使药液渗透到人体的五脏六腑、全身经络，达到祛风除湿、排汗排毒、活血化瘀的功效，对防治风湿、妇科疾病、皮肤疾病和伤风感冒等疾病尤为有效。不同体质特征的人要配上不同的药方，而这些药方自古只能族内自传。瑶族药浴大致有188种药方，主治47类疾病，日常用来洗浴的草药有20多种，有草本，也有灌木枝叶。[②]此药物洗浴无副作用，对人体内脏、血液和神经系统有益无害。瑶族药浴有很多礼仪，一般客人先洗，然后按先男后女、先老后幼的次序逐一洗浴。每当有客人进寨，乡亲们都会用油茶和药浴热情款待远方的客人，这是瑶族人接待嘉宾的最高礼仪。[③]

---

① 《瑶族医药（药浴疗法）》，中国非物质文化遗产网，http://www. ihchina. cn/Article/Index/detail?id=14883，检索日期：2019 年 9 月 7 日。

② 《藏在大山里的神秘瑶浴》，贵州文明网，http://gz. wenming. cn/zt/20170504_yzyy/20170504_wz/201705/t20170518_4249998. shtml，检索日期：2019 年 9 月 7 日。

③ 《贵州之最古老的洗浴方式——瑶族药浴》，贵州文明网，http://gz. wenming. cn/zt/20170504_yzyy/20170504_wz/201705/t20170518_4249990. shtml，检索日期：2019 年 9 月 7 日。

Item 2: the Medicine of the Yao Nationality (the Therapy of Medicated Bath)

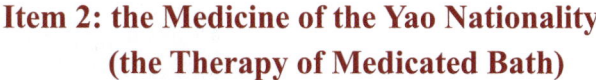

Item Serial Number: 974	Item ID Number: IX-14	Released Date: 2008 (Batch 2)	Category: Traditional Medicine
Affiliated Province: Guizhou Province	Type: New Item	Application Province or Unit: Congjiang County, Guizhou Province	

The Therapy of Medicated Bath of the Yao nationality is a traditional health preservation and curative treatment method for the Yao people to strengthen their bodies, resist wind and cold, eliminate fatigue and prevent diseases through medicated bath in Gaopo Yao Stockaded Village, Congjiang County, Guizhou Province. It is an original health protection prescription created by the Yao ancestors, only handed down within the family.

The Therapy of Medicated Bath of the Yao nationality is a treatment of fumigation bath and immersion. First, a variety of medicinal herbs are boiled at high temperature into liquid medicine and poured into a fir barrel. Then, people sit in the barrel for immersion, so that the liquid medicine can penetrate their viscera and their main and collateral channels, achieving the efficacy of dispelling wind and dampness, sweating and detoxifying, promoting blood circulation and removing blood stasis. It is especially effective in the prevention and treatment of rheumatism, gynecological diseases, skin diseases, colds and other diseases. People with different physical characteristics should be given different prescriptions, and these prescriptions can only be handed down within the family since ancient times. There are 188 kinds of prescriptions for the Medicated Bath of the Yao nationality, which can mainly cure 47 kinds of diseases. There are more than 20 kinds of herbal medicines for daily bath, including herbs and the branches and leaves of shrubs. This kind of medicated bath has no side effects and is beneficial to human viscera, blood and nervous system. There is much etiquette for the Medicated Bath of the Yao nationality. Generally, guests bathe first, and then hosts bathe one by one in the order of men before women and the old before the young. Whenever guests enter the stockaded village, villagers will warmly entertain guests from afar with oil tea and medicated bath, which is the highest etiquette for the Yao people to receive distinguished guests.

第3项：
苗医药（骨伤蛇伤疗法）

治愈骨折的草药——四块瓦
the Medicinal Herb for Fracture Healing—Sikuaiwa Herb
(*Lysimachia paridiformis Franch.* in Latin)

项目序号：975	项目编号：IX-15	公布时间：2008（第二批）	类别：传统医药
所属地区：贵州省	类型：新增项目	申报地区或单位：贵州省雷山县	

  贵州雷山县的苗医是治疗骨伤和蛇伤的行家。2006年，雷山县卫生局组织调查的113名苗医中，就有47名苗医擅长治疗上下肢骨、肋骨、颅骨和锁骨等外伤骨折，15名苗医擅长治疗毒蛇咬伤，6名能兼治这两种伤患。[1]

  雷山苗医常采用的治疗方法有十余种，其中，外治法别具特色，著名疗法有薰蒸疗法、滚蛋疗法、化水疗法（含有巫文化成分）、捣药外敷疗法、推擦、掐痧并放血疗法、热敷疗法等[2]，治疗骨伤及蛇虫咬伤非常有效。骨伤蛇伤疗法的药用鲜草药，其治疗简单、疗程短、疗效好。骨伤主要采用捣药外敷疗法，即将骨折病人正骨（复位，固定）后，捣烂药物（或用酒糟伴药）外敷患者伤处，在靠近关节活动处用小块木板捆绑固定。[3]治愈骨折的主要草药有九节茶、野葡萄根、泡桐树根皮和四块瓦等；著名的骨伤药有柏林接骨散药，该药具有"活血化瘀、清热解毒、消肿止痛、接骨生肌、舒筋活络、促进骨痂生长和愈合的功效"。[4]治疗蛇伤的主要草药有冰球子、降龙草、半边莲、蜂斗菜和山乌龟等。疗程3～5天，取适量鲜草药一味，捣烂用凉开水调后用消

---

① 《苗医药（骨伤蛇伤疗法）》，中国非物质文化遗产网，http://www.ihchina.cn/Article/Index/detail?id=14885，检索日期：2019年8月9日。

② 雷山县苗学研究会中国民博苗族文化雷山研究中心，《雷山苗族医药》，北京：中国文化出版社，2011年，第26页。

③ 潘定发，《雷山苗族医药再调查》，载《中国山地民族研究集刊》，2016年第1期，第126-137页。

④ 张东海、张立，《苗药柏林接骨散治疗伤疾举隅》，载《中国民族医药杂志》，2007年第2期，第25页。

毒药棉沾药水擦拭伤口四周，3～4 小时擦拭一次；同时，口服鲜草药 2～3 味，煨成水煎剂，每次服用 30 毫升，一日三次。[①] 苗族骨伤蛇伤疗法的传承方式主要是祖传和师授。

Item 3: the Medicine of the Miao Nationality (the Therapies for Bone Injuries and Snakebites)

Item Serial Number: 975	Item ID Number: IX-15	Released Date: 2008 (Batch 2)	Category: Traditional Medicine
Affiliated Province: Guizhou Province	Type: New Item	Application Province or Unit: Leishan County, Guizhou Province	

The Miao doctors in Leishan County of Guizhou Province are experts in treating bone injuries and snakebites. The survey conducted in 2006 by the Public Health Bureau of Leishan County shows that of the 113 Miao doctors in Leishan, 47 are good at treating the traumatic fractures of upper and lower limbs, ribs, skulls and clavicles, etc., 15 are good at treating snakebites, and six can treat both.

The Miao doctors in Leishan County often adopt more than ten therapeutic methods, among which external therapies have unique characteristics. The famous therapeutic methods are fumigation therapy, egg-rolling therapy, Huashui therapy (containing witch culture), external application therapy by mashing medicinal herbs, massage, therapy of Qiasha (also called Jiusha, a popular treatment for sunstroke or other febrile diseases by repeatedly pinching a patient's neck, etc. to achieve congestion) and bloodletting, hot compress therapy, etc. These methods are very effective for treating broken bones and snakebites. The medicines of **the Therapies for Bone Injuries and Snakebites** are fresh medicinal herbs, having the advantages of simple and short-time treatment with good curative effects. For bone injuries, external application therapy by mashing medicinal herbs is mostly adopted. That is, after bone-setting (the resetting and fixation of broken bones) is done for fracture patients, medicinal herbs are mashed (or mixed with distiller's grains) to be applied externally to the injured area, and then the part near the joint is bound

① 雷山县苗学研究会中国民博苗族文化雷山研究中心，《雷山苗族医药》，北京：中国文化出版社，2011 年，第 348 页。

and fixated with small wooden boards. The main medicinal herbs used to cure bone fractures are Glabrous Sarcandra Herb, wild grape roots, the bark of paulownia roots, Sikuaiwa Herb (*Lysimachia paridiformis Franch.* in Latin), etc. The famous medicine for bone injury is Bailin Bone-setting Powder, which has the efficacy of "promoting blood circulation and removing blood stasis, clearing away heat and toxic material, subsiding swellings and relieving pains, setting broken bones and regenerating muscles, relaxing muscles and activating main and collateral channels, as well as promoting callus growth and healing". The main medicinal herbs used to cure snakebites are Bingqiuzi Herb (*Oreorchis patens* in Latin), Xianglongcao Herb (*Hemiboea subcapitata Clarke* in Latin), Chinese lobelia, Fengdoucai Herb (*Petasites japonicus* in Latin), Shanwugui Herb (*Stephania cepharantha Hayata* in Latin), etc. The course of treatment is 3-5 days. Appropriate quantities of one kind of the fresh medicinal herbs are mashed and put into cool boiled water to get mixed. After that, the area around the wound is wiped with the disinfectant cotton wool that has been soaked with the medicinal liquid, once every 3-4 hours. At the same time, the patient should drink the medicinal liquid made from 2-3 fresh medicinal herbs 30 ml each time, three times a day. **The Therapies for Bone Injuries and Snakebites** of the Miao nationality are mainly handed down through the instructions of ancestors and masters.

九节茶药的原料——九节茶
the Raw Material of Jiujiecha Medicine—Glabrous Sarcandra Herb

第 4 项：
苗医药（九节茶药制作工艺）

项目序号：975	项目编号：Ⅸ-15	公布时间：2008（第二批）	类别：传统医药
所属地区：贵州省	类型：新增项目	申报地区或单位：贵州省黔东南苗族侗族自治州	

　　九节茶药是药膏型药剂，以九节茶为主要原料制成，是来源于贵州省黔东南苗族侗族自治州锦屏县、榕江县、黄平县等地的苗医经验方，其方剂来源于锦屏县苗医杨氏家族。

　　九节茶药的处方主要为：九节茶 1500 克、野葡萄根 1200 克、水三七 1000 克、水冬瓜 800 克、滚山珠 500 克、螃蟹 500 克、白蜡 500 克。其制作工艺有备料、炸料、制膏和贮藏。首先按处方将药称量配齐，滚山珠、螃蟹、白蜡单放，然后将九节茶、水冬瓜、水三七和野葡萄根等药物碎断成细块，将滚山珠、螃蟹碾成细粉过 80 ～ 100 目细罗筛。之后，取茶籽油 1500 克，倒入锅内加热，将九节茶、水冬瓜、水三七和野葡萄根等炸枯至黄色，去渣过滤。再将 500 克白蜡加入药油内溶化，倒入缸中待温，将滚山珠、螃蟹粉兑入，搅匀即成药膏。最后将制成的九节茶药膏贮藏在搪瓷缸或陶瓷罐内，密封置室内阴凉处。九节茶药的功效是散血退肿、续筋接骨，主治骨折、跌打损伤瘀肿等。①

Item 4: the Medicine of the Miao Nationality (the Craft of Making Jiujiecha Medicine)

Item Serial Number: 975	Item ID Number: Ⅸ-15	Released Date: 2008 (Batch 2)	Category: Traditional Medicine

① 《苗医药（九节茶药制作工艺）》，中国非物质文化遗产网，http://www.ihchina.cn/Article/Index/detail?id=14884，检索日期：2019 年 8 月 8 日。

·贵州省·国家级非物质文化遗产文献资料汇编（汉英对照）

The Documentary Compilation of the State-level Intangible Cultural Heritage of Guizhou Province (Chinese-English Versions)

Affiliated Province: Guizhou Province	Type: New Item	Application Province or Unit: Qiandongnan Miao and Dong Autonomous Prefecture, Guizhou Province

Jiujiecha Medicine is an ointment type medicament made with Glabrous Sarcandra Herb as the main raw material. It comes from an empirical prescription of the Miao doctors in Jinping County, Rongjiang County, Huangping County, etc. of Qiandongnan Miao and Dong Autonomous Prefecture, Guizhou Province. Its prescription is offered by the Yang family of the Miao doctor in Jinping County.

The main formulas of **Jiujiecha Medicine** are: 1500-gram Glabrous Sarcandra Herb, 1200-gram wild grape roots, 1000-gram pseudo-ginseng, 800-gram Shuidonggua (*Adina racemosa* in Latin), 500-gram Gunshan Bead (also called Gunshan Worm), 500-gram crabs and 500-gram white wax. Its production process consists of preparing materials, frying materials, making ointments and storage. First, enough quantities of raw materials are prepared according to the prescription, with Gunshan Bead (also called Gunshan Worm), crabs and white wax put aside. Then, Glabrous Sarcandra Herb, Shuidonggua (*Adina racemosa* in Latin), pseudo-ginseng and wild grape roots are cut up into small sections. Next, Gunshan Bead (also called Gunshan Worm) and crabs are ground into fine powder, and then sieved by using a sifter with 80-100 grids. After that, 1,500-gram tea seed oil is poured into a pot and heated. Then, Glabrous Sarcandra Herb, Shuidonggua (*Adina racemosa* in Latin), pseudo-ginseng and wild grape roots are put into the oil to get fried until they turn yellow, with dregs removed. At this time, 500-gram white wax is put into the medicinal oil to be dissolved, and then is poured into a jar till it gets warm. After that, the powder of Gunshan Bead (also called Gunshan Worm) and crabs is added to it, mixed thoroughly, and made into the ointment. Finally, the ointment of **Jiujiecha Medicine** is stored in enamel cups or ceramic jars, sealed, and placed in a cool indoor area. The curative effects of **Jiujiecha Medicine** are to disperse blood and reduce swelling, to connect fractured tendons and bones, as well as to treat fractures, traumatic injuries, blood stasis and swelling, etc.

过路黄药材
the Medicinal Herb of Guoluhuang Medicine

第 5 项：

侗医药（过路黄药制作工艺）

项目序号：976	项目编号：IX-16	公布时间：2008（第二批）	类别：传统医药
所属地区：贵州省	类型：新增项目	申报地区或单位：贵州省黔东南苗族侗族自治州	

　　"天、地、气、水、人"五位一体的思想是侗医学术思想的核心。侗医把疾病分为二十四大症、七十二小疾，广泛涉及内科、外科、妇科、儿科和骨伤等疾病，对伤科正骨、刀箭枪伤及蛇虫咬伤更是卓有成效。过路黄药制作工艺便是侗族传统医药的精华，在炮制工艺及检查病因、病机，诊断、用药和养生保健等方面都独具特色。

　　过路黄药制作工艺是侗族人民在长期使用药用生物资源、矿物资源的过程中积累和创造的、依靠口传方式传承的民间医药知识。过路黄，拉丁语为 *Lysimachia christiniae Hance*，属于报春花科珍珠菜属植物，是黔东南侗族医药中普遍应用的天然药用植物，全草供药用，有止血、抗菌、抗病毒和消炎等功效。根据不同病症，按照不同的方法进行采摘，或全草入药、或部分入药，配以其他草药制成所需的剂型，主要剂型有过路黄鲜药汁、鲜药敷剂，复方过路黄煎剂、酒剂和膏剂等。侗医把过路黄药广泛用于治疗尿路结石、胆囊炎、胆结石、黄疸性肝炎、水肿、跌打损伤、毒蛇咬伤及毒蕈和药物中毒，外敷治火烫伤及化脓性炎症等疾病。[①]

Item 5: the Medicine of the Dong Nationality
(the Craft of Making Guoluhuang Medicine)

Item Serial Number: 976	Item ID Number: IX-16	Released Date: 2008 (Batch 2)	Category: Traditional Medicine

---

① 《侗医药（过路黄药制作工艺）》，中国非物质文化遗产网，http://www.ihchina.cn/Article/Index/detail?id=14888，检索日期：2019 年 8 月 7 日。

贵州省 国家级非物质文化遗产文献资料汇编（汉英对照）

The Documentary Compilation of the State-level Intangible Cultural Heritage of Guizhou Province (Chinese-English Versions)

Affiliated Province: Guizhou Province	Type: New Item	Application Province or Unit: Qiandongnan Miao and Dong Autonomous Prefecture, Guizhou Province

The five-in-one concept of "the heaven, the earth, Qi (vital energy), water and human" is the core of the academic thought of **the Medicine of the Dong Nationality**. The Dong doctors divide diseases into 24 major ones and 72 minor ones, which widely involve the diseases of internal medicine, surgery, gynaecology, pediatrics, bone injuries, etc. **The Medicine of the Dong Nationality** is especially effective for bonesetting, wounds caused by knives, arrows and gunshots, snakebites and insect bites. **The Craft of Making Guoluhuang Medicine** is the essence of the traditional medicine of the Dong nationality, which has unique features in processing craft, examining the causes of diseases, pathogenesis, diagnosis, medicine usage, health preserving, etc.

The Craft of Making Guoluhuang Medicine is a folk medical knowledge accumulated and created by the Dong people in the process of the long-term use of medicinal biological and mineral resources, which is inherited through oral transmission. Guoluhuang Herb, *Lysimachia christiniae Hance* in Latin, is a plant of Lysimachia in primrose family, a natural medicinal plant widely used in **the Medicine of the Dong Nationality** in Qiandongnan Miao and Dong Autonomous Prefecture. The whole herb is used for medicine and has the effects of hemostasis, antibiosis, resisting viruses, diminishing inflammation, etc. According to different diseases, it is picked by using different methods. Either the whole herb or part of it is used as medicine, supplemented with other herbs and made into the required dosage form. The main dosage forms are the fresh medicinal juice of Guoluhuang Herb, its fresh medicine of external application, as well as the compound decoction, liquor extract and ointment of Guoluhuang Herb, etc. The Dong doctors use Guoluhuang Medicine widely in the treatment of urinary stones, cholecystitis, gallstones, jaundice hepatitis, edemas, traumatic injuries, snakebites, poisonous mushroom poisoning and drug poisoning. The external application of Guoluhuang Medicine can be used to cure burns, scalds, suppurative inflammation, etc.

第6项：
中医传统制剂方法
（廖氏化风丹制作技艺）

廖元和堂化风丹
Huafeng Pill of Liaoyuanhe Hall

项目序号：443	项目编号：IX-4	公布时间：2008（第二批）	类别：传统医药
所属地区：贵州省	类型：扩展项目	申报地区或单位：贵州省遵义市红花岗区、汇川区	

　　廖氏化风丹创制人廖耀寅依托贵州大娄山丰富的药材资源和板桥古镇的流通便宜，承袭祖业行医济世，于明崇祯十七年（1644）研制出具有息风通络、镇惊豁痰和开窍醒脑功能的"化风丹"。

　　廖氏化风丹在工艺上借鉴白酒发酵窖藏工艺，将核心药物处理制成药母，另将15味中药材用不同方法炮制后，与药母合磨成粉，制成丸剂，再将朱砂水与麝香研磨后的混合剂均匀涂于丸剂表面，经附着后烘干即成。化风丹为朱红色丸剂，剖面呈棕黄色，味辛。对四时瘴气、中风偏瘫、小儿高热惊风、癫痫和面肌麻痹有特效。因功效确切，在川、黔、滇、桂广为流传，被誉为"居家旅行之必备圣药"。1710年，廖家正式将此药命名为"廖元和堂化风丹"。其独特的组方配伍和多样化的药物炮制手法在中药制作中属独创。在化风丹的传承过程中，坚持"救人不论贫富，施药不分贵贱"的行医准则，体现出较高的人文理念价值。①

Item 6: the Traditional Preparation Methods of Chinese Medicine (the Craft of Making the Liao Family's Huafeng Pill)

Item Serial Number: 443	Item ID Number: IX-4	Released Date: 2008 (Batch 2)	Category: Traditional Medicine

---

① 《中医传统制剂方法（廖氏化风丹制作技艺）》，中国非物质文化遗产网，http://www.ihchina.cn/Article/Index/detail?id=14802，检索日期：2019年9月8日。

贵州省·国家级非物质文化遗产文献资料汇编（汉英对照）

The Documentary Compilation of the State-level Intangible Cultural Heritage of Guizhou Province (Chinese-English Versions)

Affiliated Province: Guizhou Province	Type: Extended Item	Application Province or Unit: Honghuagang District and Huichuan District, Zunyi City, Guizhou Province

Relying on the abundant medicinal material resources in the Dalou Mountain and on the convenient transportation in Banqiao ancient township in Guizhou Province, Liao Yaoyin, the founder of the Liao Family's Huafeng Pill, inherited his ancestors' profession to practice medicine to save people. In the 17th year during the reign of Emperor Chongzhen of the Ming Dynasty (1644), he developed "Huafeng Pill", which has the functions of dispelling wind, dredging the main and collateral channels, relieving convulsion, eliminating phlegm, resuscitating and refreshing.

Drawing on the craft of liquor fermentation and cellaring, **the Craft of Making the Liao Family's Huafeng Pill** goes: the core drug is processed into Mother drug, and 15 Chinese medicinal herbs are processed by using different methods; then, they are ground into powder together with Mother drug, and made into pills; next, cinnabar water and musk are ground into a mixture, evenly coated on the surface of the pills; after the mixture is attached and dries, the Liao Family's Huafeng Pill is finished. Huafeng Pill is a kind of vermilion pill, with brownish yellow cross section and pungent taste. It is especially effective for four-season miasma, stroke hemiplegia, infantile febrile convulsion, epilepsy and facial paralysis. Because of its precise efficacy, it is widely spread throughout Sichuan, Guizhou, Yunnan and Guangxi, acclaimed as "the essential medicine for home and travel". In 1710, the Liao family officially named this medicine "Huafeng Pill of Liaoyuanhe Hall". Its unique combination of prescriptions and diversified drug-processing techniques are original in the production of traditional Chinese medicine. In the process of inheriting Huafeng Pill, the Liao family adheres to the medical practice principles of "saving people regardless of being rich or poor, and using medicines irrespective of high or low price", which reflects its high humanistic value.

第7项:
布依族医药
（益肝草制作技艺）

蒲公英：益肝草制作的药材之一
Dandelions：One of the Medicinal Herbs for Making Liver-protecting Herb Medicine

项目序号：1356	项目编号：IX-22	公布时间：2014（第四批）	类别：传统医药
所属地区：贵州省	类型：新增项目	申报地区或单位：贵州省贵定县	

贵州省贵定县天然中药材资源丰富，有厚朴、黄皮、木通、楼子、八角枫、栀子、南五味子、朱砂根、天麻、石斛、杜仲、野党参、何首乌、胆草、天冬、银花、桔梗和灵芝等，益肝草就是由当地的多味药材加工炮制而成，主要用于防治肝病。

采药前，要在野外举行祭祀仪式，由布依族寨老主持，以祈求除病消灾为目的，摆设净茶净酒，在锣鼓、木鱼等交响节奏声中，边唱诵边烧纸，以雄鸡血献祭土地，药师面向东方，净手合掌，祭拜祖师。祭祀仪式结束后，即刻采药，务必在上午10时前完成。接着，将采摘的地耳草、酸汤杆、黄栀子、客蚂叶和蒲公英等鲜药洗净、晒干，用碓、擂钵研磨备用。后用瓦罐熬制，加入特配秘方，20分钟后即可完成。所有制药器具皆为木、石材质，不沾铁器，以保证药物的疗效。采药器具有锄头、镰刀和背篓等；制药器具有簸箕、筛子、碓、擂钵、甑子和土罐。由于布依族没有文字，益肝草制作技艺只能靠师徒口口相传。益肝草制作技艺是布依族先民顺应自然、防止疾病所积累的地方性技艺，其成本相对低廉。①

① 《国家级非物质文化遗产：布依族医药（益肝草制作技艺）》，中国布依网，https://www.buyizu.cn/h-nd-396.html?groupId=101&_ngc=-1，检索日期：2019年8月8日。

Item 7: the Medicine of the Buyi Nationality (the Craft of Making Liver-protecting Herb Medicine)

Item Serial Number: 1356	Item ID Number: IX-22	Released Date: 2014 (Batch 4)	Category: Traditional Medicine
Affiliated Province: Guizhou Province	Type: New Item	Application Province or Unit: Guiding County, Guizhou Province	

Guiding County in Guizhou Province is rich in natural resources of Chinese medicinal herbs, including Houpu (*Magnolia officinalis* in Latin), Huangpi (*Clausena lansium* in Latin), Mutong (*Akebia* in Latin), Louzi (*Trichosanthes* in Latin), Bajiaofeng (*Alangium chinense* in Latin), gardenia, South Wuweizi (*Kadsura longipedunculata* in Latin), Zhushagen (*Ardisia crenata* Sims in Latin), Tianma (*Gastrodia elata* in Latin), Shihu (*Dendrobium nobile* in Latin), Duzhong (*Eucommia ulmoides* in Latin), wild codonopsis, Heshouwu (*Pleuropterus multifloru* in Latin), Dancao Herb (*Ajuga pantantha* in Latin), Radix Asparagi, honeysuckle, Jugeng (*Platycodon grandiflorus* in Latin) and Lingzhi (*Ganoderma lucidum* in Latin). The Liver-protecting Herb Medicine is made from many local herbs, which is mainly used for the prevention and treatment of liver disease.

Before the collection of medicinal herbs, a sacrificial ceremony should be held outdoors, which is presided over by Zhailao (a head of a stockaded village) of the Buyi nationality, with the purpose of praying for the elimination of diseases and disasters. With clean tea and liquor prepared, the pharmacist burns paper money while singing to the symphonic rhythm of gongs, drums and the Wooden Fish (a percussion instrument of a hollow wooden block, originally used by Buddhist priests to beat rhythm when chanting scriptures), offering up a sacrifice to the land with cock blood. With two hands cleaned and two palms brought together, he faces the east and worships the medical ancestor. As soon as the sacrificial ceremony ends, the collection of medicinal herbs will start, which must be completed before 10:00 am. Then, the fresh herbs that have been picked, such as Di'er Grass (*Hypericum japonicum* in Latin), Suantanggan Herb (*Begonia circumlobata* Hance in Latin), yellow gardenia, Kemaye Herb (also called Cheqian Grass, *Plantago depressa* Willd. in Latin) and dandelions, are washed, dried in the sun and ground by using a mortar and pestle for later use. Next, they are boiled in an earthen pot with a special recipe added in, which will be finished in 20 minutes. All pharmaceutical tools are made of wood and stone without any iron to ensure the curative effect of the drug. The tools for collecting medicinal herbs are hoes, sickles, back baskets, etc.; while the pharmaceutical tools are dustpans, sieves, Dui (a special tool made of stone and wood for hulling rice), mortar and pestle, Zengzi (a wooden container used for steaming) and earthen pots. The Buyi nationality has no written language, so **the Craft of Making Liver-protecting Herb Medicine** can only be handed down by word of mouth from master to apprentice. This craft is a local skill accumulated by the Buyi ancestors to conform to nature and prevent diseases, and its cost is relatively low.

第十章

民俗

Chapter Ten

Folk Custom

第 1-2 项：

苗族鼓藏节

苗族鼓藏节
the Drum Worship Festival of the Miao Nationality

项目序号：467	项目编号：X-19	公布时间：2006（第一批）	类别：民俗
所属地区：贵州省	类型：新增项目	申报地区或单位：贵州省雷山县	

项目序号：467	项目编号：X-19	公布时间：2014（第四批）	类别：民俗
所属地区：贵州省	类型：扩展项目	申报地区或单位：贵州省榕江县	

　　鼓藏节是苗族以血缘宗族为单位的祭鼓活动。据《苗族古歌》记载，人类祖先姜央过鼓藏节是为了祭祀创世的蝴蝶妈妈。传说蝴蝶妈妈是枫树所生，故

苗族崇拜枫树。由于祖宗的老家在枫树心里，用枫树做成的木鼓就成了祖宗安息的地方，祭祖便成了祭鼓。苗族最高的神是祖先，是生命始祖枫树和蝴蝶妈妈。鼓藏节就是祭祀神枫树和蝴蝶妈妈。

鼓藏节每十二年举办一次，原每次持续四年，现在改为持续三年。苗族聚族而居，以血统宗族形成的地域组织"鼓社"为单位维系其生存发展。鼓是祖先神灵的象征，所以鼓藏节的仪式活动都以鼓为核心来进行。鼓藏节的仪式由鼓社组织的领导"鼓藏头"操办，"鼓藏头"由群众选举产生。鼓藏节第一年二月申日举办"招龙"仪式。全鼓社男女老幼集中到迎龙场的枫香神树脚，由"鼓藏头"在五彩宝辇下主持"招龙"仪式。第一年的七月寅日举办"醒鼓"仪式。第二年十月卯日举办"迎鼓"仪式。第三年的四月吉日，举办"审牛"仪式。第四年十月丑日，举行杀猪祭鼓仪式，称为"白鼓节"，是鼓藏节的结束仪式。怀念祖先、尊老爱幼、和睦相处、勤劳俭朴、富裕安康等是鼓藏节的祷告主题。[①]

 **Items 1-2: the Drum Worship Festival of the Miao Nationality**

Item Serial Number: 467	Item ID Number: X-19	Released Date: 2006 (Batch 1)	Category: Folk Custom
Affiliated Province: Guizhou Province	Type: New Item	Application Province or Unit: Leishan County, Guizhou Province	

Item Serial Number: 467	Item ID Number: X-19	Released Date: 2014 (Batch 4)	Category: Folk Custom
Affiliated Province: Guizhou Province	Type: Extended Item	Application Province or Unit: Rongjiang County, Guizhou Province	

The Drum Worship Festival is an activity of the Miao Nationality to offer sacrifices to drums based on consanguineous clans. According to *The Ancient Song of the Miao Nationality*, Jiang Yang, the ancestor of human kind, held **the Drum Worship Festival** to offer sacrifices to the Mother Butterfly who created the world. It's said that the maple tree gave birth to the Mother Butterfly, so the Miao people

---

① 《苗族鼓藏节》，中国非物质文化遗产网，http://www.ihchina.cn/Article/Index/detail?id=14960，检索日期：2019 年 8 月 3 日。

worship it. Since their ancestral home is the maple tree, the wooden drum made of it has become the resting place for their ancestors. Thus, to offer sacrifices to ancestors is to offer sacrifices to drums. The highest god of the Miao nationality is its ancestors, namely, the maple tree and the Mother Butterfly, which are the earliest ancestors of life. **The Drum Worship Festival** is to offer sacrifices to the divine maple tree and the Mother Butterfly.

This festival is held once every twelve years, each lasting four years. Now it has been changed to last three years. The Miao people live together and maintain its survival and development through the regional organization, "the drum commune", which is formed on the basis of consanguineous clans. The drum is the symbol of ancestral gods, so the ritual activities of **the Drum Worship Festival** are carried out with the drum as the core. The ceremony of **the Drum Worship Festival** is conducted by "the Guzang Leader" of the drum commune, who is elected by the masses. On the day of Shen (the ninth of the Twelve Earthly Branches) in the 2nd lunar month of the first year of **the Drum Worship Festival**, a ceremony of "dragon summoning" is held. All men and women, old and young, in one drum commune gather at the foot of the sacred maple tree on Yinglong Square, and "the Guzang Leader" presides over the ceremony of "dragon summoning" in a Baonian Chariot. On the day of Yin (the third of the Twelve Earthly Branches) in the 7th lunar month of the first year, a ceremony of "drum awakening" is held. On the day of Mao (the fourth of the Twelve Earthly Branches) in the 10th lunar month of the second year, a ceremony of "drum welcoming" is held. On the auspicious day in the 4th lunar month of the third year, a ceremony of "cattle examining" is held to remove the evil spirit of the cattle with Bamao Grass. On the day of Chou (the second of the Twelve Earthly Branches) in the 10th lunar month of the fourth year, a ceremony of killing pigs and offering sacrifices to the drum is held, known as "the White Drum Festival", which is the ending ceremony of **the Drum Worship Festival**. The praying themes of **the Drum Worship Festival** are the remembrance of ancestors, respect for the elderly and love for the young, harmonious coexistence, industry and frugality, prosperity and good health, etc.

水族端节赛马活动
the Horse Racing at the Duan Festival (New Year) of the Shui Nationality

第 3 项：
水族端节

项目序号：468	项目编号：Ⅹ-20	公布时间：2006（第一批）	类别：民俗
所属地区：贵州省	类型：新增项目	申报地区或单位：贵州省三都水族自治县	

　　端节是水族最盛大的传统节日，相当于汉族的春节。在水族历法年底、岁首的谷熟时节举行，以庆贺丰收、辞旧迎新，节期对应农历八月至十月。端节以亥日为主干推算过节日期，过节批次多，古代分九批，今分七批，首尾间隔约五十天。

　　端节主要活动为祭祀和赛马。除夕与初一相连的两顿饭忌荤食素，但不忌鱼虾。赛马大会是端节活动的最高潮。赛马的地点叫"端坡"或"年坡"，人们吃过年酒后从各村寨赶来这里。青年人赶端坡不只为了看赛马，他们还把这盛大的聚会看成是物色情侣的机会。跑马前要举行一个简便的祭典。跑道中央设一供席，上摆各种各样的祭品，由寨中德高望重的长者主祭。祭典完毕，寨老跃身上马在跑道上遛一圈，宣告赛马开始。水族赛马形式独特，叫作"挤马"。指挥者一声号令，骑手扬鞭策马，在山谷互相冲闯，在抗争中挤出山谷向坡顶冲去，先到远坡顶者为胜。端节是历时最长、批次最多的具有民族特色的年节。登高赛马是南方民族年节中独有的现象。同时，端节是水族斗牛舞、铜鼓舞、芦笙舞和对歌等诸多民间艺术起源、传承和发展的重要文化空间。[①]

---

① 《水族端节》，中国非物质文化遗产网，http://www.ihchina.cn/Article/Index/detail?id=14962，检索日期：2019 年 8 月 3 日。

Item 3: the Duan Festival (New Year) of the Shui Nationality

Item Serial Number: 468	Item ID Number: X-20	Released Date: 2006 (Batch 1)	Category: Folk Custom
Affiliated Province: Guizhou Province	Type: New Item	Application Province or Unit: Sandu Shui Autonomous County, Guizhou Province	

The Duan Festival (New Year) is the grandest traditional festival of the Shui nationality, equivalent to the Spring Festival of the Han nationality. It is held to celebrate the harvest and welcome the new year at the end and the beginning of the year by the calendar of the Shui nationality, corresponding to the 8th lunar month to the 10th lunar month. The dates of celebrating **the Duan Festival (New Year)** are calculated with the day of Hai (the twelfth of the Twelve Earthly Branches) as the main trunk, and it is celebrated in many batches. In ancient times, the Shui people celebrated the festival in nine batches, and now in seven batches. The interval between the beginning and the end of the festival is about 50 days.

The main activities held at **the Duan Festival (New Year)** are offering sacrifices and horse racing. For the two meals between the Lunar New Year's Eve and the Lunar New Year's Day, meat dishes are forbidden except fish and shrimp, while vegetarian food is allowed. The meeting of horse racing is the climax of **the Duan Festival (New Year)**. The place for holding it is called "Duanpo Slope" or "Nianpo Slope". After the new year feasts and drinking, people arrive here from all stockaded villages. Young people go to Duanpo Slope not only because they want to watch horse racing, but also because they regard it as an opportunity to find lovers. A simple sacrificial ceremony will be held before horse racing. In the center of the racetrack, there is an altar with various offerings placed on it. The ceremony is mainly presided over by the venerable elders in the stockaded village. After the sacrificial ceremony, Zhailao (a head of a stockaded village) jumps onto one horse and takes a ride around the track for a round, announcing the start of the horse racing. The horse racing of the Shui nationality is unique in form, which is called "the jostling of horses". With a command from the commander, the riders whip their horses, rushing towards each other in the valley. During the struggle, they jostle out of the valley and rush towards the top of the slope. The one who reaches the top of the far slope first is the winner. **The Duan Festival (New Year)** is the longest festival to celebrate the New Year that has ethnic characteristics, with celebration batches being the most. Climbing high and horse racing are unique phenomena in the new-year festivals of the ethnic groups in southern China. At the same time, **the Duan Festival (New Year)** is an important cultural space for the origin, inheritance and development of many folk arts, such as the Bullfight Dance, the Bronze Drum Dance, Lusheng Dance and antiphonal singing of the Shui nationality.

贵州省·国家级非物质文化遗产文献资料汇编（汉英对照）

The Documentary Compilation of the State-level Intangible Cultural Heritage of Guizhou Province (Chinese-English Versions)

第4项：布依族查白歌节

吹木叶：布依族查白歌节活动之一

Blowing Muye (leaves)：One of the Activities at the Zhabai Singing Festival of the Buyi Nationality

项目序号：469	项目编号：X-21	公布时间：2006（第一批）	类别：民俗
所属地区：贵州省	类型：新增项目	申报地区或单位：贵州省	

布依族查白歌节每年农历六月二十一日在贵州顶效镇查白村举行。

查白歌节源于布依族口传民间故事《查郎与白妹》。相传古时候，查白场（原名虎场坝）的查郎救了白妹的命，两人遂成为情深意长的伴侣。白岩寨头人野山猫为抢夺白妹，害死了查郎。白妹放火烧死野山猫后投入火海殉情，与查郎一同变成白仙鹤比翼双飞，变成紫云歌仙。人们为了纪念这对忠贞的夫妇，将查郎和白妹的姓连在一起，把虎场坝改名为"查白场"，将六月二十一日定为"查白歌节"。届时，男女老少汇集查白场，同吃狗肉汤锅、五色糯米饭和冤枉坨，并在查白树下悼念查郎、白妹，到查白井取水净心，到查白庙敬香。这一天，查姓村民要请摩公或端公主持祭祀活动，中老年人在查白树下用布依古歌唱查白，祭查白。布依青年男女穿着节日盛装到查白桥、查白河、松林坡、查白洞和查白井等风物景点去吹木叶、打花包、浪哨交友。夜晚各农户家坐满亲友，通宵喝酒、唱歌。到二十二日，青年男女互送信物后依依不舍地离去。查白歌节不仅是纪念性节日，更是布依族青年谈情说爱和求婚择偶的独特时机。①

Item 4: the Zhabai Singing Festival of the Buyi Nationality

Item Serial Number: 469	Item ID Number: X-21	Released Date: 2006 (Batch 1)	Category: Folk Custom

---

① 《布依族查白歌节》，中国非物质文化遗产网，http://www.ihchina.cn/Article/Index/detail?id=14963，检索日期：2019 年 8 月 3 日。

Affiliated Province: Guizhou Province	Type: New Item	Application Province or Unit: Guizhou Province

The Zhabai Singing Festival of the Buyi Nationality is held in Zhabai Village, Dingxiao Township, Guizhou Province on the 21st day of the 6th lunar month every year.

The Zhabai Singing Festival originated from an orally-transmitted folktale of the Buyi nationality, "Zha Lang and Bai Mei". Legend has it that, in ancient times, Zha Lang from Zhabai Field (formerly called Huchang Dam) saved Bai Mei's life, and they became affectionate partners. However, the headman of Baiyan Stockaded Village, Wild Bobcat, killed Zha Lang in order to snatch Bai Mei to be his wife. After Bai Mei set fire and killed Wild Bobcat, she threw herself into the sea of fire and died for love. Zha Lang and Bai Mei became a couple of white cranes, flying side by side, and finally turned into Purple-cloud Song Immortals. In order to commemorate this faithful couple, the Buyi people put the surnames of Zha Lang and Bai Mei together, changed Huchang Dam into "Zhabai Field", and set the 21st day of the 6th lunar month as "the Zhabai Singing Festival". When the festival comes, all people, male and female, old and young, will gather at Zhabai Field to eat dog-meat soup, five-color glutinous rice and Yuanwang Lump (colored glutinous rice lumps). They will mourn Zha Lang and Bai Mei under Zhabai Tree, go to Zhabai Well to fetch water and purify their hearts, and go to Zhabai Temple to burn incense. On that day, villagers with the surname of Zha will invite Mogong (the master of the Mo Sutra of the Buyi Nationality) or Duangong (a wizard) to preside over sacrificial activities. The middle-aged and old people will sing in praise of and offer sacrifices to Zha Lang and Bai Mei through singing the Ancient Song of the Buyi Nationality under Zhabai Tree. Young men and women of the Buyi nationality wear festival costumes, and go to scenic spots of Zhabai Bridge, the Zhabai River, the Pine Forest Slope, Zhabai Cave, Zhabai Well, etc. to blow Muye (leaves), play with Huabao (cube-shaped embroidered bags), have a love affair and make friends. At night, every farmer's house is filled with friends and relatives, who drink and sing throughout the night. On the 22nd day, young men and women give each other their keepsakes and leave reluctantly. The Zhabai Singing Festival is not only a commemorative festival, but also a unique opportunity for Buyi youth to have a love affair, choose spouses and make a proposal.

第 5 项：
苗族姊妹节

苗族姊妹节
the Sisters' Festival of the Miao Nationality

项目序号：470	项目编号：X-22	公布时间：2006（第一批）	类别：民俗
所属地区：贵州省	类型：新增项目	申报地区或单位：贵州省台江县	

　　苗族姊妹节是贵州省台江县苗族人民的传统节日，每年农历三月十五日至十七日举行，届时苗族青年男女穿上节日盛装，欢度佳节。

　　台江苗族姊妹节以青年妇女为中心，以展示歌舞、服饰、游方，吃姊妹饭和青年男女交换信物为主要活动内容。吃姊妹饭是这个节日的重要礼仪事项。按本地人的说法，吃了姊妹饭，防止蛀虫叮咬。姊妹饭也是姑娘们送给情侣以表达情意的信物，是节日中最为重要的标志。下田撮鱼捞虾是姊妹饭活动之一，一个寨子的姑娘与另一个寨子的小伙子相约，通过撮鱼捞虾等风俗活动谈情说爱，寻找意中人。踩鼓是整个社区参与节日活动的重要方式，姑娘们在父母的精心打扮下，身着节日盛装聚向鼓场踩鼓，从鼓场上可以看出谁的服饰艳丽，谁的银饰既美又多，苗族人以此方式展示自己的服饰文化。晚上青年男女游方对歌，谈情说爱，男方向女方讨姊妹饭，姑娘们在姊妹饭里藏入信物以表达对男方的感情。姊妹节是社区内人们走亲访友、文化娱乐和社会交往的活动舞台。[①]

Item 5: the Sisters' Festival of the Miao Nationality

Item Serial Number: 470	Item ID Number: X-22	Released Date: 2006 (Batch 1)	Category: Folk Custom

① 《苗族姊妹节》，中国非物质文化遗产网，http://www.ihchina.cn/Article/Index/detail?id=14964，检索日期：2019 年 8 月 11 日。

Affiliated Province: Guizhou Province	Type: New Item	Application Province or Unit: Taijiang County, Guizhou Province

The Sisters' Festival of the Miao Nationality is a traditional festival of the Miao people in Taijiang County, Guizhou Province. It is held from the 15th day to the 17th day of the 3rd lunar month every year, during which young men and women of the Miao nationality put on holiday attire to celebrate the festival.

The Sisters' Festival of the Miao Nationality in Taijiang County focuses on young women, with displaying songs, dances and costumes, Youfang (developing a romantic relationship between men and women of the Miao nationality), eating the Sisters' Meal and exchanging keepsakes between young men and women as its main activities. Eating the Sisters' Meal is an important item of etiquette at this festival. According to the local saying, eating the Sisters' Meal can keep the local people away from insect bites. The Sisters' Meal is also the keepsake that is given by girls to their lovers to express their affections, which is the most important symbol at the festival. Going to the field to catch fish and shrimp is one of the activities for eating the Sisters' Meal. Girls from one stockaded village make an appointment with young men from another to find their Mr. Right by flirting with each other when taking part in the folk-custom activities of catching fish and shrimp. Dancing to a drum is an important way for the whole community to participate in festival activities. Girls, dressed up finely by their parents, wear festival attire and gather at the Drum Square to dance around a drum. From the Drum Square, people can see whose costumes are gorgeous and whose silver ornaments are both beautiful and abundant. In this way, the Miao people display their costume culture. In the evening, young men and women sing in antiphonal style and develop a romantic relationship. Young men ask girls for the Sisters' Meal, and girls hide keepsakes in the meal to express their affections for the young men. The Sisters' Festival is a flatform for people to visit relatives and friends, and have cultural entertainment and social interaction within a community.

第 6-7 项：

侗族萨玛节

榕江侗族萨玛节
the Sama Festival of the Dong Nationality in Rongjiang County

项目序号：473	项目编号：X-25	公布时间：2006（第一批）	类别：民俗
所属地区：贵州省	类型：新增项目	申报地区或单位：贵州省榕江县	

项目序号：473	项目编号：X-25	公布时间：2008（第二批）	类别：民俗
所属地区：贵州省	类型：扩展项目	申报地区或单位：贵州省黎平县	

　　侗族萨玛节是南部侗族现存最古老的传统节日，是侗族母系氏族社会时期风俗的遗留，流传于贵州省榕江县、黎平县、从江县及周边侗族地区，以榕江县车江侗族萨玛节为代表。

　　"萨玛"是侗语译音，"萨"即祖母，"玛"意为大，"萨玛"意为"大祖母"，是整个侗族（特别是南部方言地区）共同祖先神灵的化身。侗族认为祖先神威巨大，能赋予人们力量去战胜敌人、战胜自然、战胜灾害，赢得村寨安乐、五谷丰登、人畜兴旺，故对之虔诚崇拜，奉为侗族的社稷神。萨玛又是传说中的古代女英雄，在侗族古代社会的政治、军事和文化等方面占有重要地位。萨玛节（祭萨）一般在农历正月、二月举行，有时也根据生产、生活或其他重大活动情况改为其他月份举行。祭萨的规模，一般为各村（团寨）各祭，有的也邀请邻村、数村或相邻片区联祭。参祭人员各地不同，许多地方是全寨男女老少一齐参加。榕江三宝侗乡各村寨，则以已婚妇女为主体（有少数德高望重的男性寨老参加）。故榕江三宝侗乡的祭萨活动，带有远古母系氏族社会的遗风。祭萨后，活动参加者绕寨一周，最后到达固定的耶坪，围成圆圈，手拉手跳起舞来，齐声高唱赞颂萨玛的"耶歌"。萨玛节对侗人的思想观念产生了很深的影响，先辈"至善"的美德对侗族的兴旺发达有举足轻重的作用。①

---

① 《侗族萨玛节》，中国非物质文化遗产网，http://www.ihchina.cn/Article/Index/detail?id=14967，检索日期：2019 年 8 月 5 日。

Items 6-7: the Sama Festival of the Dong Nationality

Item Serial Number: 473	Item ID Number: X-25	Released Date: 2006 (Batch 1)	Category: Folk Custom
Affiliated Province: Guizhou Province	Type: New Item	Application Province or Unit: Rongjiang County, Guizhou Province	

Item Serial Number: 473	Item ID Number: X-25	Released Date: 2008 (Batch 2)	Category: Folk Custom
Affiliated Province: Guizhou Province	Type: Extended Item	Application Province or Unit: Liping County, Guizhou Province	

The Sama Festival of the Dong Nationality is the oldest existing traditional festival of the Dong nationality in the southern region. It is a legacy of the customs of the Dong matriarchal clan society, spread in Rongjiang County, Liping County, Congjiang County and the surrounding areas inhabited by the Dong nationality in Guizhou Province, which is represented by **the Sama Festival of the Dong Nationality** in Chejiang Township, Rongjiang County.

"Sama" is a transliteration of the Dong language. "Sa" refers to the grandmother, "ma" means great and "Sama" means "great grandmother", who is the incarnation of the common ancestor deity of the entire Dong nationality (especially in the southern dialect area). The Dong people believe that their ancestor has great divine power, who can endow people with strength to defeat enemy, nature and disasters, to bring peace and happiness to stockaded villages, and to gain a bumper grain harvest and the prosperity of human and livestock. Therefore, they worship their ancestor devoutly and regard her as the god of the land and grain of the Dong nationality. Sama is also a legendary ancient heroine, who has played an important role in politics, military and culture of the ancient Dong society. The Sama Festival (worshipping Sama) is usually held in the 1st and the 2nd lunar months, but sometimes it is held in other months according to production, life or other major activities. Generally, the activity of worshipping Sama is held in each village (stockaded village). Sometimes, neighboring villages, several villages or adjacent areas are invited to hold the worshipping activity together. The participants vary from place to place. In many places, all men and women, old and young, in the whole stockaded village

贵州省·国家级非物质文化遗产文献资料汇编（汉英对照）

The Documentary Compilation of the State-level Intangible Cultural Heritage of Guizhou Province (Chinese-English Versions)

participate. In each stockaded village in Sanbao Dongxiang of Rongjiang County, married women are the main body of participation (a small number of highly respected male Zhailao, heads of stockaded villages, take part in). Therefore, the activity of worshipping Sama there bears the relic of ancient matriarchal clan society. After the worshipping activity, all participants walk around the stockaded village for a round, and finally arrive at the fixed place, Yeping Square. They form a circle, and dance hand in hand, singing "Yege Song" that eulogizes Sama in chorus. The Sama Festival has had a very deep influence on the Dong People's ideology, and the virtue of "supreme goodness" of their ancestors plays an important role in the prosperity of the Dong nationality.

仡佬族毛龙节：闹新春

the Maolong (legendary dragon) Festival of the Gelao Nationality: Celebrating the Spring Festival

项目序号：474	项目编号：X-26	公布时间：2006（第一批）	类别：民俗
所属地区：贵州省	类型：新增项目	申报地区或单位：贵州省石阡县	

　　石阡县的仡佬毛龙节是以仡佬族民间"龙神"信仰为主的一种信仰民俗活动，起源于古代仡佬的"竹王"崇拜和生殖崇拜。每年大年三十夜至正月十五、十六举行，主要流传于贵州省石阡县龙井、汤山等乡镇的宴明、龙凤等仡佬族村寨。

　　龙崇拜是仡佬毛龙节的核心。其基本要素包括"龙"信仰、附属图腾信仰、扎艺、玩技和念诵等五方面。其中，"龙"信仰主要包括传统故事、敬龙仪式、敬龙场合和用品及敬龙神诵词；附属图腾信仰主要包括"竹王"崇拜、盘瓠崇拜、民间佛道崇拜和原始崇拜；扎艺主要包括选材（竹篾、彩纸）和工艺等；玩技主要有"二龙抢宝""懒龙翻身""单龙戏珠""天鹅抱蛋""倒挂金钩""犀牛望月""螺丝旋顶"；念诵主要包括"开光""请水""烧龙"等仪式的念诵及"开财门"和"敬财神"等表演时的诵唱。[①]

Item 8: the Maolong (legendary dragon) Festival of the Gelao Nationality

Item Serial Number: 474	Item ID Number: X-26	Released Date: 2006 (Batch 1)	Category: Folk Custom

---

① 《仡佬毛龙节》，中国非物质文化遗产网，http://www.ihchina.cn/Article/Index/detail?id=14969，检索日期：2019 年 8 月 5 日。

贵州省 国家级非物质文化遗产文献资料汇编（汉英对照）

The Documentary Compilation of the State-level Intangible Cultural Heritage of Guizhou Province (Chinese-English Versions)

Affiliated Province: Guizhou Province	Type: New Item	Application Province or Unit: Shiqian County, Guizhou Province

The Maolong (legendary dragon) Festival of the Gelao Nationality in Shiqian County is a folk belief activity, which is mainly based on the belief in "the god of dragon" among the Gelao people, originating from the ancient Gelao people's worship of "the King of Bamboo" and their reproductive worship. It is held from the Chinese New Year's Eve to the 15th and the 16th days of the first month of the lunar calendar every year, mainly spread in the villages of Yanming, Longfeng, etc. inhabited by the Gelao nationality in Longjing and Tangshan townships of Shiqian County, Guizhou Province.

Dragon worship is the core of **the Maolong (legendary dragon) Festival of the Gelao Nationality**. Its basic elements consist of five aspects: "dragon" beliefs, accessory totem beliefs, weaving skills, performing skills and recitation. Among them, "dragon" beliefs mainly include traditional stories; the ceremonies, occasions and offerings for dragon worship; as well as the recitation of words for worshipping the god of dragon. Accessory totem beliefs mainly include the worship of "the King of Bamboo", the worship of Panhu (a character in ancient Chinese mythology), the folk worship of Buddhism and Taoism, as well as the primitive worship. Weaving skills involves the selection of the materials (thin bamboo slices and colored paper) for making the dragon and the craft of weaving the dragon. Performing skills refers to the skills for the performance of the dragon, such as "Two Dragons Snatch Treasures", "Lazy Dragons Turn Over", "One Dragon Plays with Beads", "A Swan Embraces Eggs", "Hanging Upside Down on the Golden Hook", "Rhinoceros Watch the Moon" and "Screws Revolve on the Top". Recitation mainly includes the recitation at the ceremonies of "Kaiguang (an activity to endow a certain object with the divine power through a special ritual)", "inviting water", "burning the dragon", etc., and the chanting during the performances of "opening the door of wealth", "honoring the god of wealth", etc.

第 9 项:
水书习俗

水书
the Shui Writing

项目序号:518	项目编号:X-70	公布时间:2006(第一批)	类别:民俗
所属地区:贵州省	类型:新增项目	申报地区或单位:贵州省黔南布依族苗族自治州	

　　水书是水族先民创制的一种独具一格的雏形文字,是水族民间知识、民间文化的综合记录与反映,涉及天文历法、原始信仰、伦理道德、生产生活等诸多方面,主要流传于西南地区的水族聚居地。

　　水书的文字符号体系独特,既有类似甲骨文、金文的汉字,也有众多的象形文字符号,还有段落表义的图画文字。其字数少(仅数百字),文字符号体系独特,文本不能独立表达意义,要靠能看懂读通和会使用水书的"祭师"(水书先生)据水书所载相关条目,结合口传内容做出解释才能具有意义。几千年来,水书靠一代代的水书先生通过口传、手抄的形式流传下来。水书习俗是水书形成、发展和传承并以此构成与水族生活相关的习俗。水书习俗的传承方式形成了水书的两大组成部分:(1)用水族雏形古文字编著的手抄本;(2)通过水书先生口传心授来弥补因文字发展不完善而无法记录的大量要义、仪式和祝词等。水书各类卷本繁多,主要有诵读卷本和应用卷本两大类。水书被誉为"水族的百科全书",水族人民的丧葬、祭祀、婚嫁、营建、出行、占卜和生产,均由水书先生从水书中查找出依据,然后严格按照其制约行事。水书先生与水书的结合是传承水族传统文化的重要前提。①

Item 9: the Custom of the Shui Writing

Item Serial Number: 518	Item ID Number: X-70	Released Date: 2006 (Batch 1)	Category: Folk Custom

---

① 《水书习俗》,中国非物质文化遗产网,http://www.ihchina.cn/Article/Index/detail?id=15068,检索日期:2019 年 8 月 5 日。

贵州省 国家级非物质文化遗产文献资料汇编（汉英对照）

The Documentary Compilation of the State-level Intangible Cultural Heritage of Guizhou Province (Chinese-English Versions)

Affiliated Province: Guizhou Province	Type: New Item	Application Province or Unit: Qiannan Buyi and Miao Autonomous Prefecture, Guizhou Province

The Shui Writing is a unique embryonic writing created by ancestors of the Shui nationality. It is a comprehensive record and reflection of the folk knowledge and culture of the Shui nationality, involving many aspects, such as astronomical calendar, primitive belief, ethics and morality, production and living, which is mainly spread in the southwestern area inhabited by the Shui nationality.

The system of characters and symbols of the Shui Writing is unique. In this system, there is not only a kind of Chinese characters similar to oracle bone inscriptions and bronze inscriptions, but also many hieroglyphic symbols. Besides, there is pictographic writing that expresses meanings within one paragraph. The number of characters of the Shui Writing is limited (only a few hundred), and its text can't express meanings independently. Only the "priest" (a master of the Shui Writing), who can use it, is able to read and interpret its meaning. Only according to relevant items recorded in the Shui Writing together with the content orally transmitted, can he make a meaningful explanation. For thousands of years, it has been handed down by generations of masters of the Shui Writing through oral transmission and hand writing. **The Custom of the Shui Writing** refers to the customs concerning the formation, development and inheritance of the Shui Writing, and those related to the Shui People's life. Its way of imparting and inheriting leads to the two major components of the Shui Writing: (1) the handwritten copy compiled by using the embryonic ancient characters of the Shui nationality; (2) a large number of key points, ceremonies and congratulatory speeches that are handed down through the oral instructions of masters of the Shui Writing to compensate for those that can't be recorded due to the imperfect development of characters. There are many kinds of volumes of the Shui Writing, mainly including reading volumes and application volumes, acclaimed as "an encyclopedia of the Shui nationality". Masters of the Shui Writing find out the foundation concerning the Shui people's funerals, sacrifices, marriages, house building, travelling, divination and farming from the Shui Writing. Then, the Shui people strictly follow the constraints to act. The combination of masters of the Shui Writing and the Shui Writing is an important prerequisite for imparting and inheriting the traditional culture of the Shui nationality.

苗族独木龙舟节现场
the Scene of the Dumu Dragon Boat Festival of the Miao Nationality

第10项：
苗族独木龙舟节

项目序号：982	项目编号：X-75	公布时间：2008（第二批）	类别：民俗
所属地区：贵州省	类型：新增项目	申报地区或单位：贵州省台江县	

　　台江苗族独木龙舟节是贵州苗族的一个传统节日，每年农历五月二十四至二十七举行，流行于贵州省台江县、施秉县清水江两岸和台江县巴拉河下游两岸。节日期间，苗族群众聚集在清水江中游施洞镇塘坝村河段举行划龙舟大赛，比赛规模盛大，赛事礼仪独具一格。

　　苗族世代信巫事神，造龙舟时选龙树、砍龙树都要挑吉日，祭拜天地山水诸神。苗族以鼓作为氏族或部落的代表，每届以民主方式选举产生的氏族首领称为"鼓主"（又称为"鼓头"），一般是具有组织管理能力、德高望重的长者，施洞苗族每届龙舟赛事都在鼓主的主持下进行。划龙舟时"鼓头"头戴礼帽，身穿古礼服，端坐击鼓。由男童装扮的"童女"全身新衣银饰，与"鼓头"对坐打锣。36个桡手统一身着民族新装，头戴马尾丝编制、后缀燕尾银片的斗笠，轮桨点水，口唱飞歌，迅速将龙舟划向前方。节日期间，苗族家家备好鸡鸭鹅和几百斤米，盛情接待八方来客，表现出朴实善良、热情好客的风尚。苗族独木龙舟节反映了苗族多神的巫教信仰。①

---

① 《苗族独木龙舟节》，中国非物质文化遗产网，http://www.ihchina.cn/Article/Index/detail?id=15096，检索日期：2019 年 8 月 6 日。

Item 10: the Dumu Dragon Boat Festival of the Miao Nationality

Item Serial Number: 982	Item ID Number: X-75	Released Date: 2008 (Batch 2)	Category: Folk Custom
Affiliated Province: Guizhou Province	Type: New Item	Application Province or Unit: Taijiang County, Guizhou Province	

The Dumu Dragon Boat Festival of the Miao Nationality in Taijiang County is a traditional festival of the Miao nationality in Guizhou Province. It is held from the 24th to the 27th days of the 5th lunar month every year, popular along both banks of the Qingshui River in Taijiang and Shibing counties, and those of the lower reaches of the Bala River in Taijiang County of Guizhou Province. During the festival, the Miao people gather at the river segment of Tangba Village in Shidong Township, the middle reaches of the Qingshui River, to hold the dragon boat race. The scale of the race is grand, and its ceremonial is unique.

The Miao people believe in witchcraft for generations. When they choose dragon trees and cut them down to make dragon boats, they will choose an auspicious day to worship the gods of the heaven, the earth, mountains and rivers. The Miao people take drums as the representative of clans or tribes. The clan leader elected democratically in each session is called "the drum master" (also known as "the drum head"), who is generally the elder with organizational management ability and of noble character and high prestige. Each dragon boat race of the Miao nationality in Shidong Township is presided over by him. When rowing the dragon boat, "the drum head" wears a top hat, puts on ancient ceremonial dress, and sits upright to beat the drum. A boy, dressed up as a "girl" in new clothes and with silver ornaments, sits opposite "the drum head" and beats the gong. Thirty-six oarsmen, all dressed in new ethnic costumes, wearing Douli (a bamboo hat) made of horsetail and suffixed with swallowtail silver slices, paddle in water in unison and quickly row the dragon boat forward while singing the Flying Song. During the festival, the Miao families prepare chickens, ducks, geese and rice of several hundred *jin* (a Chinese unit of weight, with one *jin* equal to 0.5 kilogram) to warmly receive tourists from all parts of the world, showing a simple, kind and hospitable custom. **The Dumu Dragon Boat Festival of the Miao Nationality** reflects the Miao people's multi-deity belief in Shamanism.

苗族跳花节现场
the Scene of the Tiaohua (dancing around the flower tree) Festival of the Miao Nationality

第11项：苗族跳花节

项目序号：983	项目编号：X-76	公布时间：2008（第二批）	类别：民俗
所属地区：贵州省	类型：新增项目	申报地区或单位：贵州省安顺市	

　　苗族跳花节是贵州苗族群众为祝愿风调雨顺、五谷丰登、六畜兴旺而举行的一种民俗活动，于每年正月初七至初九举行。每年约有五万多人到坡上参加跳花，其中以安顺市瓦窑村的跳花坡活动最具规模。

　　跳花活动从正月初六开始前期工作，在德高望重的寨老主持下，用多种万年青树枝组成一棵花树，交给上年接花树后生下孩子的户主，户主在唢呐的吹打声中再将花树从家内直送到山顶。正月初七跳花节来临，各地苗族男女云集跳花坡。未婚男青年男扮女装吹芦笙；已婚男青年背上背扇和棉被，将银饰、绣花等物品挂于棉被上，吹着芦笙参与活动；小孩则背背扇参加跳花。正月初九下午跳花结束后，结婚多年未生子女的夫妇将花树接到家中供奉。如有男女青年在跳花活动中彼此相中，男方便可请人到女方家提亲。苗族跳花节是苗族群众生活中不可缺少的重要组成部分。[①]

Item 11: the Tiaohua (dancing around the flower tree) Festival of the Miao Nationality

Item Serial Number: 983	Item ID Number: X-76	Released Date: 2008 (Batch 2)	Category: Folk Custom

---

① 《苗族跳花节》，中国非物质文化遗产网，http://www.ihchina.cn/Article/Index/detail?id=15097，检索日期：2019年8月7日。

·贵州省·国家级非物质文化遗产文献资料汇编（汉英对照）

The Documentary Compilation of the State-level Intangible Cultural Heritage of Guizhou Province (Chinese-English Versions)

Affiliated Province: Guizhou Province	Type: New Item	Application Province or Unit: Anshun City, Guizhou Province

The Tiaohua (dancing around the flower tree) Festival of the Miao Nationality is a folk activity held by the Miao people in Guizhou Province to pray for timely wind and rain, a bumper grain harvest and thriving livestock, which is held from the 7th to the 9th days of the first month of the lunar calendar. More than 50,000 people go to the hillside to take part in the activity of dancing around the flower tree every year, among which the activity of dancing at the Flower Hillside in Wayao Village of Anshun City has the largest scale.

The preliminary work of the activity of dancing around the flower tree starts on the 6th day of the first lunar month. First of all, presided over by the respected Zhailao (a head of a stockaded village), a flower tree is made by using various evergreen branches, and then is handed over to the head of the household who gave birth to a child after receiving the flower tree last year. Then, the head of the household carries the flower tree from home to the top of the hill to the accompaniment of Suona Horn (a woodwind instrument). When the festival begins on the 7th day of the first lunar month, men and women of the Miao nationality from various regions come together in crowds to dance at the Flower Hillside. Unmarried young men are dressed up as women and play Lusheng Musical Instruments; married men carry Beishan (special straps for carrying infants and young children) and quilts on their backs, with silver ornaments, embroidery and other items hung on the quilt, and play Lusheng Musical Instruments to participate in the activity; and children participate in the activity of dancing around the flower tree by carrying Beishan (special straps for carrying infants and young children) on the back. After the activity is over in the afternoon of the 9th day of the first lunar month, couples who have been married for many years but still have no children take the flower tree home to make offerings. If a young man and a young girl fall in love with each other during the activity, the man can ask a matchmaker to go to the girl's house to make a proposal. **The Tiaohua (dancing around the flower tree) Festival of the Miao Nationality** is an indispensable part in the Miao people's life.

过苗年盛况
the Grand Occasion of the New Year of the Miao Nationality

第12项：
苗年

项目序号：990	项目编号：X-83	公布时间：2008（第二批）	类别：民俗
所属地区：贵州省	类型：新增项目	申报地区或单位：贵州省丹寨县、雷山县	

　　苗年，即苗族新年，是苗族最隆重的传统节日，一般在秋收完毕、一年农活结束时举行，各地过年的时间不同，从农历九月至正月不等。

　　在贵州省清水江、都柳江流域聚居的苗族从古至今一直使用着与汉族农历不同的苗历，苗历岁首即为苗年。当地过苗年需通过协商按顺序进行，这使得不同苗寨可以在不同月份轮流成为节日狂欢的中心区域。在贵州省丹寨县及其周边县市，苗族"嘎闹"支系的四个亚支系有过苗年的习俗。其中"尤"支系主要居住在丹寨北部、凯里南部和麻江东部，"恭"支系主要居住在丹寨境内、凯里南部和剑河、台江、黄平、麻江的部分地区，"白领苗"支系主要居住在丹寨南部、三都北部，"清江苗"支系主要居住在雷山西部、丹寨东部。苗年是苗家一年劳作的结束与欢乐的开始，苗年期间人们走村串寨，你迎我往、杀年猪、打糯米粑、祭祖、吃团年饭、喝串寨酒、跳芦笙舞，部分地区还举行斗牛、斗鸟和赛歌等活动，喜庆活动一个又一个，芦笙盛会一寨接一寨，欢乐一直持续到早春二月的翻鼓节。[①]苗族群众过苗年的主要目的有：（1）悼念五千多年前在部落大战中罹难的苗族始祖蚩尤；（2）庆祝一年劳作的收获；（3）祭祀祖宗神灵及苗族视为保护神的枫木、竹木、岩妈、水井等。

---

① 《苗年》，中国非物质文化遗产网，http://www.ihchina.cn/Article/Index/detail?id=15118，检索日期：2019年9月7日。

·贵州省·国家级非物质文化遗产文献资料汇编（汉英对照）

The Documentary Compilation of the State-level Intangible Cultural Heritage of Guizhou Province (Chinese-English Versions)

Item 12: the New Year of the Miao Nationality

Item Serial Number: 990	Item ID Number: X-83	Released Date: 2008 (Batch 2)	Category: Folk Custom
Affiliated Province: Guizhou Province	Type: New Item	Application Province or Unit: Danzhai County and Leishan County of Guizhou Province	

The New Year of the Miao Nationality, or the New Year of the Miao people, is the grandest traditional festival of the Miao nationality. It is usually held when autumn harvest and farm work come to an end every year, but the time for celebrating the festival varies from place to place, usually from the 9th to the 1st lunar months.

The Miao people living in the Qingshui River and the Duliu River basins of Guizhou Province have been using the calendar of the Miao nationality different from the lunar calendar of the Han nationality since ancient times. In the calendar of the Miao nationality, the beginning of the year is the New Year. The local celebration of **the New Year of the Miao Nationality** needs to be carried out in order through negotiation, which makes different Miao stockaded villages take turns to become the center of festival revelries in different months. In Danzhai County and its surrounding counties and cities of Guizhou Province, the four sub-branches of "Ganao" branch of the Miao nationality have the custom of celebrating **the New Year of the Miao Nationality**. Among them, the sub-branch of "You" mainly lives in the north of Danzhai County, the south of Kaili City and the east of Majiang County; the sub-branch of "Gong" mainly lives in Danzhai County, the south of Kaili City, as well as some areas in Jianhe, Taijiang, Huangping and Majiang counties; the sub-branch of "White-collar Miao" mainly lives in the south of Danzhai County and the north of Sandu County; and the sub-branch of "Qingjiang Miao" mainly lives in the west of Leishan County and the east of Danzhai County. **The New Year of the Miao Nationality** means the end of the Miao people's one year of manual labor and the beginning of their joy. During the festival, the Miao people are busy with visiting relatives from village to village, or welcoming visitors and seeing them off. They kill pigs, make glutinous rice cakes, worship their ancestors, have reunion dinners, visit other villages to drink liquor, and perform Lusheng Dance. In some areas, activities such as bullfighting, bird fighting and singing competitions will also be held. Festive activities are held one after another, Lusheng galas are held in one stockaded village after another, and joys never stop until the Drum Festival in the 2nd lunar month in early spring. The main purposes of the Miao people to celebrate **the New Year of the Miao Nationality** are as follows: (1) to mourn Chiyou, the earliest ancestor of the Miao people who died in a tribal war more than 5,000 years ago; (2) to celebrate the harvest after a year's manual labor; (3) to offer sacrifices to the gods of ancestors, as well as the maple tree, bamboo, the Rock Mother, the well, etc., which are regarded as protective gods by the Miao nationality.

苗族百鸟衣
the Hundred-bird Costume of the Miao Nationality

第13项：
　　　　苗族服饰

丹寨县雅灰乡送陇村石光林百鸟衣
Shi Guanglin's the Hundred-bird Costume in Songlong Village,
Yahui Township, Danzhai County

项目序号：513	项目编号：X-65	公布时间：2008（第二批）	类别：民俗
所属地区：贵州省	类型：扩展项目	申报地区或单位：贵州省桐梓县、安顺市西秀区、关岭布依族苗族自治县、纳雍县、剑河县、台江县、榕江县、六盘水市六枝特区、丹寨县	

　　苗族文化最鲜明、最具体的表现就是多姿多彩的民族服饰，其中各地苗族男性服饰大同小异，而苗族妇女服饰则最具代表性，各地差异较大。

　　桐梓县妇女上衣多采用对开襟样式，下身穿蜡染百褶裙和挑花围裙，袖子套上挑花袖筒，小腿裹多层挑花绑腿。

　　安顺市西秀区的苗族妇女通常将头发梳成绾髻，盘于半月形红木梳或小木梳上，也可用银链外绕，或包上青色蜡染镶边布，折成尖顶，上插银簪。上身穿两襟交叉相合的短衣或斜开襟短衣，袖口及领口有花边或彩边装饰，衣服上绣或染各类花鸟图案；下身着长裙或百褶裙，配以织锦系腰，围裙多用蜡染或刺绣镶边。

关岭苗族妇女服饰分衣裙和头饰两部分。衣裙上衣的领扁、坎肩和衣袖上的三条大小不一、图纹各异的刺绣图案象征苗族故地黄河、长江和沅江，其中不同的几何图形代表三大流域内纵横交错的阡陌田园。裙子中央的大型图案象征心手相连的苗族同胞，上衣前胸和后背呈长方形的大型彩色刺绣图案中，不同的花纹分别表示太阳、星星、鲜花等。围腰上三条垂直呈"川"字形的绣花图案分别代表三大苗族方言。

纳雍县箐苗妇女将头饰插在盘成"V"状、形似牛角的高髻上。纳雍箐苗头饰具有"鬏首""触角"等"族徽"标志。纳雍全刺绣服饰工艺技巧精湛、制作流程古朴，堪称苗族服饰中的精品。

剑河县苗族妇女服饰有十二大类，近百种款式，单是刺绣就有二十多种，针法多样，服饰图案造型丰富多彩、古朴神秘，构图丰满严谨，形象主次分明，色彩装饰对比强烈，具有独特的审美价值和鲜明的民族风格。

台江县苗族妇女服饰按当地方言划分，包括方你型、方纠型、方白型、方秀型、方南型、方翁型、方厘型、八香型和翁芒型九类，款式百余种。刺绣针法主要有平绣、锦上绣、破线绣、辫绣和盘绣等二十多种。构图有对称式、左右式、中心式等，艺术上体现变异、夸张的特点，主次分明，一幅构图就是一个故事，被史学家称为"穿在身上的史书"。

摆贝苗族服饰"百鸟衣羽毛裙"是榕江县苗族妇女服饰中最有代表性的一种。其衣裙图案以百鸟造型为主体，龙凤形象穿插其间，反映了对鸟图腾的崇拜。衣襟、衣袖、围腰、裙子、下摆等布满其他图案。服饰制作需经滚、轧、揉、舂捶等多道工序，在此过程中交替使用蜡染、织花、刺绣等多种工艺，制作细腻，富有创意。

六盘水市六枝特区梭戛箐苗妇女服饰以手工技艺为主制作的彩色蜡染和挑花刺绣两种服饰均采用天然原材料，其独特的图案、线条和多种表意、象征符号成为箐苗文化的重要组成部分。

丹寨县以苗族嘎闹支系为主体，其"雅灰型"的百鸟衣突出了苗族古服的原貌，以刺绣或蜡染技艺展示其对鸟图腾的崇拜，将鸟纹表现得淋漓尽致。"百鸟衣""锦鸡服"和"蜡染古装"等集中体现了鸟崇拜的族群意识。①

---

① 《苗族服饰》，中国非物质文化遗产网，http://www.ihchina.cn/Article/Index/detail?id=15047，检索日期：2019 年 9 月 8 日。

贵州省 国家级非物质文化遗产文献资料汇编（汉英对照）

The Documentary Compilation of the State-level Intangible Cultural Heritage of Guizhou Province (Chinese-English Versions)

Item 13: the Costumes of the Miao Nationality

Item Serial Number: 513	Item ID Number: X-65	Released Date: 2008 (Batch 2)	Category: Folk Custom
Affiliated Province: Guizhou Province	Type: Extended Item	Application Province or Unit: Tongzi County, Xixiu District of Anshun City, Guanling Buyi and Miao Autonomous County, Nayong County, Jianhe County, Taijiang County, Rongjiang County, Liuzhi Special Region of Liupanshui City, and Danzhai County of Guizhou Province	

The most distinctive and specific expression of the Miao culture is the varied and colorful ethnic costumes. Among them, the male Costumes of the Miao Nationality vary slightly in various regions, while the female Costumes of the Miao Nationality are the most representative, with significant differences in various places.

The upper outer garments of women in Tongzi County are mostly Duijin tops with two fronts of the upper garments opposite each other. They wear batik pleated skirts and cross-stitch aprons on the lower body. Outside their sleeves are cross-stitch outer sleeves. Their lower legs are wrapped around multi-layered cross-stitch leggings.

Women of the Miao nationality in Xixiu District of Anshun City usually comb their hair into buns, coiling it around the half-moon-shaped red wood combs or small combs. They can also wrap their hair around silver chains or cyan batik cloth with lace, coiling it into a pointed top, with silver hairpins inserted. They wear short tops with two fronts crossed and overlapped, or with slanted Yijin (two fronts of an upper garment). Their cuffs and necklines are decorated with lace or colorful edges, and their tops are embroidered or dyed with all kinds of flower and bird patterns. On their lower bodies are long skirts or pleated skirts, with brocade belts around the waists. Their aprons are often rimmed with batik or embroidery patterns.

The female Costumes of the Miao Nationality in Guanling County consist of tops, skirts and headwear. The three embroidery patterns with different sizes and designs on the collars, vests and sleeves of the tops symbolize the Yellow River, the Yangtze River and the Yuanjiang River, the old haunts of the Miao nationality. The different geometric figures within them represent the crisscross fields within the three major river basins. The large pattern in the center of the skirt symbolizes the

Miao compatriots united by hearts and hands. In the large-scale rectangular colored embroidery patterns on the front and back of the tops, different patterns represent the sun, stars, flowers, etc. respectively. On the aprons, the three vertical embroidery patterns that are in the shape of the Chinese character " 川 " represent the three Miao dialects.

Jingmiao women in Nayong County insert their headwear into the V-shaped buns similar to the shape of ox horns. Jingmiao headwear in Nayong County has the symbol of "family emblems", such as "hemp-tied hair buns" and "antennas". The fully-embroidered costumes in Nayong County are exquisite in craftsmanship, and simple and unsophisticated in production procedure, which are regarded as the best of **the Costumes of the Miao Nationality**.

The female Costumes of the Miao Nationality in Jianhe County have twelve categories and nearly 100 styles, with more than 20 embroidery techniques alone. The embroidery methods are diverse, and the clothing patterns are rich and colorful, quaint and mysterious. The composition of the patterns is full and rigorous, with images of clear priorities and a sharp contrast in color decoration, which has unique aesthetic value and distinct ethnic style.

According to local dialects, the female Costumes of the Miao Nationality in Taijiang County are divided into nine types: Fangni type, Fangjiu type, Fangbai type, Fangxiu type, Fangnan type, Fangweng type, Fangli type, Baxiang type and Wengmang type, with more than 100 styles. There are more than 20 kinds of embroidery methods, such as flat embroidery, brocade embroidery, thread-split embroidery, braiding embroidery and coiling embroidery. With clear priorities, the composition of patterns includes symmetrical type, left-and-right type and central type, reflecting the characteristics of variation and exaggeration in art. Each pattern tells a story, so **the Costumes of the Miao Nationality** are called "a history book worn on the body" by historians.

"The Hundred-bird Costume and Feather Skirt", the costume of the Miao nationality in Baibei Village, is the most representative of the female Costumes of the Miao Nationality in Rongjiang County. The patterns on the top and the skirt are mainly designed in the shape of a hundred birds, with the images of dragons and phoenixes interspersed among them, reflecting the worship of bird totem. Yijin (two fronts of an upper garment), sleeves, aprons, skirts and lower hems are covered with other patterns. Its making needs to go through many procedures, such as rolling, pressing hard, kneading and pounding. During the process, the crafts of batik, flower

贵州省·国家级非物质文化遗产文献资料汇编（汉英对照）

The Documentary Compilation of the State-level Intangible Cultural Heritage of Guizhou Province (Chinese-English Versions)

weaving and embroidery are used alternately, making the costume very delicate and creative.

Jingmiao women's costumes in Suojia Township of Liuzhi Special Region of Liupanshui City are mainly made by hand. The two kinds of costumes, colored batik costumes and cross-stitch embroidery costumes, are made of natural raw materials. Their unique patterns and lines, and diversified ideographic and symbolic symbols have become an important part of Jingmiao culture.

Ganao branch of the Miao nationality is the major group of the Miao people in Danzhai County. Its "Yahui-type" Hundred-bird Costume highlights the original appearance of the ancient costume of the Miao nationality, showing its worship of bird totem through the embroidery or batik technique and exhibiting bird patterns incisively and vividly. "The Hundred-bird Costume", "the Golden Pheasant Costume" and "the Batik Ancient Costume" are the concentrated reflection of the ethnic consciousness of bird worship.

第14项：
布依族"三月三"

贞丰布依族"三月三"：祭山求雨祈福
"the Double Third Festival" of the Buyi Nationality in Zhenfeng County:
Offering Sacrifices to the Mountain to Pray for Rain and Blessings

项目序号：1202	项目编号：X-127	公布时间：2011（第三批）	类别：民俗
所属地区：贵州省	类型：新增项目	申报地区或单位：贵州省贞丰县、望谟县	

　　"三月三"是布依族具有民族特色的传统节日，主要流行于贞丰、望谟县等县的布依族村寨。

　　农历三月初三正是农耕生产即将开始，春旱较严重，蚊蝇害虫正在萌动，火灾事故较频发的时节。每当这个时候，贞丰县布依族人民要举行祭祀活动，通过舞草龙扫寨驱邪消灾、杀猪宰牛祭山拜神求雨、上山"躲虫"祈福等，表达人们对农业丰收、家宅平安的企盼。"三月三"也是贞丰布依族青年男女对唱情歌、寻亲择偶的节日。①望谟县布依族的"三月三"是当地一年中最隆重的节日，人们要到山中祭祀山神和祖宗。节日前夕，村民们采来黄饭花、枫叶和紫蕃藤，用这些植物的汁浸泡糯米，做成红、黄、黑、紫和白五色花米饭。布依族人相信吃了五色花米饭后会人丁兴旺，身体强健。绣球是"三月三"中男女青年用来传达情爱的信物，姑娘们在节前赶制。绣球的表面用十二片花瓣连接成一个圆球形，每一片花瓣代表一年中的某个月份，上面绣有当月的花卉，象征着纯洁的爱情。节日当天，各家准备酒肉数十斤，糯饭成担，上山祭祖，下午宴请亲友，酒饭后，男女对歌。歌词皆即兴发挥，歌声是条红线，姑娘会将绣球赠与意中人，他则报之以手帕或毛巾，遂订秦晋之好。②

---

① 《布依族"三月三"》，中国非物质文化遗产网，http://www.ihchina.cn/Article/Index/detail?id=15284，检索日期：2019 年 8 月 7 日。

② 《布依族"三月三"》，中国非物质文化遗产网，http://www.ihchina.cn/Article/Index/detail?id=15285，检索日期：2019 年 8 月 6 日。

·贵州省·国家级非物质文化遗产文献资料汇编（汉英对照）

The Documentary Compilation of the State-level Intangible Cultural Heritage of Guizhou Province (Chinese-English Versions)

Item 14: "the Double Third Festival" of the Buyi Nationality

Item Serial Number: 1202	Item ID Number: X-127	Released Date: 2011 (Batch 3)	Category: Folk Custom
Affiliated Province: Guizhou Province	Type: New Item	Application Province or Unit: Zhenfeng County and Wangmo County of Guizhou Province	

"The Double Third Festival" is a traditional festival of the Buyi nationality with ethnic characteristics, mainly popular in Buyi stockaded villages in Zhenfeng County, Wangmo County, etc.

The 3rd day of the 3rd lunar month is the time when farming is about to begin, spring drought is serious, mosquitoes and flies are sprouting, and fire accidents are frequent. When the time comes, the Buyi people in Zhenfeng County will hold sacrificial activities. They express their hope for a good agricultural harvest and a peaceful life by dancing the Straw-woven Dragon to sweep away evil spirits and eliminate disasters, killing pigs and cattle to worship mountains and gods and to pray for rain, and going up the mountain to "keep away from insects" and to pray for blessings. "The Double Third Festival" is also a festival for young Buyi men and women in Zhenfeng County to sing love songs and look for lovers and spouses. **"The Double Third Festival" of the Buyi Nationality** in Wangmo County is the grandest festival of the year in the local area, during which people go up the mountain to worship the mountain god and their ancestors. Before the festival, villagers collect the Yellow Rice Flower (*Buddleja officinalis* in Latin), maple leaves and wisteria flowers, and soak glutinous rice in the juice of these plants to make the five-color rice of red, yellow, black, purple and white. The Buyi people believe that eating the five-color rice can make their populations flourishing, and their bodies strong and healthy. The Embroidered Ball is a keepsake used by young men and women at "the Double Third Festival" to convey their love, which is made by girls before the festival. The twelve petals on its surface are connected into a spherical shape, each petal representing a certain month of the year with the flower of that month embroidered on it, symbolizing pure love. On the day of the festival, each family prepares meat and liquor of several dozen *jin* (a Chinese unit of weight, with one *jin* equal to 0.5 kilogram), and a lot of glutinous rice. They go up the mountain to worship their ancestors. In the afternoon, they entertain friends and relatives. After the meal, young men and women sing songs in antiphonal style. All lyrics are improvised. The sound of singing acts as a red string which binds a couple of man and woman destined to marry. A girl will give her Embroidered Ball to her Mr. right, and he will return her with a handkerchief or a towel. At last, the two families will form a marriage alliance.

讨葱蒜活动
the Activity of Asking for Scallions and Garlic

第15项：
三月三（报京三月三）

项目序号：460	项目编号：X-12	公布时间：2014（第四批）	类别：民俗
所属地区：贵州省	类型：扩展项目	申报地区或单位：贵州省镇远县	

　　报京三月三是贵州省黔东南苗族侗族自治州镇远县独有的侗族传统节日，又名"播种节"，俗称"讨葱蒜"。其被称为"播种节"有两层含义：（1）农历三月将开始进行播种；（2）农历三月是男女青年播种爱情的好时光，男女青年借此机会互相认识了解，沟通感情。

　　三月初三当天清晨，镇远县报京寨未出嫁的姑娘们相约到寨边的水田中、溪沟里捞鱼虾，燃起篝火烧烤或煮酸辣汤锅，与前来讨笆篓的侗族男青年一起享用。在野炊过程中打情骂俏，看似不经意的姑娘们则暗自选择心上人。野炊结束，姑娘们到菜园里扯葱蒜，再拿到寨中池塘清洗。然后按照当地风俗，手提竹篮列队在古树下站好，等候心上人来讨取。男青年们看准心仪的姑娘，走过去讨要。得到竹篮后，拉起姑娘撒腿就跑。午时，大寨的各入口处都有侗族妇女把关，外寨客人要喝上一口"拦门酒"才得以放行。寨老与贵宾相携进入芦笙场，人们手拉手随着芦笙节奏，围成一圈又一圈缓缓踏步起舞。晚饭吃"龙席"，长长的桌子放着美味佳肴，主客分两边围坐。饮酒时，要唱酒歌调节气氛。晚上，人们来到花坡和竹林中的大树下，观看青年男女们吹木叶、唱情歌，直到深夜。[1]

---

[1] 徐世钊，《国家非遗："报京三月三"》，http://www.qdnrbs.cn/qdngs/2017-12/23/139_5542.htm，检索日期：2019 年 7 月 31 日。

Item 15: the Double Third Festival (the Baojing Double Third Festival)

Item Serial Number: 460	Item ID Number: X–12	Released Date: 2014 (Batch 4)	Category: Folk Custom
Affiliated Province: Guizhou Province	Type: Extended Item	Application Province or Unit: Zhenyuan County, Guizhou Province	

The Baojing Double Third Festival is a unique traditional festival of the Dong nationality in Zhenyuan County, Qiandongnan Miao and Dong Autonomous Prefecture, Guizhou Province, also called "the Sowing Festival", commonly known as "Asking for Scallions and Garlic". To call it "the Sowing Festival" has two meanings: first, sowing will begin in the third month of the lunar calendar; second, the third month of the lunar calendar is a good time for young men and women to sow love, so they take this opportunity to get to know each other and develop a romantic relationship.

In the morning of the Double Third Festival, unmarried girls in Baojing Stockaded Village of Zhenyuan County make an appointment to go to the paddy fields and streams by the village to catch fish and shrimp. They ignite a bonfire to make barbecue food or boil sour and spicy soup, and enjoy the food with the young men of the Dong nationality who come to beg for Balou (small baskets made of bamboo strips used to hold fish and shrimp). During the picnic, they flirt with each other, and the seemingly casual girls select their sweethearts in secret. When the picnic is over, girls will go to the vegetable garden to pluck scallions and garlic, and clean them in the village pond. Then, according to the local custom, girls stand in line under the ancient tree with bamboo baskets in hands, waiting for sweethearts to come and ask for them. Young men walk over to the girls they like and ask for the bamboo baskets. After a young man gets the bamboo basket, he will take the girl's hand and run away with her. At noon, all entrances to the stockaded village are guarded by the Dong women. Visitors from other stockaded villages have to drink a mouthful of "the Entrance-blocking Liquor" before they are allowed to enter it. Zhailao (a head of a stockaded village) and distinguished guests walk together to Lusheng Square, and then all people hold hands and dance slowly in circles to the rhythm of Lusheng Musical Instruments. The dinner is called "the Dragon Feast". With delicious foods

· **贵州省** · 国家级非物质文化遗产文献资料汇编（汉英对照）

The Documentary Compilation of the State-level Intangible Cultural Heritage of Guizhou Province (Chinese-English Versions)

put on long tables, hosts and guests sit on both sides. When drinking liquor, they will sing toasting songs to adjust the atmosphere. In the evening, people walk to the Flower Hillside, standing under big trees in the bamboo forest to listen to young men and women blowing Muye (leaves) and singing love songs until late at night.

榕江侗族欢庆侗年
Celebrating the New Year of the Dong Nationality in Rongjiang County

第16项：

侗年

项目序号：1205	项目编号：X-130	公布时间：2011（第三批）	类别：民俗
所属地区：贵州省	类型：新增项目	申报地区或单位：贵州省榕江县	

　　侗年是侗族感谢祖先保佑的传统节日，也是侗族家人团圆、庆贺丰收的节日，同时又是侗族文化大展示的节日，主要流行于贵州省榕江县乐里七十二寨、寨蒿四十八寨等侗族地区。

　　侗年在侗家人聚居的各村寨基本上都是按照传统规定轮流举行，具有广泛的群众性和民间传承性。节日期间，各家或杀猪宰羊，或杀鸡杀鸭，请客访友，宴饮作乐。节日前一天，备豆腐、鱼虾，当晚用酸水煮熟，经一夜冷却成"冻菜"，节日当天便以"冻菜"祭祀祖先。这天，侗家备好各种酸菜、冻鱼和糍粑以馈亲友，叫"吃杨粑"。过农历大年时，对方要如数还礼，称为"还杨粑"。侗年最重要的仪式是"斗莎"（即唱祭祖歌），目的是祭祀祖先，这也是老人们传承民族优秀传统文化的一种形式。无论是小孩、成人，还是青年人新婚伊始，老人们都要通过"斗莎"教育下一代为人处世、明辨是非、勤俭持家、尊老爱幼等。[1]

---

① 《侗年》，中国非物质文化遗产网，http://www. ihchina. cn/Article/Index/detail?id=15288，检索日期：2019 年 8 月 5 日。

贵州省·国家级非物质文化遗产文献资料汇编（汉英对照）

The Documentary Compilation of the State-level Intangible Cultural Heritage of Guizhou Province (Chinese-English Versions)

Item 16: the New Year of the Dong Nationality

Item Serial Number: 1205	Item ID Number: X-130	Released Date: 2011 (Batch 3)	Category: Folk Custom
Affiliated Province: Guizhou Province	Type: New Item	Application Province or Unit: Rongjiang County, Guizhou Province	

The New Year of the Dong Nationality is a traditional festival for the Dong people to thank their ancestors for blessings, to have family reunions and to celebrate the harvest. Besides, it is also a festival to display the Dong culture. It is mainly spread in areas inhabited by the Dong people, such as the seventy-two stockaded villages in Leli Township and the forty-eight stockaded villages in Zhaihao Township of Rongjiang County, Guizhou Province.

The New Year of the Dong Nationality is basically held in turn in stockaded villages where the Dong people live according to traditional rules, which has the features of extensive mass and folk inheritance. During the festival, pigs and sheep, or chickens and ducks are killed in all families. The Dong people treat guests to feasts, visit friends, wine and dine, and have great fun. On the day before the festival, tofu, fish and shrimps are prepared and cooked in sour water that night. After one night's cooling, they become "frozen dishes". On the day of the festival, these "frozen dishes" are offered to ancestors. On this day, the Dong families prepare all kinds of pickled vegetables, frozen fish and glutinous rice cakes, and send them to friends and relatives, which is called "eating Yangba Cake". When the Lunar New Year comes, the other party should repay them in full, which is called "repaying Yangba Cake". The most important ceremony in **the New Year of the Dong Nationality** is "Dousha" (singing ancestral worship songs). Its purpose is to worship ancestors. Besides, it's also a form for the old people to pass down the excellent traditional ethnic culture. The elderly will educate the next generation, whether they are children, adults or young couple who have just got married, to conduct themselves in society, to distinguish right from wrong, to be industrious and thrifty in managing a household, to respect the old and cherish the young, etc. through "Dousha" (singing ancestral worship songs).

四十八寨歌节
the Singing Festival of 48 Stockaded Villages

第17项：
歌会（四十八寨歌节）

项目序号：1209	项目编号：X-134	公布时间：2011（第三批）	类别：民俗
所属地区：贵州省	类型：新增项目	申报地区或单位：贵州省天柱县	

　　四十八寨歌节是流传在贵州天柱县境内的民间歌会，包括十三个歌场。从农历三月开始到九月结束，每个歌场每年赶一次，开场时间多是月中属"戊"的日子。每到集会时间，山坡上、公路旁人山人海，歌声此起彼伏。

　　四十八寨歌节歌场众多，包括侗族区、苗族区和苗侗汉杂居区。歌词、唱腔丰富，有河边调、高坡调、青山调和阿哩调等。不管哪个区域哪个腔，均用侗语演唱，因此各种腔各寨都能听懂、会唱。歌场上一般以村寨或家族为单位组成"歌堂"。歌堂以侃歌为主。人们以歌会友，比文才、比肚才、比口才。除了唱侗族传统山歌，还唱大量以汉族历史故事为题材的套歌，如"唱三国""唱说唐""穆桂英挂帅""唱毛红玉英""唱洛阳桥"等。唱古歌、叙事歌是歌场对歌最大的特色。叙事歌是侃歌的主要内容，往往通过对人对事的歌唱讲一个故事，这类歌最受人们喜爱。各村寨均有一定影响力的歌手、歌师。一些老歌师没有进过学堂，但记忆力超群、出口成歌，对三国、凤姣李旦和梁祝等历史故事传说歌谣倒背如流。[①]四十八寨歌节也是侗苗群众聚会玩山、唱歌、交友、恋爱的传统民族歌会，是他们业余文化生活的重要场所。[②]

---

① 《歌会（四十八寨歌节）》，中国非物质文化遗产网，http://www. ihchina. cn/Article/Index/detail?id=15293，检索日期：2019 年 8 月 8 日。

② 王砂砂，《天柱：四十八寨歌节值得期待》，http://www. gzfwz. org. cn/xwdt/201804/t20180416_3122758. html，检索日期：2019 年 8 月 8 日。

贵州省·国家级非物质文化遗产文献资料汇编（汉英对照）

The Documentary Compilation of the State-level Intangible Cultural Heritage of Guizhou Province (Chinese-English Versions)

Item 17: the Singing Gathering (the Singing Festival of 48 Stockaded Villages)

Item Serial Number: 1209	Item ID Number: X-134	Released Date: 2011 (Batch 3)	Category: Folk Custom
Affiliated Province: Guizhou Province	Type: New Item	Application Province or Unit: Tianzhu County, Guizhou Province	

The Singing Festival of 48 Stockaded Villages is a folk singing gathering spread in Tianzhu County, Guizhou Province, consisting of 13 song fields. It is held on each song field once a year from the 3rd to the 9th lunar months, mostly starting with the day of "Wu" (the fifth of the Ten Heavenly Stems) in a month. Whenever the time for gathering comes, there are a sea of people on the hillside and beside the road, with the singing rising one after another.

The many song fields of **the Singing Festival of 48 Stockaded Villages** include the area of the Dong nationality, the area of the Miao nationality, and the mixed residential area of the Miao, Dong and Han nationalities. Rich in lyrics and singing tones, the songs have riverside tune, high slope tune, green hill tune, Ali tune, etc. In whichever area or tune, songs are all sung in the Dong language, so people from all stockaded villages can understand and sing them. On the singing field, different "singing halls" are usually formed with villages or families as units. These "singing halls" are mainly for people to get together and sing songs. People make friends through singing, competing in literary talent, wisdom and eloquence. In addition to the traditional Mountain Songs of the Dong nationality, there are also a large number of Taoge (a series of songs) with historical stories of the Han nationality as the theme, such as "The Singing of the Three Kingdoms", "The Singing of the Tang Dynasty", "Mu Guiying Takes Command", "The Singing of Mao Hong and Yu Ying" and "The Singing of the Luoyang Bridge". Singing ancient songs and narrative songs is the greatest feature of the antiphonal singing on song fields. Narrative songs are the main songs for people to get together and sing, which usually tell a story through the singing of people and events. This kind of songs are the most popular among the people. In each village, there are singers and vocalists with certain influence. Some old vocalists have never been to school, but they have excellent memory, and can sing songs extemporaneously. They can recite ballads concerning historical stories and legends fluently, such as The Three Kingdoms, Feng Jiao and Li Dan, as well as Liang Shanbo and Zhu yingtai. **The Singing Festival of 48 Stockaded Villages** is also a traditional ethnic singing gathering for the Dong and Miao people to get together, climb mountains, sing songs, make friends and fall in love, so it is an important place for their amateur cultural life.

第18项：
月也

侗族月也
Yueye Activity of the Dong Nationality

项目序号：1213	项目编号：X-138	公布时间：2011（第三批）	类别：民俗
所属地区：贵州省	类型：新增项目	申报地区或单位：贵州省黎平县	

月也，侗语意为"集体出访做客"，一般在春节期间或秋后的农闲时节（农历正月和八月）举行，是侗族传统交际联谊活动，流传于贵州省的黎平县、从江县和榕江县的侗族地区。

月也活动规模盛大，侗寨男女老幼都身着节日盛装参加，寨中"歌队""芦笙队"和戏班子一同参与。月也时间长短由其内容决定，一般每家派一名代表参加。由寨中有威望的人率领，集体到某友好村寨拜访。甲寨客人快到乙寨时，乙寨众人要到寨口迎接，同时用日常生产工具或生活用具等设置重重路障。双方摆开歌阵，对唱拦路歌。主队用歌提问，客队用歌回答，答对一次撤除一个路障。如答错，客队就燃放鞭炮，表示歉意和敬意，主队就尽撤路障，迎客入寨，参加联欢活动。期间，宾主白天或演侗戏，或赛芦笙，或踩歌堂；晚上则到鼓楼对唱大歌，或欣赏"嘎锦"（侗族曲艺）直到深夜；之后，两寨青年男女还要到月堂里行歌坐夜直至天亮。宾主如此欢度3～5日始散。离别时，主寨还要以猪羊馈赠。视收成情况，次年或若干年后，此寨再到彼寨回访。在侗族月也习俗中，集体做客是活动的形式，文化展示是活动的内容，情感交流是活动的目的。①

---

① 《月也》，中国非物质文化遗产网，http://www.ihchina.cn/Article/Index/detail?id=15297，检索日期：2019年8月6日。

Item 18: Yueye Activity

Item Serial Number: 1213	Item ID Number: X-138	Released Date: 2011 (Batch 3)	Category: Folk Custom
Affiliated Province: Guizhou Province	Type: New Item	Application Province or Unit: Liping County, Guizhou Province	

Yueye Activity, meaning "to pay a group visit to the neighboring village" in the Dong language, is generally held during the Spring Festival or in the slack season after autumn (the 1st and the 8th lunar months). It is a traditional social activity for promoting fellowship of the Dong nationality, spread in areas inhabited by the Dong people in Liping County, Congjiang County and Rongjiang County of Guizhou Province.

Yueye Activity is a large-scale event. Men and women, old and young, of the Dong nationality are all dressed in festival costumes to participate in it, together with "the singing team", "Lusheng team" and the theatrical troupe in the stockaded village. The length of this activity is determined by its content, and the participants are generally one representative from one family. Led by a prestigious person in the stockaded village, they pay a group visit to another stockaded village that is in good relationship with theirs. When guests from Village A arrive at Village B, all people from Village B welcome them at the entrance to the stockaded village. At the same time, they set up many roadblocks with daily production tools or household goods, and then the two sides form two singing line-ups, singing road-blocking songs in antiphonal style. The host line-up asks a question by singing songs, and the visiting line-up answers the question by singing songs. If the latter answers one question correctly, one roadblock will be removed. If the answer is wrong, the visiting line-up will set off firecrackers to express its apology and respect. Then, the host line-up removes all roadblocks, and welcomes the guests into the stockaded village to participate in the get-together. During the activity, in the daytime, visitors and hosts perform Dong Opera, hold contests of playing Lusheng Musical Instruments, or sing and dance in singing halls; at night, they go to the Drum Tower to sing Al Laox of the Dong Nationality in antiphonal style, or enjoy "Gajin" (a kind of Quyi art of the Dong nationality) until late. After that, young men and women of the two stockaded villages go to the Moon Hall to sing songs and sit until daybreak. The guests and

贵州省 国家级非物质文化遗产文献资料汇编（汉英对照）

The Documentary Compilation of the State-level Intangible Cultural Heritage of Guizhou Province (Chinese-English Versions)

hosts spend 3-5 days together joyfully, and then the guests say goodbye to the hosts. At the time of departure, pigs and sheep will be given as presents to guests by the host stockaded village. People from Village B will visit Village A the next year or several years later depending on the harvest situation. In the custom of **Yueye Activity** of the Dong nationality, group visiting is the form of the activity, cultural display is its content, and emotional exchange is its purpose.

第19项：苗族栽岩习俗

苗族栽岩
Planted Rocks of the Miao Nationality

项目序号：1217	项目编号：X-142	公布时间：2011（第三批）	类别：民俗
所属地区：贵州省	类型：新增项目	申报地区或单位：贵州省榕江县	

苗族有一种栽岩（将一块长方形的石条埋入泥中，半截露出地面）的公众议事和立法活动，即栽岩习俗，这是苗族议榔制的产物。苗族议榔制是历史上苗族社会组织的一种，议榔制可以由一个鼓社、一个寨或几个寨，乃至整个地区组成，苗族习惯法称为议榔规约。每次议榔会议前，先由寨头们商议议榔内容，然后召开群众大会，宣布议定的议榔规约，由大会通过，之后在会址竖石一块（即栽岩），表示该议榔规约坚如磐石，不可更改。议榔栽岩是苗族的口碑条款规约，规范苗人的行为，有很强的约束力。

议榔的目的是维护苗人正常的生产和生活，表现形式是用赌咒的方式颁布条款规约。一旦颁布，靠赌咒的"魔力"和寨老及群众的互相监督来实施条款规约。岩是规约的载体，过去栽的岩无文字，规约和款项由议榔师向族人、寨老或群体宣布并通过后，就自然保存于人们头脑中。有触犯相关规约的案件时，族老或寨民就以案件轻重处罚相关的银两，重犯都是以杀头修榔。议榔栽岩有一寨的议榔，有数寨联合的议榔，有区域性或族群的议榔；还有多人的议榔，个人的议榔；有关于习俗、友谊、防护的议榔，也有驱邪、划分界线等的议榔。①

---

① 《苗族栽岩习俗》，中国非物质文化遗产网，http://www.ihchina.cn/Article/Index/detail?id=15311，检索日期：2019年8月8日。

Item 19: the Rock-planting Custom of the Miao Nationality

Item Serial Number: 1217	Item ID Number: X-142	Released Date: 2011 (Batch 3)	Category: Folk Custom
Affiliated Province: Guizhou Province	Type: New Item	Application Province or Unit: Rongjiang County, Guizhou Province	

The Miao nationality has an activity of planting rocks (burying a rectangular rock bar in the mud, half exposed to the ground) in which people publicly discuss official business and enact legislation, which is called "the rock-planting custom". It is the result of Yilang system of the Miao nationality. This system is a kind of social organization of the Miao nationality in history, which can be composed of a drum commune, a stockaded village or several stockaded villages, and even the whole region. The customary law of the Miao nationality is called Yilang Stipulation. Before each Yilang meeting, leaders of the stockaded villages will discuss the content for the meeting first, and then hold a mass meeting to announce the agreed Yilang Stipulation and pass it at the meeting. After that, a rock will be erected (namely, planting a rock) at the site of the meeting, indicating that this Yilang Stipulation is as firm as a rock and cannot be changed. Yilang Rock Planting belongs to oral terms and stipulations of the Miao nationality, which regulates the Miao people's behavior, having strong binding force.

The purpose of Yilang system is to maintain the normal production and life of the Miao people, and its manifestation is to promulgate terms and stipulations by means of swearing. Once promulgated, the terms and stipulations will be implemented by the "magic power" of swearing and the mutual supervision of Zhailao (a head of a stockaded village) and the masses. Rocks are the carriers of stipulations. In the past, there were no words on the planted rocks. Since Yilang master's announcement of the passing of the terms and stipulations to clansmen, Zhailao (a head of a stockaded village) or the masses, they were naturally kept in the Miao people's minds. If there were cases of violating relevant stipulations, clan elders and villagers would punish the offenders with certain forfeits (silver) according to the degree of seriousness of the cases, and a felon would be beheaded. Yilang Rock Planting includes one-stockaded-village Yilang, several-stockaded-village Yilang, regional or ethnic Yilang, multiple-people Yilang, personal Yilang, custom Yilang, friendship Yilang, protection Yilang, as well as exorcism Yilang, boundary-demarcation Yilang, etc.

彝族火把节
the Torch Festival of the Yi Nationality

第20项：火把节（彝族火把节）

项目序号：458	项目编号：X-10	公布时间：2011（第三批）	类别：民俗
所属地区：贵州省	类型：扩展项目	申报地区或单位：贵州省赫章县	

彝族火把节是贵州省赫章县彝族最隆重的传统节日，每年农历六月二十四日举行。[1]

彝族火把节是根据彝族十月太阳历来定的，一年以 10 个月计算，一个月以 36 日记日，以北斗星斗柄指向定季节，斗柄正下指南为大寒，在期间过十月年节，即彝族十月年。斗柄正上指北为大暑，在期间过新年，即火把节，又叫"星回节"。此后，该仪式经发展演变，增加了歌舞表演、服饰展示、斗牛、赛马、摔跤、打陀螺和荡秋千等活动，成为今天的火把节。火把节期间，活动丰富多彩，有赛马、摔跤、斗牛、斗羊和古歌对赛等；青年男女们借此机会展示自己绚丽多彩的服饰与高超的才艺，赛装与选美活动有序展开；夜幕降临，彝族家家户户点燃火把，进行象征性的驱虫活动，而后人们围着篝火，在唢呐、笛子和月琴的伴奏下，围成圈子跳起《阿西里西》《撒麻舞》《撒荞舞》《乌蒙彝舞》等舞蹈。[2]

---

① 《火把节（彝族火把节）》，中国非物质文化遗产网，http://www.ihchina.cn/Article/Index/detail?id=14948，检索日期：2019 年 8 月 7 日。

② 涂敏、陈康清，《国家级非物质文化遗产——赫章彝族"火把节"》，http://gz.people.com.cn/n/2014/0812/c344113-21963045.html，检索日期：2019 年 8 月 8 日。

Item 20: the Torch Festival (the Torch Festival of the Yi Nationality)

Item Serial Number: 458	Item ID Number: X-10	Released Date: 2011 (Batch 3)	Category: Folk Custom
Affiliated Province: Guizhou Province	Type: Extended Item	Application Province or Unit: Hezhang County, Guizhou Province	

The Torch Festival of the Yi Nationality is the most solemn traditional festival of the Yi nationality in Hezhang County, Guizhou Province, held on the 24th day of the 6th lunar month every year.

When to hold **the Torch Festival of the Yi Nationality** depends on the Ten-month Solar Calendar, in which a year has 10 months and a month has 36 days. The direction of the Big Dipper's handle determines the season. When it points directly down to the south, the season is Dahan (the coldest). During this period, the Yi people celebrate the Ten-month New Year Festival, that is, the Ten-month New Year of the Yi nationality. When it points directly up to the north, the season is Dashu (the hottest). During this period, the Yi people celebrate the New Year, namely **the Torch Festival**, or "the Xinghui Festival". Later, this ceremony has undergone evolution, and activities, such as singing-and-dancing performances, costume displays, bullfighting, horse racing, wrestling, whipping tops and playing on the swings, have been added, thus becoming **the Torch Festival** of today. During **the Torch Festival**, rich and colorful activities are held, such as horse racing, wrestling, bullfighting, goat fighting and antiphonal singing competition of ancient songs. Young men and women take this opportunity to show their gorgeous costumes and superb talents, with costume competition and beauty pageant going on orderly. As night falls, every Yi family lights torches to carry out the symbolic activity of repelling insects. After that, accompanied by Suona Horn (a woodwind instrument), flutes and Yueqin (a four-stringed plucked musical instrument with a full-moon-shaped sound box), people perform dances of "Axi Lixi", "Sama Dance", Saqiao Dance", "Wumengyi Dance", etc. in circles around the bonfire.

第21项：
农历二十四节气
（石阡说春）

石阡说春
Shiqian Spring Saying

项目序号：516	项目编号：X-68	公布时间：2011（第三批）	类别：民俗
所属地区：贵州省	类型：扩展项目	申报地区或单位：贵州省石阡县	

　　"说春"是石阡侗族人民世代流传下来的一种在立春时节扮装"春官"说唱歌谣、劝农劳作的民俗表演活动，祝福风调雨顺、丰衣足食。"春官"是周代一种职官，执掌农耕事务。后世民间出现扮装"春官"的说唱艺人在农村走家串户表演，形成一种劝农祈福的"春官送春"习俗。说唱者被俗称为"春倌"。清乾隆石阡府志已有当地说春习俗的记载。石阡侗族吸收了这一习俗并传承至今。

　　"说春"在每年立春时开始，春分时结束。说春词实际是唱，有简单的曲调，各地不一。"说春"分为"说正春"和"说野春"。"说正春"有固定春词，内容主要是说"二十四个农事节气""渔樵耕读"，内容涵盖历史、地理、人文等方面。"说野春"又称为"说耍耍春""说花花春"，内容丰富、灵活多变，主要段子名目有《开财门》《颂主人》《说茶》《见子打子》等。"春倌"手端春牛，凡到说春之家，均要散发一张农历、一张财神春贴，意在劝农春耕，祝福主人吉祥如意。石阡说春是我国源远流长的农业文明传统民俗仪式的宝贵遗存。①

---

① 《农历二十四节气（石阡说春）》，中国非物质文化遗产网，http://www.ihchina.cn/Article/Index/detail?id=15062，检索日期：2019 年 8 月 8 日。

Item 21: the Twenty-four Solar Terms of the Lunar Calendar (Shiqian Spring Saying)

Item Serial Number: 516	Item ID Number: X-68	Released Date: 2011 (Batch 3)	Category: Folk Custom
Affiliated Province: Guizhou Province	Type: Extended Item	Application Province or Unit: Shiqian County, Guizhou Province	

"Spring Saying" is a kind of folk performance activity passed down from generation to generation by the Dong people in Shiqian County, in which the dressed-up "Chunguan (the official in charge of spring affairs)" talks and sings ballads to urge farmers to do farm work at the Beginning of Spring, wishing for timely wind and rain, and for ample food and clothing. "Chunguan (the official in charge of spring affairs)" was a kind of official post in charge of farming affairs in the Zhou Dynasty. Folk talking-and-singing artists who dress up as "Chunguan (the official in charge of spring affairs)" have emerged in later generations, and perform it from house to house in rural areas, thus forming a custom of "Chunguan delivering a message of spring" to urge farmers to start farming and to pray for blessings. The talking-and-singing artists are commonly called "the messenger of spring". The local custom of Spring Saying has been recorded in *The Annals of Shiqian Prefecture* during the reign of Emperor Qianlong of the Qing Dynasty. The Dong people in Shiqian County have absorbed this custom, imparting and inheriting it up to now.

"Spring Saying" starts at the Beginning of Spring and ends at the Spring Equinox each year. The words of Spring Saying are actually sung with simple tunes, varying from place to place. "Spring Saying" is divided into "formal Spring Saying" and "informal Spring Saying". "Formal Spring Saying" has fixed librettos, and its content is mainly about "the 24 Farming Solar Terms" and "Fishermen, Woodcutters, Farmers and Intellectuals", covering history, geography, humanities, etc. "Informal Spring Saying" is also called "Making Fun of Spring" or "Telling Funny Stories of Spring", with rich and flexible content. The main segments include "Opening the Door of Wealth", "Praising the Owner", "Talking about Tea" and "Making Fun of Whatever One Sees". "The messenger of spring" holds a wooden carving of cattle in hand. At whichever home he arrives, he will send out a lunar calendar and a spring sticker of the God of Wealth. The purpose is to urge farmers to start spring farming and to wish the hosts happiness and good luck. **Shiqian Spring Saying** is a precious legacy of the traditional folk rituals of China's long-standing agricultural civilization.

第22项：
仡佬族三幺台习俗

仡佬族三幺台习俗
the Sanyaotai (three-feast) Custom of the Gelao Nationality

项目序号：1363	项目编号：X-150	公布时间：2014（第四批）	类别：民俗
所属地区：贵州省	类型：新增项目	申报地区或单位：贵州省道真仡佬族苗族自治县	

　　仡佬族三幺台习俗是仡佬族民间一种最隆重的食俗礼仪。"三"指三台席。"幺台"是务川、道真仡佬族苗族自治县的方言，有"结束""完成"之意。三幺台指一台宴席要经历三道程序才算完成。

　　作为仡佬族食俗中最高级别的宴席，三幺台由茶席、酒席和饭席三轮席组成。第一台为茶席，意为"接风洗尘"，让远道而来的宾客先喝一碗油茶，以米粑、米花糖、粽子、饼子、糖食、核桃、花生、板栗、瓜子等果品糕点佐饮，饮完撤去碗盘，只留筷子；第二台为酒席，又称"八仙醉酒"，意为酒桌上的主人和宾客如神仙般快乐，以猪的心、肝、舌、耳、腰花、肚片、香肠、瘦肉片以及卤鸡等冷菜、卤菜佐食，饮完撤去杯盘，只留筷子；第三台为饭席，又称"四方团圆"，意为四方来客团团圆圆、亲如一家，以烧白、猪头、肚扣、酥肉、木耳、黄花、笋子、海带和灰豆腐果等搭配米饭食用。仡佬族的婚丧嫁娶、祝寿、立房和节日庆典场合，三幺台都是一项不可或缺的食俗活动。[①] 三幺台宴席其间，坐席的方向、碗筷的排列、上菜的次序等均有严格要求，这是仡佬饮食文化中的"礼"，更是仡家人内在的伦理精神，贯穿在饮食活动过程中。[②]

---

① 周菁，《仡佬族食俗"三幺台"价值探讨》，载《贵州民族研究》，2015年第5期，第114-117页。

② 吴思，《仡佬族非物质文化遗产三幺台》，载《当代贵州》，2016年第16期，第50-51页。

Item 22: the Sanyaotai (three-feast) Custom of the Gelao Nationality

Item Serial Number: 1363	Item ID Number: X−150	Released Date: 2014 (Batch 4)	Category: Folk Custom
Affiliated Province: Guizhou Province	Type: New Item	Application Province or Unit: Daozhen Gelao and Miao Autonomous County, Guizhou Province	

The Sanyaotai (three-feast) Custom of the Gelao Nationality is the most ceremonious dietary etiquette among the Gelao people. "San" refers to three feasts, and "yaotai" is the dialect in Gelao and Miao Autonomous Counties of Wuchuan and Daozhen, meaning "to end" and "to finish". Sanyaotai (three-feast) means that a banquet can only be finished after three procedures.

As a banquet of the highest level in the dietary custom of the Gelao nationality, Sanyaotai (three-feast) consists of three feasts, namely tea feast, liquor feast and meal feast. The first is the tea feast, with the implication of "welcoming and washing off the dust of the guests". Guests from afar are invited to drink a bowl of oil tea, supplemented with fruit, dim sum and cakes, such as rice cakes, pop-rice candies, Zongzi (glutinous rice dumpling), pancakes, sugar food, walnuts, peanuts, chestnuts and sunflower seeds. After the tea feast, bowls and plates are taken away, with chopsticks left only. The second is the liquor feast, also known as "Eight Immortals' Drinking", which implies that hosts and guests at the table are as happy as immortals. It is supplemented with cold dishes and pot-stewed meat, such as pig's hearts, livers, tongues, ears, kidneys, tripe slices, sausages, lean pork slices and pot-stewed chicken. After the liquor feast, cups and plates are taken away, with chopsticks left only. The third is the meal feast, also called "All Parties' Reunion", which implies that guests from all directions get together, as close as one family. The dishes are Shaobai (steamed pork), pig head meat, pig's tripe slices, crisp meat, Mu'er (edible tree fungus), daylilies, bamboo shoots, sea-tangle, gray tofu balls, etc., served with rice. On the occasions of the weddings, funerals, birthday celebrations, house building and holiday celebrations of the Gelao nationality, Sanyaotai (three-feast) is an indispensable activity concerning dietary customs. During the course of Sanyaotai (three-feast), there are strict requirements for the direction of seats, the arrangement of bowls and chopsticks, and the order of serving dishes. This is the "etiquette" of the Gelao food culture and the ethical spirit of the Gelao people, running through the process of the dietary activity.

第23项：
布依族服饰

布依族妇女服饰
Women's Costume of the Buyi Nationality

项目序号：1370	项目编号：X-157	公布时间：2014（第四批）	类别：民俗
所属地区：贵州省	类型：新增项目	申报地区或单位：贵州省	

　　布依族服饰的原材料以棉为主，颜色多为青、蓝、白，刺绣图案多为花草和几何图形，使用丝线颜色以红、绿、蓝、黄和紫为主。

　　布依族服饰分为普通生活装和盛装。普通生活装只有头帕、上衣和裤子，并且上衣的领和袖无刺绣花边装饰。[①]盛装由上衣、裤子、长衫、裙子、花鞋、腰带、围胸、头帕和首饰构成。布依族男子服饰的式样各地基本相同，多包头帕，头帕有条纹和纯青两种；衣服为对襟短衣，一般是内白外青或蓝，裤子为长裤；老年男性多穿大袖短衣或青、蓝长衫，脚上穿布统袜。布依族妇女大多着大襟短衣，部分着百褶长裙。在布依族聚居的扁担山一带，少女喜穿滚边短衣，系绸缎腰带，头戴织锦头帕，以粗发辫盘扎头巾，额上为织锦图案和数圈发辫，下穿裤子，着绣花鞋。青年女性穿蜡染百褶裙，斜襟短衣，绣花盘肩，用各种花线沿衣肩绣成两排小正方形的半圆形图案，领圈两边抛花织锦，颜色醒目；衣袖中间为织锦，上下两段是蜡染；衣服下摆为一寸左右的织锦镶边，胸前戴绣花或织锦长围腰，系浅色绸缎腰带；头戴织锦头巾，耳边垂着一束各色线做成的耍须。已婚者的头饰戴"更考"，以竹笋壳和布匹制成，形如撮箕，前圆后矩。每逢盛大节日或宴会时，妇女均喜佩带各式耳环、戒指、项

---

① 杨浩、陈亚林，《布依族服饰独具一种文化之美》，载《黔西南日报》，2019年2月12日第8版。

圈、发簪和手镯等银饰。^①

 ## Item 23: the Costumes of the Buyi Nationality

Item Serial Number: 1370	Item ID Number: X-157	Released Date: 2014 (Batch 4)	Category: Folk Custom
Affiliated Province: Guizhou Province	Type: New Item	Application Province or Unit: Guizhou Province	

The raw materials of **the Costumes of the Buyi Nationality** are mainly cotton, with colors usually being cyan, blue and white. Their embroidery patterns are mostly flowers, plants and geometric figures, and the colors of the silk threads adopted are mainly red, green, blue, yellow and purple.

The Costumes of the Buyi Nationality are divided into plain clothes for daily wearing and splendid attire. The former only consists of kerchiefs, tops and trousers, and there is no decoration of embroidery lace on the collars and sleeves of the tops. The latter consists of tops, trousers, long gowns, skirts, embroidered shoes, waist belts, chest aprons, kerchiefs and ornaments. The styles of Buyi men's costumes are basically the same everywhere, usually including kerchiefs. There are two types of kerchiefs: striped ones and pure cyan ones. Their clothes are Duijin short tops with two fronts of the upper garments opposite each other, white inside and cyan or blue outside, and their trousers are long. The elderly men mostly wear short tops with large sleeves, or cyan and blue long gowns, with cloth stockings on their feet. Most Buyi women wear short tops with big Yijin (two fronts of an upper garment), and some wear long pleated skirts. In the area of the Biandan Mountain inhabited by the Buyi people, young girls like wearing short tops with embroidered and rolled edges and tying silk waist belts, with brocade headscarves on their heads and wrapped around their thick braids. On their foreheads are brocade patterns and several circles of braids. They wear trousers and embroidered shoes. Young women wear batik pleated skirts and short tops with slanted Yijin (two fronts of an upper garment) and embroidered shoulders. They use various colored threads to embroider

---

① 《布依族服饰文化》，安龙县人民政府网，http://www. gzal. gov. cn/zxfw/xxlyfw/fsmq/201810/t20181025_3242781. html，检索日期：2018 年 7 月 25 日。

two rows of small within-square semicircular patterns along the shoulder and floral patterns on both sides of the collar, which are eye-catching in color. The middle parts of the tops and sleeves are made of brocade, and the upper and lower parts are made of batik. The lower hems of the tops are brocade lace with a length of about one *cun* (a Chinese unit of length, with one *cun* roughly equal to 1.3 inches). They wear long embroidered or brocade aprons on the chest, and tie light-colored satin waist belts. On their heads are brocade kerchiefs, with a bunch of silk whiskers made of various colored threads hanging around their ears. The married women wear "Gengkao headwear", which is made of bamboo shoot shells and cloth and shaped like a dustpan, round at the front and rectangular at the back. At every grand festival or banquet, women like wearing all kinds of silver jewelry, such as earrings, rings, necklaces, hairpins and bracelets.

侗族妇女服饰
Women's Costume of the Dong Nationality

第24项：侗族服饰

项目序号：1371	项目编号：X-158	公布时间：2014（第四批）	类别：民俗
所属地区：贵州省	类型：新增项目	申报地区或单位：贵州省黔东南苗族侗族自治州	

　　侗族服饰多用自种的棉花、自纺自织自染的侗布为衣料，细布、绸缎多做盛装配饰。侗族服饰多为青、紫、黑、蓝、白和浅蓝等色，分不同的季节和场合穿用。

　　侗族服饰主要分为男子服饰、妇女服饰和儿童童装三种。侗族男子服饰主要有两种款式：（1）对襟窄裤式；（2）右衽短衣宽裤式。此外，每逢盛大节庆时，侗族男子还穿着特制服饰，如"芦笙踩堂"的百鸟衣，"抢花炮"的武士装束，"抬官人"的芦笙衣饰等，并"以金鸡羽插髻"为饰。侗族妇女服饰包括衣、裙、裤、鞋、头巾、发饰和首饰。按不同地区，侗族妇女服饰可分为六种类型：（1）对襟裙装式；（2）对襟裤装式；（3）交襟左衽裙装式；（4）交襟左衽裤装式；（5）右衽大襟裙装式；（6）右衽大襟裤装式。此外，侗族妇女佩戴的银器首饰也是其服饰风格的重要部分。日常便装的首饰主要有头替、银梳、耳环和手镯，对襟裙装还有胸兜挂链以及悬于背上的S型银垂和六面银花等饰品。侗族童装一般是根据各地区大人的服饰款式加以剪裁制作，更加简单方便，特别是女孩的服饰款式，基本上是母亲服饰款式的简化。5～6岁以下男孩着小筒开档裤，穿对襟式便衣。女孩穿裙或裤式便装，蓄长发挽髻，脚穿各式绣花童鞋。在头顶，侗族儿童还会戴各种精致的童帽，如狗头绣花帽、狮头绣花帽、猫头绣花帽、兔头绣花帽及鱼尾绣花帽等，这是侗族原始

贵州省 国家级非物质文化遗产文献资料汇编（汉英对照）

The Documentary Compilation of the State-level Intangible Cultural Heritage of Guizhou Province (Chinese-English Versions)

风俗习惯的遗传。[①]

Item 24: the Costumes of the Dong Nationality

Item Serial Number: 1371	Item ID Number: X-158	Released Date: 2014 (Batch 4)	Category: Folk Custom
Affiliated Province: Guizhou Province	Type: New Item	Application Province or Unit: Qiandongnan Miao and Dong Autonomous Prefecture, Guizhou Province	

The Costumes of the Dong Nationality mostly use self-planted cotton and self-spin, self-woven and self-dyed Dong cloth as clothing materials, with fine cloth and satin as accessories of the splendid attire. They are often in cyan, purple, black, blue, white, light blue, etc., worn in different seasons and on different occasions.

The Costumes of the Dong Nationality are mainly divided into three kinds: Men's Costumes, Women's Costumes and Children's Costumes. Men's Costumes of the Dong Nationality mainly have two styles: Duijin tops with two fronts of the upper garments opposite each other and narrow-legged trousers, and Youren short tops with the left fronts of the upper garments covering the right ones and wide-legged trousers. Besides, at every grand festival celebration, the Dong men will wear specially-made costumes, such as the Hundred-bird Costumes for "Lusheng Caitang Dance", warrior costumes for "Scrambling for Huapao (fireworks)" and Lusheng costumes for "Taiguanren (carrying Guanren disguised by young kids on sedan chairs around the village to pray for timely wind and rain, prosperity as well as safety)", with "golden pheasants' feathers inserted in hair buns" as the decoration. Women's Costumes of the Dong Nationality include clothes, skirts, trousers, shoes, headscarves, hair accessories and ornaments. They can be divided into six types according to different regions: (1) Duijin tops with two fronts of the upper garments opposite each other and skirts; (2) Duijin tops with two fronts of the upper garments opposite each other and trousers; (3) Jiaojin Zuoren tops with the right fronts of the upper garments covering the left ones and skirts; (4) Jiaojin Zuoren tops with the right fronts of the upper garments covering the left ones and trousers; (5) Youren big-Yijin tops with the left

① 石佳能，《侗族服饰文化简论》，载《贵州民族研究》，1998年第2期，第89-96页。

fronts of the upper garments covering the right ones and skirts; (6) Youren big-Yijin tops with the left fronts of the upper garments covering the right ones and trousers. In addition, the silver ornaments worn by the Dong women are also an important part of their clothing style. The ornaments for daily casual clothes mainly include headwear, silver combs, earrings and bracelets. For Duijin tops with two fronts of the upper garments opposite each other and skirts, there are also other accessories, such as Xiongdou (an embroidered undergarment covering the chest and abdomen) and chains, as well as S-shaped silver pendants and six-sided silver flowers which hang from the back. Children's Costumes of the Dong Nationality are generally cut and made according to the styles of adults' costumes in various regions, which is done more easily and conveniently. In particular, girls' costume styles are basically the simplification of their mothers'. Boys under the age of 5-6 wear narrow-legged trousers with a split crotch and Duijin-style casual clothes with two fronts of the upper garments opposite each other. Girls wear casual clothes of skirts or trousers, with their long hair in buns and their feet wearing various embroidered children's shoes. On their heads, the Dong children also wear various exquisite children's hats, such as Dog's Head-embroidered Hat, Lion's Head-embroidered Hat, Cat's Head-embroidered Hat, Rabbit's Head-embroidered Hat and Fish's Tail-embroidered Hat, which is the inheritance of the primitive customs and habits of the Dong nationality.

迎汪公
Welcoming Wanggong Deity

第25项：
民间信俗
（屯堡抬亭子）

项目序号：992	项目编号：X-85	公布时间：2014（第四批）	类别：民俗
所属地区：贵州省	类型：扩展项目	申报地区或单位：贵州省安顺市西秀区	

　　屯堡抬亭子，即"迎汪公"，又叫"迎神""迎菩萨"，主要流传于贵州省安顺市西秀区所辖七眼桥、大西桥一带的屯堡村寨，已沿袭数百年。

　　屯堡村寨民间宗教信仰中的神灵颇多，以祭祀汪公最为普遍和隆重。屯堡人受先祖江南的区域文化"祭汪公"活动影响，视汪公为先祖神，每逢正月十八汪公诞日，到汪公庙内献祭，祈汪公保佑丰衣足食，清吉平安。而鲍屯、吉昌屯的村民则要在正月十七、十八、十九这三日抬汪公游村，民间称这一活动为"抬汪公"，也称为"抬亭子"。"抬亭子"当天，村民在汪公庙前举行隆重的祭祀仪式后，抬着汪公像在屯中巡游，道路两旁，屯堡人家摆上供品，点烛上香，燃放爆竹迎接。巡游队伍中，还有古装花车、腰鼓队和地戏队等，充满了浓郁的屯堡民俗风情。[①]屯堡抬亭子活动将古代江淮地区的社火民俗活动完整地保存了下来。

---

① 王砂砂，《贵州安顺"屯堡抬亭子"》，http://www.gzfwz.org.cn/xwdt/201804/t20180416_3122257.html，检索日期：2019年8月8日。

Item 25: the Folk-belief Custom (Lifting Up Wanggong Deity's Shrine of Tunpu Villages)

Item Serial Number: 992	Item ID Number: X-85	Released Date: 2014 (Batch 4)	Category: Folk Custom
Affiliated Province: Guizhou Province	Type: Extended Item	Application Province or Unit: Xixiu District, Anshun City, Guizhou Province	

Lifting Up Wanggong Deity's Shrine of Tunpu Villages, also known as "Welcoming Wanggong Deity", "Welcoming the Deity" or "Welcoming the Bodhisattva", is mainly spread in Tunpu villages in Qiyanqiao Township and Daxiqiao Township under the jurisdiction of Xixiu District, Anshun City, Guizhou Province. It has been passed down for hundreds of years.

There are many deities in the folk religious beliefs of Tunpu villages, among which the most common and ceremonious is offering sacrifices to Wanggong Deity. Influenced by their ancestors' regional cultural activity of "offering sacrifices to Wanggong Deity" in regions south of the Yangtze River, the Tunpu people regard Wanggong as their ancestral god. On the 18th day of the first month of the lunar calendar, Wanggong Deity's birthday, villagers go to Wanggong Deity's Temple to offer sacrifices, praying for his blessing of adequate food and clothes, tranquility, auspiciousness and safety. People in Baotun Village and Jichang Village carry Wanggong Deity on a three-day tour in the village on the 17th, the 18th and the 19th days of the first month of the lunar calendar. Villagers call this activity as "Lifting Up Wanggong Deity", or "Lifting Up Wanggong Deity's Shrine". On this day, after a solemn sacrificial ceremony in front of Wanggong Deity's Temple, villagers carry Wanggong's statue on a tour in the village. The Tunpu people place sacrificial offerings on both sides of the road, light candles and incense, and set off firecrackers to welcome it. In the parade team, there are also ancient-style festooned carts, a Waist Drum team and a Ground Opera team, which are full of rich Tunpu folk custom. The activity of **Lifting Up Wanggong Deity's Shrine of Tunpu Villages** has completely preserved the folk activity of Shehuo in ancient Changjiang-Huaihe area.

贵州省·国家级非物质文化遗产文献资料汇编（汉英对照）

The Documentary Compilation of the State-level Intangible Cultural Heritage of Guizhou Province (Chinese-English Versions)

刊刻款文的石碑——法石
the Stone of Law—a stone tablet with inscriptions of Kuan texts

第26项：规约习俗（侗族款约）

项目序号：1217	项目编号：X-142	公布时间：2014（第四批）	类别：民俗
所属地区：贵州省	类型：扩展项目	申报地区或单位：贵州省黎平县	

　　侗族款约是侗族社会以氏族血缘关系为核心，以地域为纽带的组织形式，款规款约是款组织为了规范成员的行为制定的一系列制度规定。流传于贵州省的侗族群体中间。

　　"款"是古代侗族地区的民间自治与自卫组织，有大款、中款和小款之分："大款为整个侗族地区所订立"①；"中款为局部地区，一般为几个洞联合订立"②；"小款一般是一个洞（几个村寨）根据大款、中款所定的原则又加以具体化，补充订立一些实施细节的条款"③。不论大款、中款或小款，"都有款场（立法和执法的场所）、法石（刊刻款文的石碑），'立碑戒告，万古不移'，使侗款法律化、制度化"④。侗族款约的形式除了款规中的款词外，还有相关的一些活动，如讲款活动、款首和款社内部的聚会议款，款与款之间的互相交往等。侗族款约有十种：族源款、款坪款、约法款、出征款、英雄款、创世款、习俗款、祝赞款、请神款和祭祀款。族源款是记述各个族群历史的款词；款坪款是记述各个款组织的区划和村寨范围的款词；约法款记述的是各款组织制定的规章约法及维护社区社会秩序的共同规约条款；出征款是款组织集结款众抗御外来强暴，出征前的盟誓款词；英雄款是颂扬、缅怀侗族历史英雄人物，记述英雄的功绩和战斗历程的款词；创世款是叙述世间万物和人类起源的款词；习俗款是介绍侗族各种风俗习惯来历的款词；祝赞款是款社之间

---

① 《黎平县志》编纂委员会，《黎平县志》，成都：巴蜀书社，1989年，第147页。

② 同上。

③ 同上。

④ 同上。

交往互相祝福、赞颂的款词；请神款是进行合款仪式活动邀请诸神参与助款神威的款词；祭祀款有两种，一是悼词，二是神祭款和送神款。① 侗族款约使得侗族社会保持长期的和谐平稳，由此将侗族神秘的传统文化很好地传承至今。

Item 26: the Stipulation Custom (Kuan Stipulation of the Dong Nationality)

Item Serial Number: 1217	Item ID Number: X-142	Released Date: 2014 (Batch 4)	Category: Folk Custom
Affiliated Province: Guizhou Province	Type: Extended Item	Application Province or Unit: Liping County, Guizhou Province	

Kuan Stipulation of the Dong Nationality is an organizational form in the Dong society centered on the blood relationship of clans and linked by regions. All clauses of Kuan Stipulation are a series of institutional stipulations formulated by Kuan organizations to regulate the behavior of their members, spread among the Dong people in Guizhou Province.

"Kuan" is a self-governing and self-defensive folk organization in ancient Dong areas, which is divided into three kinds: big Kuan, medium Kuan and small Kuan. "Big Kuan is concluded for the whole area of the Dong nationality"; "medium Kuan is concluded for local areas, usually for several Dong (stockaded villages)"; and "small Kuan is usually the clauses further concretized and supplemented for implementation details by one Dong (several stockaded villages) according to the principles set by big Kuan and medium Kuan". No matter whether it is big Kuan, medium Kuan or small Kuan, "there is a Kuan Site (the place of legislation and law enforcement) and a Stone of Law (a stone tablet with inscriptions of Kuan texts). 'Erecting a stone tablet to warn people, with no change forever' can make **Kuan Stipulation of the Dong Nationality** legalized and institutionalized." Its forms include Kuan texts and some related activities, such as activities of publicizing Kuan Stipulation, meetings of Kuan leaders and those within Kuan communities for discussing Kuan Stipulation, and the

① 班裕思，《"侗族款约"入选国家非遗名录唤醒了黎平县的民族传统文化记忆》，http://www. gzfwz. org. cn/xwdt/201804/t20180416_3122883. html，检索日期：2019 年 7 月 25 日。

贵州省 国家级非物质文化遗产文献资料汇编（汉英对照）

The Documentary Compilation of the State-level Intangible Cultural Heritage of Guizhou Province (Chinese-English Versions)

mutual intercourse between different Kuan organizations. **Kuan Stipulation of the Dong Nationality** is divided into ten kinds: Kuan of Ethnic Origin, Kuan Concerning the Locations of Kuan Organizations, Kuan of Regulations, Kuan of Going Out to Battle, Kuan of Heroes, Kuan of the Creation, Kuan of Customs, Kuan of Blessing and Praising, Kuan of Inviting the Deity and Kuan of Offering Sacrifices. Kuan of Ethnic Origin is the Kuan texts that record the history of each ethnic group; Kuan Concerning the Locations of Kuan Organizations is the Kuan texts that record the regional division and village scope of each Kuan organization; Kuan of Regulations records the rules and regulations formulated by each Kuan organization, and the common stipulations for maintaining the social order of communities; Kuan of Going Out to Battle is the Kuan texts about the pledge made by the masses who are gathered by Kuan organizations before going out to battle for the purpose of resisting external violence; Kuan of Heroes is the Kuan texts that praise and commemorate the historical heroes of the Dong nationality and those that record their exploits and fighting histories; Kuan of the Creation is the Kuan texts that narrate the origins of all things in the world and human beings; Kuan of Customs is the Kuan texts that introduce the origins of all customs and habits of the Dong nationality; Kuan of Blessing and Praising is the Kuan texts that are concerned with the mutual blessing and praise between Kuan communities; Kuan of Inviting the Deity is the Kuan texts used for inviting the deities to participate in the ceremonial activity of combining different Kuan organizations and to endow them with divine power; and Kuan of Offering Sacrifices is divided into two kinds: one is the eulogy, and the other is Kuan of Offering Sacrifices to the Deity and Kuan of Seeing Off the Deity. **Kuan Stipulation of the Dong Nationality** has made the Dong society keep long-term harmony and stability, thus making the mysterious traditional culture of the Dong nationality passed down quite well up to now.

附录 Appendixes

一、词汇表 Glossary

第一批：Batch 1

第二批：Batch 2

第三批：Batch 3

第四批：Batch 4

新增项目：New Item

扩展项目：Extended Item

项目序号：Item Serial Number

项目编号：Item ID Number

公布时间：Released Date

类别：Category

所属地区：Affiliated Province

类型：Type

申报地区或单位：Application Province or Unit

民间文学：Folk Literature

传统音乐：Traditional Music

传统舞蹈：Traditional Dance

传统戏剧：Traditional Opera

曲艺：Quyi (a general term for all Chinese talking-and-singing art forms)

传统体育、游艺与杂技：Traditional Sports, Recreations and Acrobatics

传统美术：Traditional Fine Arts

传统技艺：Traditional Craft

传统医药：Traditional Medicine

民俗：Folk Custom

二、贵州省国家级（1—4 批）非物质文化遗产项目名称汉英对照
The Chinese-English Versions of the Names of the State-level Intangible Cultural Heritage Items of Guizhou Province (Batches 1-4)

第一章　民间文学　Chapter One　Folk Literature

苗族古歌：The Ancient Song of the Miao Nationality

刻道：*Kheik Det (carved song stick) Epic*

仰阿莎：*Yang'asha Poem*

布依族盘歌：Pange Songs of the Buyi Nationality

珠郎娘美：*Zhulang and Niangmei Folktale*

苗族贾理：Jaxlil of the Miao Nationality

亚鲁王：*King Yalu*

第二章　传统音乐　Chapter Two　Traditional Music

侗族大歌：Al Laox of the Dong Nationality

侗族琵琶歌：Pipa Songs of the Dong Nationality

铜鼓十二调：Twelve Tunes of the Bronze Drum

苗族民歌（苗族飞歌）：Folk Songs of the Miao Nationality (Flying Songs of the Miao Nationality)

布依族民歌（好花红调）：Folk Songs of the Buyi Nationality (Haohuahong Tune)

芦笙音乐（苗族芒筒芦笙）：Lusheng Music (Mangtong and Lusheng of the Miao Nationality)

布依族勒尤：Leyou Musical Instrument of the Buyi Nationality

多声部民歌（苗族多声部民歌）：Polyphonic Folk Songs (Polyphonic Folk Songs of the Miao Nationality)

彝族民歌（彝族山歌）：Folk Songs of the Yi Nationality (Mountain Songs of the Yi Nationality)

土家族民歌：Folk Songs of the Tujia Nationality

第三章　传统舞蹈　Chapter Three　Traditional Dance

芦笙舞（锦鸡舞）：Lusheng Dance (the Golden Pheasant Dance)

芦笙舞（鼓龙鼓虎－长衫龙）：Lusheng Dance (the Dragon-and-tiger Dance in Long Gowns)

芦笙舞（滚山珠）：Lusheng Dance (Gunshanzhu Dance)

苗族芦笙舞：Lusheng Dance of the Miao Nationality

木鼓舞（反排苗族木鼓舞）：the Wooden-drum Dance (Fanpai Wooden-drum
　　Dance of the Miao Nationality)

毛南族打猴鼓舞：the Monkey Drum Dance of the Maonan Nationality

瑶族猴鼓舞：the Monkey Drum Dance of the Yao Nationality

彝族铃铛舞：the Small Bell Dance of the Yi Nationality

布依族高台狮灯舞：the High-platform Lion Lantern Dance of the Buyi Nationality

铜鼓舞（雷山苗族铜鼓舞）：the Bronze-drum Dance (Leishan Bronze-drum Dance
　　of the Miao Nationality)

阿妹戚托：Amei Qituo Dance

布依族转场舞：Zhuanchang Dance of the Buyi Nationality

第四章　传统戏剧　Chapter Four　Traditional Opera

思南花灯戏：Sinan Lantern Opera

花灯戏：the Lantern Opera

侗戏：Dong Opera

布依戏：Buyi Opera

彝族撮泰吉：Cuotaiji Opera of the Yi Nationality

傩戏（德江傩堂戏）：Nuo Opera (Dejiang Nuotang Opera)

傩戏（仡佬族傩戏）：Nuo Opera (Nuo Opera of the Gelao Nationality)

傩戏（荔波布依族傩戏）：Nuo Opera (Libo Nuo Opera of the Buyi Nationality)

傩戏（庆坛）：Nuo Opera (Qingtan)

安顺地戏：Anshun Ground Opera

木偶戏（石阡木偶戏）：the Puppet Play (Shiqian Puppet Play)

黔剧：Guizhou Opera

第五章　曲艺　Chapter Five　Quyi (a general term for all Chinese talking-and-
singing art forms)

布依族八音坐唱：Bayin Sitting-and-singing of the Buyi Nationality

第六章　传统体育、游艺与杂技　Chapter Six　Traditional Sports, Recreations
and Acrobatics

赛龙舟：the Dragon-boat Racing

·贵州省·国家级非物质文化遗产文献资料汇编（汉英对照）

The Documentary Compilation of the State-level Intangible Cultural Heritage of Guizhou Province (Chinese-English Versions)

第七章　传统美术　Chapter Seven　Traditional Fine Arts

苗绣（雷山苗绣）：Miao Embroidery (Leishan Miao Embroidery)

苗绣（花溪苗绣）：Miao Embroidery (Huaxi Miao Embroidery)

苗绣（剑河苗绣）：Miao Embroidery (Jianhe Miao Embroidery)

苗绣：Miao Embroidery

水族马尾绣：the Horsetail Embroidery of the Shui Nationality

苗族剪纸：Paper Cutting of the Miao Nationality

剪纸（水族剪纸）：Paper Cutting (Paper Cutting of the Shui Nationality)

泥塑（苗族泥哨）：Clay Sculpture (Clay Whistles of the Miao Nationality)

侗族刺绣：the Embroidery of the Dong Nationality

第八章　传统技艺　Chapter Eight　Traditional Craft

苗族蜡染技艺：the Batik Craft of the Miao Nationality

蜡染技艺：the Batik Craft

蜡染技艺（黄平蜡染技艺）：the Batik Craft (Huangping Batik Craft)

苗寨吊脚楼营造技艺：the Craft of Constructing Diaojiao Buildings (pile dwellings) of Miao Stockaded Villages

苗族芦笙制作技艺：the Craft of Making Lusheng Musical Instruments of the Miao Nationality

民族乐器制作技艺（苗族芦笙制作技艺）：the Craft of Making National Musical Instruments (the Craft of Making Lusheng Musical Instruments of the Miao Nationality)

玉屏箫笛制作技艺：the Craft of Making Yuping Xiao and Flutes

苗族银饰锻制技艺：the Craft of Making Silver Ornaments of the Miao Nationality

茅台酒酿制技艺：the Craft of Making Maotai Liquor

皮纸制作技艺：the Craft of Making Bark Paper

陶器烧制技艺（牙舟陶器烧制技艺）：the Craft of Firing Pottery (the Craft of Firing Yazhou Pottery)

苗族织锦技艺：the Craft of Making Brocade of the Miao Nationality

枫香印染技艺：the Craft of Fengxiang Dip Dyeing

彝族漆器髹饰技艺：the Craft of Painting Lacquerware of the Yi Nationality

侗族木构建筑营造技艺：the Craft of Constructing Wooden Structures of the Dong Nationality

银饰制作技艺（苗族银饰制作技艺）：the Craft of Making Silver Ornaments (the Craft of Making Silver Ornaments of the Miao Nationality)

绿茶制作技艺（都匀毛尖茶制作技艺）：the Craft of Making Green Tea (the Craft of Making Duyun Maojian Tea)

第九章　传统医药　**Chapter Nine　Traditional Medicine**

传统中医药文化（同济堂传统中药文化）：Traditional Chinese Medicine Culture (the Traditional Chinese Medicine Culture of TONGJI TANG)

瑶族医药（药浴疗法）：the Medicine of the Yao Nationality (the Therapy of Medicated Bath)

苗医药（骨伤蛇伤疗法）：the Medicine of the Miao Nationality (the Therapies for Bone Injuries and Snakebites)

苗医药（九节茶药制作工艺）：the Medicine of the Miao Nationality (the Craft of Making Jiujiecha Medicine)

侗医药（过路黄药制作工艺）：the Medicine of the Dong Nationality (the Craft of Making Guoluhuang Medicine)

中医传统制剂方法（廖氏化风丹制作技艺）：the Traditional Preparation Methods of Chinese Medicine (the Craft of Making the Liao Family's Huafeng Pill)

布依族医药（益肝草制作技艺）：the Medicine of the Buyi Nationality (the Craft of Making Liver-protecting Herb Medicine)

第十章　民俗　**Chapter Ten　Folk Custom**

苗族鼓藏节：the Drum Worship Festival of the Miao Nationality

水族端节：the Duan Festival (New Year) of the Shui Nationality

布依族查白歌节：the Zhabai Singing Festival of the Buyi Nationality

苗族姊妹节：the Sisters' Festival of the Miao Nationality

侗族萨玛节：the Sama Festival of the Dong Nationality

仡佬毛龙节：the Maolong (legendary dragon) Festival of the Gelao Nationality

水书习俗：the Custom of the Shui Writing

苗族独木龙舟节：the Dumu Dragon Boat Festival of the Miao Nationality

苗族跳花节：the Tiaohua (dancing around the flower tree) Festival of the Miao Nationality

苗年：the New Year of the Miao Nationality

苗族服饰：the Costumes of the Miao Nationality

布依族"三月三"："the Double Third Festival" of the Buyi Nationality

三月三（报京三月三）：the Double Third Festival (the Baojing Double Third Festival)

侗年：the New Year of the Dong Nationality

歌会（四十八寨歌节）：the Singing Gathering (the Singing Festival of 48 Stockaded Villages)

月也：Yueye Activity

苗族栽岩习俗：the Rock-planting Custom of the Miao Nationality

火把节（彝族火把节）：the Torch Festival (the Torch Festival of the Yi Nationality)

农历二十四节气（石阡说春）：the Twenty-four Solar Terms of the Lunar Calendar (Shiqian Spring Saying)

仡佬族三幺台习俗：the Sanyaotai (three-feast) Custom of the Gelao Nationality

布依族服饰：the Costumes of the Buyi Nationality

侗族服饰：the Costumes of the Dong Nationality

民间信俗（屯堡抬亭子）：the Folk-belief Custom (Lifting Up Wanggong Deity's Shrine of Tunpu Villages)

规约习俗（侗族款约）：the Stipulation Custom (Kuan Stipulation of the Dong Nationality)

三、一至十章中的文化负载词汉英对照
The Chinese-English Versions of the Culture-loaded Words
in Chapters 1-10

第一章　民间文学　Chapter One　Folk Literature

苗族史诗：the epic of the Miao nationality

清水江流域：the Qingshui River Basin

盘歌问答：singing in antiphonal style by asking and answering questions

歌骨歌花：singing the main song and chorus

刻木：the Carved Stick

歌棒：the Song Stick

刻木记事符号：wood-carved notations for recording events

飞云大峡谷：Feiyun Grand Canyon

《苗族开亲歌》：*Kaiqin Song of the Miao Nationality*

对唱：antiphonal singing

比兴：Bi (analogy) and Xing (borrowing) techniques

苗族美神：the god of beauty of the Miao nationality

五言韵文体：five-character literary compositions in rhyme

北盘江流域：the Beipanjiang River Basin

套歌：group songs

户外歌：outdoor songs

毕摩：Bimo (the high priest in the traditional religion of the Yi nationality)

独唱：solo singing

一人领唱众人合唱：one person leading the singing with others singing in chorus

衬词：foil words

月琴：Yueqin (a four-stringed plucked musical instrument with a full-moon-shaped sound box)

箫筒：Xiaotong flutes

木叶：Muye (leaves)

贯洞侗乡：Guandong, the area inhabited by the Dong people

娘美井：Niangmei Well

江剑坡：Jiangjian Slope

栽岩立法：planting rocks for legislation

· **贵州省** · 国家级非物质文化遗产文献资料汇编（汉英对照）

The Documentary Compilation of the State-level Intangible Cultural Heritage of Guizhou Province (Chinese-English Versions)

理老司法：performing judicial administration by leaders of stockaded villages

鼓社执法：enforcing the law through drum communes

亚鲁王国：the Kingdom of Yalu

第二章　传统音乐　Chapter Two　Traditional Music

鼓楼大歌：the Drum Tower al laox

大琵琶：Big Pipa (a plucked string instrument with a fretted fingerboard)

"桑嘎"（歌师）："Sangga" (the singer)

琵琶：Pipa (a plucked string instrument with a fretted fingerboard)

定弦：tuning up

牛腿琴：Niutui Lute (a bow-and-string instrument of the Dong nationality, named for its slender body looking like cattle's thigh)

行歌坐夜：Xingge Zuoye (singing songs while sitting through the night, a custom of the Dong nationality for young men and women to sing love songs and get to know each other)

唢呐：Suona Horn (a woodwind instrument)

皮鼓：the Leather Drum

大镲：big cymbals

滑音：the glide note

甩音：the flinging note

敬客歌：the song of respecting guests

问候歌：the song of greeting

抬爱歌：the song of favoring

"二八栏杆"："Erba Langan", which means that they have gained harmonious affections

芦笙：Lusheng Musical Instruments

祖鼓：the Ancestral Drum

布依族八音坐唱乐班：the troupes of Bayin Sitting-and-singing of the Buyi Nationality

自然换气法：natural ventilation method

循环换气法：cyclic ventilation method

宫：Gong (one of the five ancient Chinese musical notes equal to "Do" in western musical scale)

商：Shang (one of the five ancient Chinese musical notes equal to "Re" in western musical scale)

羽：Yu (one of the five ancient Chinese musical notes equal to "La" in western musical scale)

徵：Zhi (one of the five ancient Chinese musical notes equal to "Sol" in western musical scale)

角：Jue (one of the five ancient Chinese musical notes equal to "Mi" in western musical scale)

纯五度：perfect fifth

纯八度：octave

大三度：major third

大六度：major sixth

第三章　传统舞蹈　Chapter Three　Traditional Dance

麻鸟型超短裙：the Hemp Bird-type Miniskirts

跳月：the Moon Dance

锦鸡银饰：gold-pheasant silver ornaments

绣花超短百褶裙：embroidered ultra-short pleated skirts

翘尖绣花鞋：embroidered shoes with upturned tips

银角冠：the silver horn crowns

花带：the flower belts

跳月场：the Moon Dancing Field

大襟长衫：long gowns with big Jin (two fronts of an upper garment)

箐鸡翎帽：pheasant-feather hats

绣花白褂：embroidered white coats

歪梳苗支系：the Waishu Miao branch

"绕坡"活动：the activity of "circling the slope"

箐鸡舞：the Pheasant Dance

小花苗支系：the Xiaohua Miao branch

芦笙棒舞：Lusheng Stick Dance

"蒙洒"苗人：the "Mengsa" Miao people

木鼓：the Wooden Drum

丑年：the year of Chou (the second of the Twelve Earthly Branches)

祭鼓节：the Drum-worship Festival

铜鼓：the Bronze Drum

白裤瑶：the Baiku branch of the Yao nationality

·贵州省·国家级非物质文化遗产文献资料汇编（汉英对照）

The Documentary Compilation of the State-level Intangible Cultural Heritage of Guizhou Province (Chinese-English Versions)

饭甑：a rice steamer

共鸣箱：a sound box

笃尔帝：King Du'er

祭祀歌舞场：the Sacrificial-song Dance Hall

盘江流域：the Panjiang River Basin

三国：the Three Kingdoms

南北朝：the Northern and Southern dynasties

八仙桌：Baxian Tables (a kind of old-fashioned square table for eight people)

响器：Xiangqi (sound-making instruments)

马锣：Maluo (a kind of Chinese percussion instrument)

堂锣：Tangluo (a copper percussion instrument)

鼓藏节：the Drum Worship Festival

祭鼓舞：the Drum Worship Dance

姑娘出嫁舞：the Girl's Dance of Getting Married

跳脚舞：the Foot Dance

东方踢踏舞：the Oriental Tap Dance

晒坝场：the Threshing Ground

浪哨：Langshao activity (having a love affair)

跳转场：dancing on vacant lots

第四章　传统戏剧　**Chapter Four　Traditional Opera**

灯夹戏：the Lantern plus Opera

台灯：the Stage Lantern

傩堂戏：Nuotang Opera

湘剧：Hunan Opera

辰河戏：Chenhe Opera

旦角：Dan Character (a female role)

灯调：the lantern tune

正调：the formal tune

杂调：the miscellaneous tune

小调：the minor tune

曲牌：Qupai (the tune name of a melody)

二胡：Erhu (a two-stringed bowed instrument)

三弦：Sanxian (a three-stringed plucked musical instrument)

地灯：the Ground Lantern

元宵：the Lantern Festival

还愿：redeeming a vow to a god

愿灯：the Willing Lantern

侗琵琶：Dong Pipa (a plucked string instrument with a fretted fingerboard)

低胡：Bass Erhu (a two-stringed bowed instrument)

丑角：Chou Character (a clown)

八音坐弹：Bayin Sitting and Playing

板凳戏：the Bench Opera

尖子胡琴：Jianzi Huqin Musical Instruments

朴子胡琴：Puzi Huqin Musical Instruments

短箫：Short Xiao (a vertical bamboo flute)

木鱼：the Wooden Fish (a percussion instrument of a hollow wooden block, originally used by Buddhist priests to beat rhythm when chanting scriptures)

包包锣：Baobao Gong

小马锣：Small Maluo (a kind of Chinese percussion instrument)

生：Sheng Character (a male role in Chinese opera, usually referring to the role with a beard or a young man)

尺：*chi* (a Chinese unit of length, with one *chi* roughly equal to 13 inches)

山林老人：mountain forest elders

山神：mountain gods

坛班：altar troupes

傩坛：Nuotan Altar

山王：the Mountain King

秦童：Qintong (a role of clown in Nuo Opera)

文戏：Wenxi (operas characterized by singing and acting)

武戏：Wuxi (operas characterized by acrobatic fighting)

傩戏班子：Nuo Opera Troupe

做桃：Zuotao (making the peach)

架桥：Jiaqiao (building the bridge)

魔公：the Demon Lord

坛师：the Altar Master

庆坛：Qingtan

端公戏：Duangong Opera

贵州省 国家级非物质文化遗产文献资料汇编（汉英对照）

The Documentary Compilation of the State-level Intangible Cultural Heritage of Guizhou Province (Chinese-English Versions)

文坛：Civil Tan (altar)

武坛：Martial Arts Tan (altar)

做道场：make a Daochang (a place where the Taoist or Buddhist rites are performed)

跳端公：Duangong Dance

跳神：Tiaoshen (a sorcerer's dance in a trance)

神头：Shentou (the master of the troupe)

刻木人像：the carved wooden figure

锣鼓牌子：Gong-and-drum Paizi

头子：Touzi (role types)

高腔：high tone

平弹：Pingtan

牌子：Paizi (also called Qupai, meaning the tune name of a melody)

净：Jing Character (a male role in Chinese opera, usually with rough and bold personalities)

盔头：Kuitou (caps worn by actors)

蟒袍：the Python Robe (official robe)

撰本戏：the Compiled Benxi Play

小本子戏：the Short Benzi Play

庙会戏：the Temple-fair Play

愿戏：the Vow-fulfilling Play

众戏：the Masses Play

贵州弹词：Guizhou Tanci (a talking-and-singing art with roles performing it while sitting to the accompaniment of a dulcimer)

瓮琴：Wengqin Musical Instrument

小京胡：Small Jinghu (a traditional Chinese stringed instrument, also called Huqin Musical Instrument)

箫：Xiao (a vertical bamboo flute)

旦：Dan Character (a female role)

末：Mo Character (a middle-aged male role in Chinese opera)

丑：Chou Character (a clown)

小生：Xiaosheng (the young male role in Chinese opera)

正生：Zhengsheng (the main male role in Chinese opera)

老生：Laosheng (a male role of middle age and above in Chinese opera)

正旦：Zhengdan (the main female role in Chinese opera)

小旦：Xiaodan (a young female role in Chinese opera)

贴旦：Tiedan (a minor female role in Chinese opera)

花旦：Huadan (a young or middle-aged female role in Chinese opera often with lively or boisterous personality and a hint of comedy)

老旦：Laodan (an old female role in Chinese opera)

第五章　曲艺　Chapter Five　Quyi (a general term for all Chinese talking-and-singing art forms)

南盘江流域：the Nanpanjiang River Basin

牛骨胡：Niuguhu Musical Instrument

牛角胡：Niujiaohu Musical Instrument

葫芦琴：Huluqin Musical Instrument

葫芦胡：Huluhu Musical Instrument

刺鼓：Cigu Drum

竹鼓：the Bamboo Drum

勒朗：Lelang (a wind instrument of the Buyi nationality made of bamboo)

勒尤：Leyou Musical Instrument

闲调：the casual tune

第六章　传统体育、游艺与杂技　Chapter Six　Traditional Sports, Recreations and Acrobatics

端午、端阳：the Dragon Boat Festival

铜岩：Tongyan Rock

第七章　传统美术　Chapter Seven　Traditional Fine Arts

纸捻：Zhinian (paper rolled into slim strips)

清水江：the Qingshui River

吃牯脏：Chiguzang (also called the Drum Worship Festival, with cattle as sacrifices)

娘娘神：the Deity of Empress

灵房花：Lingfang Flowers (wreaths for the deceased)

第八章　传统技艺　Chapter Eight　Traditional Craft

榀：*pin* (a measurement unit, referring to a house frame)

·贵州省·国家级非物质文化遗产文献资料汇编（汉英对照）

The Documentary Compilation of the State-level Intangible Cultural Heritage of Guizhou Province (Chinese-English Versions)

笙斗：Shengdou (a container in Lusheng Musical Instruments where the air is
    retained and the reed is caused to vibrate)

坯、坯胎：Pi, Pitai (a product that already has the required shape but still needs
    processing)

雷公山：the Leigong Mountain

中裙苗：Zhongqun Miao (the Miao nationality wearing medium-length skirts)

寸：*cun* (a Chinese unit of length, with one *cun* roughly equal to 1.3 inches)

丈：*zhang* (a Chinese unit of length, with one *zhang* roughly equal to 131 inches)

火塘：the Fire Pit

清明：the Tomb Sweeping Day

第九章　传统医药　**Chapter Nine　Traditional Medicine**

仙灵骨葆胶囊（片）：Xianling Bone-protecting Capsules (tablets)

枣仁安神胶囊：Zaoren (kernels of wild jujubes) Tranquilizing Capsules

补肾益脑胶囊：Capsules of Tonifying Kidneys and Benefiting Brains

润燥止痒胶囊：Capsules of Moistening Dryness and Relieving Itching

心脑康胶囊：Heart-and-Brain Recovery Capsules

胶体果胶铋胶囊：Colloidal Bismuth Pectin Capsules

复方牙痛酊：Compound Toothache Tincture

滇白珠糖浆：Syrup of Dianbaizhu (*Gaultheria leucocarpa var. yunnanensis* in Latin)

诺氟沙星：Norfloxacin

复方甘草口服溶液：Compound Glycyrrhiza Oral Solution

掐痧：Qiasha (also called Jiusha, a popular treatment for sunstroke or other febrile
    diseases by repeatedly pinching a patient's neck, etc. to achieve congestion)

九节茶：Glabrous Sarcandra Herb

四块瓦：Sikuaiwa Herb (*Lysimachia paridiformis Franch.* in Latin)

柏林接骨散药：Bailin Bone-setting Powder

冰球子：Bingqiuzi Herb (*Oreorchis patens* in Latin)

降龙草：Xianglongcao Herb (*Hemiboea subcapitata Clarke* in Latin)

半边莲：Chinese lobelia

蜂斗菜：Fengdoucai Herb (*Petasites japonicus* in Latin)

山乌龟：Shanwugui Herb (*Stephania cepharantha Hayata* in Latin)

水冬瓜：Shuidonggua (*Adina racemosa* in Latin)

滚山珠：Gunshan Bead (also called Gunshan Worm)

气：Qi (vital energy)

廖氏化风丹：the Liao Family's Huafeng Pill

大娄山：the Dalou Mountain

厚朴：Houpu (*Magnolia officinalis* in Latin)

黄皮：Huangpi (*Clausena lansium* in Latin)

木通：Mutong (*Akebia* in Latin)

楼子：Louzi (*Trichosanthes* in Latin)

八角枫：Bajiaofeng (*Alangium chinense* in Latin)

南五味子：South Wuweizi (*Kadsura longipedunculata* in Latin)

朱砂根：Zhushagen (*Ardisia crenata* Sims in Latin)

天麻：Tianma (*Gastrodia elata* in Latin)

石斛：Shihu (*Dendrobium nobile* in Latin)

杜仲：Duzhong (*Eucommia ulmoides* in Latin)

何首乌：Heshouwu (*Pleuropterus multifloru* in Latin)

胆草：Dancao Herb (*Ajuga pantantha* in Latin)

天冬：Radix Asparagi

桔梗：Jugeng (*Platycodon grandiflorus* in Latin)

灵芝：Lingzhi (*Ganoderma lucidum* in Latin)

寨老：Zhailao (a head of a stockaded village)

地耳草：Di'er Grass (*Hypericum japonicum* in Latin)

酸汤杆：Suantanggan Herb (*Begonia circumlobata* Hance in Latin)

客蚂叶：Kemaye Herb (also called Cheqian Grass, *Plantago depressa* Willd. in Latin)

碓：Dui (a special tool made of stone and wood for hulling rice)

甑子：Zengzi (a wooden container used for steaming)

第十章 民俗 Chapter Ten Folk Custom

蝴蝶妈妈：the Mother Butterfly

鼓藏头：the Guzang Leader

申日：the day of Shen (the ninth of the Twelve Earthly Branches)

迎龙场：Yinglong Square

宝辇：Baonian Chariot

寅日：the day of Yin (the third of the Twelve Earthly Branches)

卯日：the day of Mao (the fourth of the Twelve Earthly Branches)

丑日：the day of Chou (the second of the Twelve Earthly Branches)

·贵州省·国家级非物质文化遗产文献资料汇编（汉英对照）

The Documentary Compilation of the State-level Intangible Cultural Heritage of Guizhou Province (Chinese-English Versions)

白鼓节：the White Drum Festival

春节：the Spring Festival

亥日：the day of Hai (the twelfth of the Twelve Earthly Branches)

除夕：the New Year's Eve

初一：the New Year's Day

端坡：Duanpo Slope

年坡：Nianpo Slope

斗牛舞：the Bullfight Dance

铜鼓舞：the Bronze Drum Dance

芦笙舞：Lusheng Dance

查白场：Zhabai Field

虎场坝：Huchang Dam

紫云歌仙：Purple-cloud Song Immortals

狗肉汤锅：dog-meat soup

五色糯米饭：five-color glutinous rice

冤枉坨：Yuanwang Lump (colored glutinous rice lumps)

查白树：Zhabai Tree

查白井：Zhabai Well

查白庙：Zhabai Temple

摩公：Mogong (the master of the Mo Sutra of the Buyi Nationality)

端公：Duangong (a wizard)

布依古歌：the Ancient Song of the Buyi Nationality

查白桥：Zhabai Bridge

查白河：the Zhabai River

松林坡：the Pine Forest Slope

查白洞：Zhabai Cave

花包：Huabao (cube-shaped embroidered bags)

浪哨：have a love affair

游方：Youfang (developing a romantic relationship between men and women of the Miao nationality)

姊妹饭：the Sisters' Meal

鼓场：the Drum Square

对歌：sing in antiphonal style

耶坪：Yeping Square

耶歌：Yege Song

竹王：the King of Bamboo

大年三十夜：the Chinese New Year's Eve

盘瓠：Panhu (a character in ancient Chinese mythology)

竹篾：thin bamboo slices

二龙抢宝：Two Dragons Snatch Treasures

懒龙翻身：Lazy Dragons Turn Over

单龙戏珠：One Dragon Plays with Beads

天鹅抱蛋：A Swan Embraces Eggs

倒挂金钩：Hanging Upside Down on the Golden Hook

犀牛望月：Rhinoceros Watch the Moon

螺丝旋顶：Screws Revolve on the Top

开光：Kaiguang (an activity to endow a certain object with the divine power through a special ritual)

请水：inviting water

烧龙：burning the dragon

开财门：opening the door of wealth

敬财神：honoring the god of wealth

甲骨文：oracle bone inscriptions

金文：bronze inscriptions

水书先生：a master of the Shui Writing

巴拉河：the Bala River

鼓主：the drum master

鼓头：the drum head

斗笠：Douli (a bamboo hat)

飞歌：the Flying Song

斤：*jin* (a Chinese unit of weight, with one *jin* equal to 0.5 kilogram)

花坡：the Flower Hillside

背扇：Beishan (special straps for carrying infants and young children)

都柳江：the Duliu River

汉族农历：the lunar calendar of the Han nationality

苗历：the calendar of the Miao nationality

糯米粑：glutinous rice cakes

翻鼓节：the Drum Festival

贵州省 国家级非物质文化遗产文献资料汇编（汉英对照）

The Documentary Compilation of the State-level Intangible Cultural Heritage of Guizhou Province (Chinese-English Versions)

岩妈：the Rock Mother

百鸟衣羽毛裙：the Hundred-bird Costume and Feather Skirt

衣襟：Yijin (two fronts of an upper garment)

百鸟衣：the Hundred-bird Costumes

锦鸡服：the Golden Pheasant Costume

蜡染古装：the Batik Ancient Costume

草龙：the Straw-woven Dragon

黄饭花：the Yellow Rice Flower (*Buddleja officinalis* in Latin)

绣球：the Embroidered Ball

播种节：the Sowing Festival

讨葱蒜：Asking for Scallions and Garlic

笆篓：Balou (small baskets made of bamboo strips used to hold fish and shrimp)

拦门酒：the Entrance-blocking Liquor

芦笙场：Lusheng Square

龙席：the Dragon Feast

糍粑：glutinous rice cakes

吃杨粑：eating Yangba Cake

还杨粑：repaying Yangba Cake

斗莎：Dousha (singing ancestral worship songs)

属"戊"的日子：the day of "Wu" (the fifth of the Ten Heavenly Stems)

套歌：Taoge (a series of songs)

踩歌堂：sing and dance in singing halls

鼓楼：the Drum Tower

"嘎锦"（侗族曲艺）："Gajin" (a kind of Quyi art of the Dong nationality)

月堂：the Moon Hall

议榔制：Yilang system

议榔规约：Yilang Stipulation

议榔栽岩：Yilang Rock Planting

议榔师：Yilang master

十月太阳历：the Ten-month Solar Calendar

北斗星：the Big Dipper

大寒：Dahan (the coldest)

十月年节：the Ten-month New Year Festival

彝族十月年：the Ten-month New Year of the Yi nationality

大暑：Dashu (the hottest)

星回节：the Xinghui Festival

唢呐：Suona Horn

立春：the Beginning of Spring

春官：Chunguan (the official in charge of spring affairs)

春倌：the messenger of spring

春分：the Spring Equinox

二十四个农事节气：24 Farming Solar Terms

渔樵耕读：Fishermen, Woodcutters, Farmers and Intellectuals

财神：the God of Wealth

米粑：rice cakes

米花糖：pop-rice candies

粽子：Zongzi (glutinous rice dumpling)

八仙醉酒：Eight Immortals' Drinking

四方团圆：All Parties' Reunion

烧白：Shaobai (steamed pork)

木耳：Mu'er (edible tree fungus)

对襟短衣：Duijin short tops with two fronts of the upper garments opposite each other

大袖短衣：short tops with large sleeves

布统袜：cloth stockings

大襟短衣：short tops with big Yijin (two fronts of an upper garment)

滚边短衣：short tops with embroidered and rolled edges

更考：Gengkao headwear

对襟窄裤式：Duijin tops with two fronts of the upper garments opposite each other and narrow-legged trousers

右衽短衣宽裤式：Youren short tops with the left fronts of the upper garments covering the right ones and wide-legged trousers

芦笙踩堂：Lusheng Caitang Dance

抢花炮：Scrambling for Huapao (fireworks)

抬官人：Taiguanren (carrying Guanren disguised by young kids on sedan chairs around the village to pray for timely wind and rain, prosperity as well as safety)

对襟裙装式：Duijin tops with two fronts of the upper garments opposite each other and skirts

对襟裤装式：Duijin tops with two fronts of the upper garments opposite each other and trousers

交襟左衽裙装式：Jiaojin Zuoren tops with the right fronts of the upper garments covering the left ones and skirts

交襟左衽裤装式：Jiaojin Zuoren tops with the right fronts of the upper garments covering the left ones and trousers

右衽大襟裙装式：Youren big-Yijin tops with the left fronts of the upper garments covering the right ones and skirts

右衽大襟裤装式：Youren big-Yijin tops with the left fronts of the upper garments covering the right ones and trousers

对襟裙装：Duijin tops with two fronts of the upper garments opposite each other and skirts

胸兜：Xiongdou (an embroidered undergarment covering the chest and abdomen)

小筒开档裤：narrow-legged trousers with a split crotch

对襟式便衣：Duijin-style casual clothes with two fronts of the upper garments opposite each other

狗头绣花帽：Dog's Head-embroidered Hat

狮头绣花帽：Lion's Head-embroidered Hat

猫头绣花帽：Cat's Head-embroidered Hat

兔头绣花帽：Rabbit's Head-embroidered Hat

鱼尾绣花帽：Fish's Tail-embroidered Hat

汪公：Wanggong Deity

汪公庙：Wanggong Deity's Temple

款组织：Kuan organizations

洞：Dong (stockaded villages)

款场：Kuan Site

法石：the Stone of Law

款文、款词：Kuan texts

款首：Kuan leaders

款社：Kuan communities

族源款：Kuan of Ethnic Origin

款坪款：Kuan Concerning the Locations of Kuan Organizations

约法款：Kuan of Regulations

出征款：Kuan of Going Out to Battle

英雄款：Kuan of Heroes
创世款：Kuan of the Creation
习俗款：Kuan of Customs
祝赞款：Kuan of Blessing and Praising
请神款：Kuan of Inviting the Deity
祭祀款：Kuan of Offering Sacrifices
神祭款：Kuan of Offering Sacrifices to the Deity
送神款：Kuan of Seeing Off the Deity

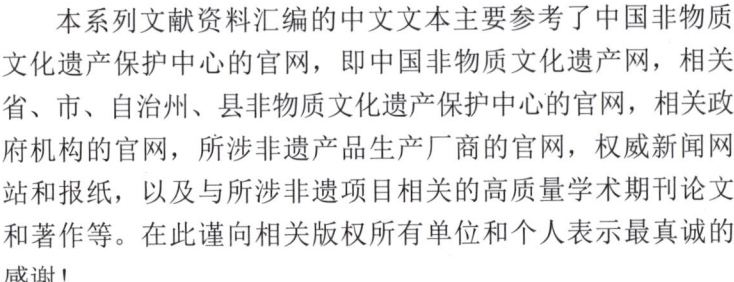

　　本系列文献资料汇编的中文文本主要参考了中国非物质文化遗产保护中心的官网，即中国非物质文化遗产网，相关省、市、自治州、县非物质文化遗产保护中心的官网，相关政府机构的官网，所涉非遗产品生产厂商的官网，权威新闻网站和报纸，以及与所涉非遗项目相关的高质量学术期刊论文和著作等。在此谨向相关版权所有单位和个人表示最真诚的感谢！

　　具体而言，《四川省国家级非物质文化遗产文献资料汇编（汉英对照）》［The Documentary Compilation of the State-level Intangible Cultural Heritage of Sichuan Province (Chinese-English Versions)］的中文文本主要参考了以下来源的资料：中国非物质文化遗产网、四川省非物质文化遗产保护中心官网、凉山彝族自治州非物质文化遗产保护中心官网、泸州市非物质文化遗产普及基地网、楚雄州图书馆彝族文献数据库系统、西昌市文化馆官网、夹江县文化馆官网、中国人民政治协商会议阿坝州黑水县委员会官网、中国旅游新闻网、腾讯网、中国新闻网、华夏经纬网、成都水井坊股份有限公司官网、普洱茶网、搜狐网、四川新闻网、人民网四川频道、《阿坝日报》、《成都日报》、《宜宾日报》、《四川日报》、《民族论坛》、《现代艺术》、《四川戏剧》、《民族艺术研究》、《四川党的建设》、《四川民族学院学报》、《本草纲目》、《情歌的故乡——康定》等。《云南省国家级非物质文化遗产文献资料汇编（汉英对照）》［The Documentary Compilation of the State-level Intangible Cultural Heritage of Yunnan Province (Chinese-English Versions)］的中文文本主要参考了以下来源的资料：中国非物质文化遗产网、云南非物质文化遗产保护网、迪庆非物质文化遗产保护、瑞丽市门户网、中国民族建筑研究会中国民族建筑网、楚雄州非遗网、中国·云龙网、蒙自市特产网、昆中药网、保山日报网、中国网、《中国青年报》、《大理日报》、《民族文学研究》、《民族艺术研究》、《民族艺术》、《民族音乐》、《玉溪师范学院学报》、《今日民族》、《建水县非物质文化遗产保护名录》（建水县文化和旅游局编）、《云南省志·医药志》、《云南档案》等。《贵州省国家级非物质文化遗产文献资料汇编（汉英对照）》［The Documentary Compilation of the State-level Intangible Cultural Heritage of Guizhou Province (Chinese-English Versions)］的中文文本主要参考了以下来源的资料：中国非物质文化遗产网、贵州省非物质文化遗产保护中心官网、黔西南州人民政府网、中国铜仁门户网、凯里市人民政府网、安龙县人民政府网、中华人民共和国国家民族事务委员会官网、贵州文明网、贵州百科信息网、多彩贵州网、中国布依网、黔东南新闻网、中华网、人民网、东方资讯网、同济堂官网、国医小镇网、《贵州民族报》、《黔西南日报》、《贵州社会科学》、《贵州民族研究》、《民族文学研究》、《贵州师范大学学报·社会科学版》、《武术研究》、《中华艺术论丛》、《贵州民族学院学报（哲社版）》、《民族学刊》、《安顺学院学报》、《中国山地民族研究集刊》、《中国民族医药杂志》、《当代贵州》、《雷山苗族医药》、《黎平县志》等。①

　　本课题 2019 年 3 月 15 日立项后，年底暴发了新冠疫情，造成课题组成员前往非遗所属地现场搜集文献资料的行程受阻。故在整个课题进行期间，课题组成员仅利用 2019 年暑假（7—8 月）和寒假（2020 年 1 月初）前往四个非遗项目所属地，即贵阳市多彩贵州城、梭戛苗族生态博物馆、中国·贵州花溪镇山布依族生态博物馆和建水县非物质文化遗产保护中心进行文献资料的搜集。在这几次行程中，相关负责人给予课题组成员热情的接待和大力的支持。可以说，这三部文献资料汇编（汉英对照）的顺利完稿离不开以下单位、个人的大力支持，在此课题组谨逐一表示最诚挚的谢意：首先，要特别感谢贵旅艺术团团长、侗族大歌国家级传承人张明超先生为课题组提供了有关侗族大歌和其他贵州省国家级非物质文化遗产的文字和图片资料，并赠与了《指掌间的舞蹈——贵州民族工艺名匠荟萃》（贵州人民出版社出版）这一本非遗著作。这些宝贵的资料为课题组完善贵州省的相关国家级非遗项目的文献资料汇编起到

---

① 由于行政调整，有些省、市、县的非物质文化遗产保护中心被调整至其他相关部门，其官网地址发生改变，导致编者原来查阅、参考、引用的文章在原网址无法查到，如四川省非物质文化遗产保护中心、凉山彝族自治州非物质文化遗产保护中心、泸州市非物质文化遗产普及基地等；有的企业官网更新，原有文章已不再展示，如成都水井坊股份有限公司官网；由于编者搜集汇编文献时间较早，有些新闻网站或其他网站进行了更新，本书中引用的某些文章在脚注标明网址已无法访问，如腾讯网、四川新闻网、华夏经纬网、人民网四川频道、保山日报网、多彩贵州网、凯里市人民政府网、贵州文明网、安龙县人民政府网、黔西南州人民政府网、中国铜仁门户网、人民网、中华人民共和国国家民族事务委员会官网、贵州百科信息网、中国民族建筑研究会中国民族建筑网、楚雄州非遗网、中国网等。另外，目前在本书编辑出版过程中还能在脚注网址查阅到的文章未来也可能会由于某种原因无法查阅，因此带来的不便敬请谅解！特此说明。

贵州省·国家级非物质文化遗产文献资料汇编（汉英对照）

The Documentary Compilation of the State-level Intangible Cultural Heritage of Guizhou Province (Chinese-English Versions)

了关键作用。其次，还要特别感谢梭嘎苗族老艺人为课题负责人提供了详细了解并亲身体验梭嘎苗族服饰的机会。再次，十分感谢建水县文化和旅游局及前建水县非物质文化遗产保护中心对本课题的大力支持。2020 年 1 月初，课题负责人和成员向晓红教授前往前建水县非物质文化遗产保护中心搜集有关建水县的国家级非物质文化遗产铓鼓舞和建水紫陶烧制技艺的文献资料，受到中心唐主任的热情接待，唐主任还赠与课题组《建水县非物质文化遗产保护名录》，为课题组完善这两个非遗项目的文献资料起到了重要作用。最后，还要感谢美国教师 Ann Fouts 女士对本系列文献资料汇编英文文本的润色及提出的修改意见。在后期的审校过程中，课题负责人多次就英译文是否表达地道、用词是否精准等问题向 Ann Fouts 女士请教，Fouts 女士对这些英译文提出了很多宝贵的修改意见，在此谨向 Ann Fouts 女士表达课题组最真诚的感谢！

李新新

2024 年 6 月 30 日于西华大学